2006/2007 EDITION

You & the Law in Spain

DAVID SEARL

SANTANA BOOKS

First published September 1985
Second edition - March 1986
Third edition - October 1987
Fourth edition - April 1988
Fifth edition - May 1989
Sixth edition - June 1990
Seventh edition - May 1993
Eigth edition - January 1996
Ninth edition - June 1997
Tenth edition - March 1999
Eleventh edition - April 2000
Twelfth edition - March 2001
Thirteenth edition - May 2002
Fourteenth edition - March 2003
Fifteenth edition - March 2004
Sixteenth edition - March 2005
2006/2007 Edition

You and the Law in Spain
Published by Ediciones Santana S.L.
Apartado 41, 29650 Mijas Pueblo (Málaga), Spain
Tel: (0034) 952 485 838. Fax: (0034) 952 485 367
E-mail: info@santanabooks.com

Printed in Spain by
Gráficas San Pancracio S.L.

ISBN: 84-89954-54-2
Depósito Legal: MA-613/2006

IMPORTANT NOTICE

You and the Law in Spain is meant as a guide to Spanish Law as it applies to foreigners. It is not, however, a substitute for personal, professional legal advice, and it cannot be a basis for any claim against the author or Ediciones Santana.

ACKNOWLEDGEMENTS

We would like to express our sincere gratitude to all those people who have taken time from their busy schedules in government offices, private practice, real estate agencies, moving companies, and on through a long list, to answer our questions and then the questions that arose from their answers.

There is always more to find out.

Among these helpful people, we offer our special thanks for service beyond the call of duty to:

Maribel Aizpurúa, sector chief at the Málaga Tax Agency office, for her endless patience with complicated tax questions, and to her entire staff.

Lawyer **Manuel Ubeda Castañeda** of Ubeda-Retana y Asociados legal services in Fuengirola, for always being on the other end of the telephone with the right answer.

Lawyer **Jorge Retana Alumbreros** of Ubeda-Retana in particular for his thorough knowledge of Spanish tax legislation affecting foreigners.

Tax Consultant **Sergio Llull Cejudo**, also of Ubeda-Retana, for his expertise on Spanish business practices and labour legislation.

Marbella Gestor **Ricardo Sánchez Bocanegra**, for his many years of experience with foreigners in Spain.

Tax Consultant and Property Administrator **Juan José López Guzmán**, for his wide familiarity with tax problems and Community issues.

Anette Skou, **Marta Rey** and **Luisa Machen** of the Mijas Department of Foreign Residents. They are ladies who help.

Fuengirola Insurance Broker **Caroline Ford**, of Brain Insurance in Fuengirola, for her help on Spanish insurance regulations.

CONTENTS

	Introduction	*9*
	What's new in this edition	*13*
Chapter 1	Moving to Spain	*17*
Chapter 2	Resident or Tourist?	*27*
Chapter 3	Buying Property	*35*
Chapter 4	Selling Property	*79*
Chapter 5	Building a home	*91*
Chapter 6	Letting and renting	*105*
Chapter 7	You and your car and On the road	*121*
Chapter 8	You and your money	*151*
Chapter 9	Taxes on property	*165*
	Forms 211-212-213-214	*182-188*
Chapter 10	Spanish income tax	*191*
Chapter 11	Working and starting a business	*207*
	What to do – Crisis advice	
Chapter 12	Employing others	*225*
Chapter 13	Birth, death, marriage and nationality	*235*
Chapter 14	Spanish wills and inheritance tax	*247*
Chapter 15	Your legal advisers	*267*
Chapter 16	You and the Spanish authorities	*279*
Chapter 17	How to complain	*295*
	Hoja de Reclamación	*296*
Chapter 18	You and your community	*303*
Chapter 19	Law of Horizontal Property in English	*317*
Chapter 20	Communities of detached villas	*355*
	Index	*370*

INTRODUCTION

YOU AND THE LAW IN SPAIN IS 21 YEARS OLD

WELCOME to the revised and expanded 2006-2007 edition of *You and the Law in Spain*. It is special because it represents our coming of age, 21 years of helping foreign residents and property owners to understand the legal system of their new country.

This is the 17th edition because in the early years *You and the Law in Spain* was not updated every year as it is now. We thank those loyal readers who have purchased every edition since the beginning.

In honour of the occasion, Spanish legislators have been very busy amending, refining and passing new laws. They have installed new traffic laws, including a points system for driving licences. They are planning major changes in the capital gains law and for income tax. They have banned smoking in work places and many public areas. They have legalised gay marriage and made divorce easier.

In response to all their activity we have prepared this special edition for our anniversary year, including new quick reference sections on what to do if you have a traffic accident, get a traffic ticket, want to make a complaint, or have other problems.

We have expanded our coverage of Spanish mortgages, buying off-plan safely and several other areas. This edition includes the complete translation into English of Spain's Horizontal Law, which regulates Communities of Property Owners, along with commentary to inform you on what really happens in practice.

They tell us that Spain is becoming more and more like its European partners to the north. As one foreign resident remarked, "Spain is no longer an exotic country". That, at least, is the theory.

In real life, foreigners who live or own property in Spain find that this country is still, as the tourist posters used to proclaim, somewhat "different".

When a foreign resident reads the law prohibiting any vehicle from producing sounds louder than a certain number of decibels then directly experiences the same motor bike screaming beneath his window again and again, he starts to wonder.

The law grants a tourist stay of 90 days only to any visitor to Spain, whether he is European Union or not. When the visitor talks to foreigners who have lived in Spain for 10 years, with no residence document, with only brief absences and no problems with the law, he wonders more.

When he is advised that there are heavy penalties for people who under-declare the value of a property transaction in order to minimise transfer taxes and then his lawyer tells him he can put much less than the real purchase price on the contract, he is totally baffled.

This 2006-2007 edition of *You and the Law in Spain* is designed to serve the tens of thousands of foreigners who take up residence or buy a holiday home in Spain every year. These foreign property purchasers have among them bought more than ten billion euros worth of Spanish real estate in recent years. According to official estimates close to 1.5 million foreigners own property in Spain. More than two million foreigners hold residence and work permits, meaning that Spain is their real home.

All these residents are confronted with an unfamiliar legal system and a language they don't usually speak. They have unusual new problems to solve and are offered opportunities of which they are often unaware.

To make their move as safe and easy as possible, they must absorb a great deal of information. This book is designed to present that information clearly and directly. Where the procedure involved is simple, our explanation is simple. When the process is complicated, we try to give at least an idea of the complications involved.

This book is not a substitute for a lawyer or a tax accountant, but it should enable you to ask your lawyer or tax accountant the right questions and to understand his answers.

I have gathered much of the information here during 30 years of attempting to answer readers' questions in magazine columns on

Spanish law and the queries posed by callers to my radio programme.

People want to know why they haven't yet received the title deed to their house, whether they can import their car into Spain, if they are liable to pay Spanish income tax, and hundreds of other things.

The answers to their questions come from Spanish lawyers, government officials, tax advisers, property experts, and on through a long list.

Experience is essential. To further complicate matters, practice varies from one autonomous region of Spain to another as the individual regions exercise their independent powers. The Valencia region does not have exactly the same inheritance tax rules as the Andalusian region. Some things are tolerated though the law suggests otherwise. Some things which appear simple and straightforward in law, turn out to be complicated in practice.

We hope the book will serve as a manual of operations in your new country. It tells you the procedures to follow when you buy a house, when you bring money into Spain, and when you want to keep your foreign-registered car here. It tells you the questions you want to ask your lawyer, your estate agent, and the man who wants to sell you insurance. The book points out some of your principal rights and obligations, such as the obligation to pay Spanish income tax once you have resided in Spain for six months in any calendar year and the right to seek employment under exactly the same conditions as Spaniards. It tells you how to get a Spanish driver's licence, whether or not you should make your maid or gardener a full-time employee and how to arrange burial in your local cemetery.

Frustration and confusion arise in any country when you buy or sell a house, or move to another town. You will get three different answers to your questions from three different Spanish authorities. Persist. Eventually it will get sorted out. Spain is not a Third World country. It is a modern industrial power whose bureaucratic system functions much like those in any other European country.

In general, Spanish authorities hope that you will like the country, bring some money into it, and live happily ever after here. They are perfectly aware that foreign residents in Spain are cashing their pension cheques in Spanish banks every month, producing prosperity for all. They do not wish to discourage this.

While this book cannot explain all the ins and outs of the Spanish legal system to you, we hope that its guidance will make your adjustment to your new country a little easier and more comfortable.

WHAT'S NEW
IN THIS EDITION

Spanish capital gains tax: good news and bad news

The good news for non-resident foreign property owners is that non-resident capital gains tax will be slashed in 2007 from its present 35 per cent to a less painful 18 per cent. This means that, as of January 1, 2007, non-resident sellers will face only half as much tax when they sell their property.

The cut comes in response to a sharp reprimand from the European Union that the rate of 35 per cent discriminated against non-resident EU property owners in Spain, when residents were taxed only 15 per cent.

The bad news is that resident property owners will be subject to the same 18 per cent tax on capital gains instead of their former 15 per cent, also starting in 2007.

These measures are contained in Spain's proposed budget for 2007, which has not yet been enacted but no one expects the Congress to vote any major changes in the government's plan.

Bad news for long-term owners

Further bad news for long-term property owners has already happened. As of January 20, 2006, a series of reductions and exemptions from capital gains tax have been cancelled.

Until January 20, 2006, a property seller who made his purchase before December 31, 1986, faced no capital gains tax at all. Those who bought after 1986, up until 1994 had a partial reduction of 11 per cent per year of ownership.

These reduction factors still apply to all profits earned before January 20, 2006. However, the long-term owners will now face capital gains tax, just like everyone else, on profits earned after January 20. The end of these exemptions which also affect other assets, like stocks, was put into effect quite stealthily and suddenly. Protests have already started against the retroactive nature of the new law.

All sellers, both resident and non-resident, still have the right to use the inflation correction factor which helps to reduce their taxable profit but never eliminates it.

Resident sellers over 65 years of age who sell their principal home continue to be exempt from capital gains if they have lived there for a minimum of three years.

See section on Taxes on Property for more details.

Driving licence by points starts in July, 2006

As of July 1, 2006, Spain's Traffic Department puts into effect a system of points for driving licences. Drivers start with 12 points and have points deducted for various infractions. See the section On the Road in Spain for discussion of the details.

A driver who loses all his points and his licence must wait for six months before he can attend the re-education course which will enable him to obtain a licence again. Repeat offenders must wait a year without a licence.

The points system is in addition to the revised Traffic Code which stiffens penalties for speeding more than 50 per cent over the posted limit and for drink driving. The Traffic Department authorities continue to lobby the Congress for even harsher measures, such as making it easier to send drunken drivers to gaol. They can presently be imprisoned, but court procedures often drag out for years.

The revised code also imposes stricter penalties for use of mobile telephones while driving and for failure to use approved child seats and harnesses.

New Valencia land-grab law — "more of the same" say victims

Early in December, 2005, the full European Parliament voted by a majority of 90 per cent to adopt a devastating report by European Commission investigators into abuses of the Valencia "land-grab" law.

This vote opens the way for the Parliament to call Valencia regional officials to testify at the European Court of Justice, under threat of EU sanctions, such as the withdrawal of subsidies to the Valencia region.

This law, the 1994 LRAU, is the *Ley Reguladora de Actividades Urbanísticas*. It allowed private developers to act with official powers to seize privately owned land, paying minimal compensation. The EU report calls abuses of the law a "clear violation of human rights".

Under pressure, the Valencia government has now enacted a new land law, unfortunately called the *LUV, Ley Urbanística Valenciana*. The law makes it just a little less difficult for victims of forced expropriation to defend themselves.

Victims of the land-grab, more than 20,000 of them, foreigners and Spaniards, have formed the *Abusos Urbanísticos No* association. They call the new law simply "more of the same" and will continue to fight it.

Their next move is aimed at the European Court of Human Rights. A major UK law firm is presenting a series of test cases. If you are a Costa Blanca property owner, you can check out this association at their very complete web site, www.aun@abusos-no.org.

See Section on Building Your Own Home for more details.

Anti-smoking law gets mixed reception

It's true. The Spanish national anti-smoking law went into effect in January of 2006. The law prohibits smoking in public places and the work place.

We have all seen smokers lighting up in Spanish airports, right under the No Smoking sign, and we have all seen office workers with butts smouldering in ashtrays on their desks, where smoking has always been prohibited.

But this time it seems they are taking it seriously. Remember that more than two-thirds of people do not smoke. With the new regulations in hand, they are uniting for the first time to condemn rebels against the law. And also, for the first time, we are beginning to see smokers going outside for a cigarette break.

The other principal effect of the law has been a booming business for sign manufacturers. This is because the law allows smaller establishments, such as your neighbourhood bar, to declare themselves as smoking zones. They must display a sign, however, which says *"Aquí se puede fumar"* (smoking permitted here). Larger areas can divide into smoking and non-smoking areas, but the smoking area can never exceed 30 per cent of the space.

Several defiant smokers have already been fined 300 Euros for violating the law, so perhaps you should not light up as soon as you get off the plane in Spain.

MOVING TO SPAIN

1

EUROPEAN UNION CITIZENS	17
PENSIONERS	17
E-121 FORM	18
NON-PENSIONERS	18
EU WORKERS	18
SPANISH CONSULATE	19
NON-EU CITIZENS	19
INCOME REQUIREMENTS	20
VISADO DE RESIDENCIA	21
IMPORTING YOUR POSSESSIONS	21
NEW RESIDENT EXEMPT FROM DUTY	22
ONE-YEAR LIMIT ON DEPOSIT	23
BRIDE'S TROUSSEAU EXEMPT	24
IMPORTING PETS	25

SPAIN's revised law for foreigners, passed in 2003, made it much easier for European Union citizens to apply for residence. Recent changes even exempt EU citizens who are working in Spain from the need to renew their present residence cards.

European Union citizens

European Union citizens coming to reside in Spain now need to present only their application form, four photographs and their passport with photocopy in order to apply for a residence card (see Chapter Two, Resident or Tourist). EU citizens no longer need to demonstrate proof of income or medical insurance.

Pensioners

Even under the revised Foreigners' Law, a European Union

pensioner still needs a residence card. They do not need to show proof of income or medical insurance, but there is one important step they should take before they leave home.

Form E-121

EU pensioners should obtain Form E-121 from their own country, which will enable them to transfer their rights to medical care to the Spanish Social Security medical system. These "E" for "European" forms are readily available in all EU countries. You must obtain it, however, in your home country before you come to Spain.

EU citizens who are not entitled to receive pensions as a result of working in their home countries will have to show that they receive regular income from some other source. They will also be required to obtain medical insurance from a company operating in Spain.

Non-pensioners

EU citizens who are not of retirement age and who do not receive a pension must also obtain medical insurance in Spain. If they are not working in Spain, they must demonstrate that they either receive a regular income or possess sufficient resources to maintain themselves.

EU workers

An EU citizen intending to work or start a business in Spain, can simply arrive in the country and begin his paperwork immediately.

EU citizens looking for work can apply for employment at the national employment service under exactly the same conditions as Spaniards. When they get a job, they can obtain their work and residence card on application. They will be required to pay into the Spanish Social Security system in return for medical care and an eventual pension.

Those intending to start a business will face a labyrinth of permits and licences, just as Spaniards themselves do, but it can all be overcome (see section on Working and Starting a Business for details.)

Consulates have information

Ask the Spanish consulate for a copy of the "C" leaflet, which explains many details about moving to Spain. The leaflet number varies from country to country but it is Leaflet C16 in the UK. This leaflet explains about importing your household goods, and gives information about driving licences, for example. It also lists requirements for obtaining the *Visado de residencia*, the residence visa, which is necessary for non-EU citizens intending to reside in Spain (see below).

Some consulates have a great deal of information available besides that contained in leaflet C16. The Spanish government produces many publications to inform visitors and investors. If you are interested in doing business in Spain, or travelling about, or in the arts, or in specific data on a certain region, be sure to ask if they have any pamphlets. They can often order them for you if they do not have them in stock.

You may also be surprised at the information available from your own government. They publish pamphlets on doing business in Spain, explaining import and export restrictions and currency controls, for example. They probably have data about what is produced and what is needed and current information about how money flows between Spain and your country.

Ask at your country's Foreign Ministry or Commerce Ministry about any subject that particularly interests you, whether it be teaching or onion farming. There is probably a government publication bearing on it.

Non-European Union citizens

First, go to the Spanish consulate in your home country. If you are from a non-EU country, you will need to obtain the *Visado de residencia*, a visa you must present when you apply for a residence permit after you have arrived in Spain.

The visa can only be obtained from the Spanish consulate in your home country before you leave for Spain.

There are, in fact, seven different types of visa, depending on whether you are a retired pensioner, an investor, an executive of a multinational company, or carrying out a cultural or sporting activity. Make sure you request the right one for your circumstances.

Second, go to your bank and make sure they understand exactly how your money is to be sent to you. Make absolutely sure they know a corresponding bank in the area of Spain where you will live. Transfers of money can take weeks when not properly handled.

There are bank branches which simply do not understand international transactions. There are others that do not have corresponding banks in your home country.

You will need to establish that the bank you choose in Spain has a working relationship with your bank at home and can readily receive funds from them. Transfers have been known to get stuck in a main office in Madrid and not reach their destination until weeks, even months later, after heated telephone calls and faxes.

Once you have a bank account in Spain, you can deposit your foreign cheques, or make direct transfers, and then write euro cheques for payments on your new property, or your rent, making money matters much easier.

Holding a Spanish bank account will work in your favour when you apply for your visa at the consulate in your country. It is not, however, strictly necessary.

For non-EU persons, this application for the visa is your first legal step towards acquiring residency in Spain. It gives the Spanish authorities a chance to examine your financial situation before they decide whether you will make a useful resident. Once you have the visa, you are practically assured of obtaining the residence permit.

Information sheets issued by Spanish consulates in various countries will show how much income you need in order to get this visa.

The Spanish consulate in Washington, DC, requires US citizens to show an income of at least $10,000 a year per person if they wish to retire in Spain.

An American wishing to start a business or invest in Spain has to demonstrate capital of about $18,000.

If you have this income, you are all right. If you haven't, do not assume that you will be denied the visa. Many other details also come into the picture. You may have capital which is not at the moment producing income, for example, or your income may not start until some future date.

The consular officials will judge each case on its merits. But they do want to be sure that you have sufficient means to support yourself in Spain. If you intend to start a business, for example, you will need to show that you are bringing into Spain enough money to do so, unless you are from an EU country.

Visado de residencia

When you are ready to apply for the visa, you will need to present a valid passport and evidence supporting your source of income. You may also be asked to show that you have made some arrangements for remitting this income to Spain.

You will also need a *Certificado penal*, a paper showing you have no prison record, issued by your local police. The Spanish consulate in your country can tell you exactly how to obtain it in your area.

You then fill out the visa application form in duplicate. If you are a couple, each of you must sign the form. Make it clear that you intend to take up residency, as this affects your right to import your furniture into Spain free of duty (see section below on "Importing Your Possessions").

You will be asked to provide a reference in Spain and one in your home country. If you have bought or rented property in Spain, your seller would make an excellent reference. Or your new bank manager or lawyer in Spain. You will need two passport photos.

You must enter Spain and have your passport stamped within 60 days of the time the visa is issued to you. So it is best to gather all your information and the necessary documents in advance, but leave the final application until a month or so before your intended departure date.

The visa sometimes is issued quickly, but it's best to ask.

NOTE: If you are a non-EU citizen already established in Spain but still on tourist status, it is possible to apply for exemption from the visa requirement so that you do not have to return to your home country. However, authorities have cracked down on this exemption and it is almost impossible to obtain.

With the visa in hand, you can then apply for duty-free import of your furniture. Your removal company should be able to handle all the paperwork involved (see the next section).

Importing your possessions

European Union citizens may skip this section, as duties on importation of household goods have disappeared with free circulation of goods within the EU. If they are moving to Spain, and bringing all their possessions, their moving company will know how to handle the forms required. For details on importing automobiles, EU citizens should see chapter on You and Your Car.

New resident free of duty

When you come to Spain from outside the EU to take up residence, the Spanish government grants you the privilege of importing your household effects and personal possessions free of customs duty. This privilege is a one-time grant and is only available to those who take out an official residence permit.

You do not have to purchase property in order to justify this privilege, but you will have to show a residence permit, and you will have to make a prior deposit, which will be returned to you within a year.

For those who wish to import furniture for a second residence or holiday home, there is a second form of importation. For this *vivienda secundaria* exemption, you need not become a resident. You must make a deposit, however, just as the resident does. The non-resident must wait two years, however, for the return of his money.

In both cases, the deposit will be about 50 per cent of the estimated value of the goods.

The conditions are that you have not been a resident in Spain during the two years prior to the importation of the goods; that your goods enter the country within three months of your own arrival in Spain; that the goods are used, being at least six months old, and that you undertake not to sell them for two years.

Under this provision you can import, among other things, furniture, books, works of art, personal effects and collections, musical instruments, food and liquor, washing machines, electric or gas cookers, refrigerators, vacuum cleaners, floor polishers, radios and television sets.

The Spanish authorities remind you that the electric current in Spain is 220 volts and 50 cycles. This difference is especially important for Americans and Canadians, who will find their stereo sound equipment needs various adaptors to function properly and that their television sets will not function at all because the European system is different from the North American television system.

All the appropriate information is presented in Spanish leaflet C16, which you should request from the Spanish consulate in your home country at the beginning of your application to come to Spain to take up residency. See section "Before You Leave". (This is leaflet C21 for Americans and its number varies from country to country.)

At the consulate or through your removal company, you fill out a form requesting the Head of the Customs Office, *La Dirección General de Aduanas*, to allow your goods to enter Spain free of duty. You will need a complete list, in duplicate, of all your possessions. The list must be in Spanish. The consulate will legalise your application and list by stamping them, for a small fee.

You can obtain the forms by writing to the nearest consulate or you can collect them in person. Your removal company should include most of this paperwork in its services. Be sure to ask them.

Removal companies

The selection of a removal company is extremely important. Some companies are familiar with the paperwork, have experienced agents at the borders and customs depots, and know how to keep your property from winding up in Barcelona in the customs shed for three months, which quite often happens when all the papers are not in order. Make enquiries among people who have moved to Spain until you find a company with satisfied clients.

There are a lot of things that can go wrong with international removals, so take your time in finding the right company. You must also present a photocopy of the first five pages of your passport, correctly legalised by the Spanish consulate, to your removal agents. They need to show this at the customs office at the Spanish border when they enter with your goods.

Make sure that your removal company guarantees delivery to your door in Spain. There have been cases where goods were held up in customs and a different removal company brought them from the Barcelona depot or a Spanish port, collecting more money for the distance travelled within Spain.

One-year time limit to recover deposit

From the time your goods enter Spain, you have one year to present a residence permit to the customs authorities and request the return of your deposit.

Be warned. If you wait more than 12 months from the time your furniture enters Spain, you will not be able to claim the return of your deposit. Some unwary foreigners have allowed the time limit to lapse and lost their deposits.

You might think that the professional customs agent employed by the removal company or by you personally to handle the deposit guaranty would inform you when this time limit was near, but you would be wrong in many cases. You yourself must be alert and must see your customs agent to make sure the procedures are correctly carried out, on time.

When you have your residence card in hand, you need to obtain a certificate from your local town hall that the furniture is still in your possession. They will send a policeman or an inspector to visit you. He will check the list against the furniture itself and sign the certificate. With this document and your residence permit — along with the receipt given you showing that this is your first application for a Spanish residence permit — you can claim the release of your deposit.

The deposit will have been made into a Spanish bank, which in turn will issue a certificate that is presented to the customs office. The certificate guarantees that the funds have been deposited in the Spanish bank for the purposes of the customs guarantee. When the customs office releases the deposit, you present that paper to the bank, which releases the funds back to you.

This deposit system also applies when a foreign non-resident purchases or rents property in Spain and wishes to import goods to furnish this property, even though the foreigner will not reside there full-time. You can do this, duty-free, by following the same procedure outlined above. This time, however, you have a time limit of two years.

At the end of the two years, you obtain the document from the town hall certifying that the goods are still in your possession, and the customs office will authorise the release of your deposit. This is called a *vivienda secundaria* plan, for a second home.

One condition for obtaining this exemption is that you must not let the property to others. It must be for your own personal and exclusive use.

Bride's trousseau exempt

A foreign woman who marries either a Spaniard or a foreigner officially resident in Spain may bring into Spain free of duty her wedding gifts and trousseau. This is not a genuine regulation, but a courtesy granted by the Customs Office upon special application. It is only granted in cases where reciprocal treatment is given to a Spanish woman who marries a citizen of another country.

Importing your pet

What about Rover? Yes, of course, you can take your faithful pet to Spain with you, but it's a bit complicated. You want to obtain the standard European Union form for a Pet Passport, whether you are coming from the EU or not.

In order to obtain this passport, you need a health certificate for your pet issued by a veterinary authorised by the appropriate ministry in your country. This certificate must be issued not more than 15 days before you enter Spain with the pet.

In addition you will need a certificate of vaccination against rabies, also issued by an authorised veterinarian. Animals less than two months old do not require this. Animals between two and three months of age must have been vaccinated not less than one month before they are imported. Animals of three months or older must have been vaccinated not less than one month and not more than 12 months before being imported. If the animal has no anti-rabies certificate, it may be quarantined for 20 days.

Finally, you will need a certificate declaring that the area in which the animal was normally kept is free from animal diseases. This certificate usually comes from your agriculture ministry.

All these certificates must be stamped and legalised by the Spanish consulate, for which they charge a small fee, and you will have your authorised pet passport.

Once you have arrived in Spain, you will want to have your pet fitted with a new microchip which gives your address in Spain. UK pet owners can now take their dogs back with them when they return home. They must start the procedures in Spain at least a month before their trip, however, in order to obtain the required certificates.

Cars, caravans and boats

For information on importing cars, caravans and boats, see the section on "You and Your Car".

GLOSSARY

Agente de Aduana – licensed customs agent
Dirección General de Aduanas – General Customs Directorate

Certificado penal – certificate of criminal record

Visado de residencia – special visa obtained from Spanish consulate for persons taking up residency.

Vivienda secundaria – second home, holiday home

RESIDENT OR TOURIST?

2

YOU AS A TOURIST   27
TOURIST STAY IS 90 DAYS   28
PERMANENCIA   28
BENEFITS OF TOURIST STATUS   29
YOU AS A RESIDENT   29
TAX ADVANTAGES FOR RESIDENTS   30
HOW TO APPLY FOR RESIDENCE   32
  EU CITIZEN   32
  NON-EU CITIZEN   32
NIE TAX IDENTIFICATION NUMBER   33
EU CITIZENS CAN VOTE   33

IF you live more or less full-time in Spain, you should hold an official residence permit. The law specifies that a person who has been present in Spain for six months must either leave the country or apply for a residence permit.

The disadvantages of being an official resident are largely imaginary, and it is becoming more and more difficult to remain on tourist status when you are really a resident.

Furthermore, some real tax savings are available for residents who sell property or who bequeath Spanish property on their deaths (see final section below on Resident Tax Savings).

Let's take a look at both possibilities.

You as a tourist

First of all, what is a tourist? When you visit Spain for a short holiday, you are a tourist. If you have a holiday home or a second home in Spain where you spend months at a time, you are still a tourist of sorts, as your principal residence is in another country.

If your principal residence is in Spain and you spend most of your time here, you can still have — technically — tourist status if you do not take out a residence permit. But the Spanish authorities are growing stricter about allowing people to retain "tourist status" when they really live full-time in Spain.

The concrete definition is this: a tourist is a person who spends less than six months in Spain in one calendar year.

The "tourist" stay in Spain for EU and non-EU citizens alike is limited to 90 days. To stay another 90 days, you are required to obtain a *permanencia*, which is an extension that is stamped in your passport (see below).

Anyone who stays more than six months must apply for a residence permit.

Some foreigners who are really resident in Spain continue to remain on tourist status by going to, say, Morocco every six months, where they have their passports stamped. They then return to Spain to begin a new period of "tourism".

There are people who have gone on for years in this way. For those who live near borders and who want to keep their official presence in Spain as undocumented as possible, this has been an acceptable practice, even if not quite cricket.

However, Spanish authorities have become stricter and people who have crossed a particular border every three months for years with no complications, now find their passports being carefully examined. Some have been stopped and ordered to obtain a residence permit. Others have been refused entry.

Permanencia: It is also possible to get further 90-day extensions, called *permanencias*. However, you are entitled to only one *permanencia* in a calendar year so — even with this extension — you have a total of six months.

When you hear old Spain hands say things like: "Don't worry about it. They have given me nine *permanencias* in a row and never made any problems about it", be aware that this was only out of the authorities´ laxity or the goodness of their hearts. It is no longer true.

The word *permanencia* means a temporary stay, not a permanent one, as you may think when comparing it to the English word. In fact, the verb *permanecer* in Spanish means "to stay" or "to remain", not "to be permanent".

You apply for this *permanencia*, which is stamped in your passport, by going to the foreign department of your local police station, or *comisaría*. You need your passport, a couple of photos, and some evidence of your ability to finance your continued stay in Spain. There is no specific cash requirement, though authorities suggest an income of €600 a month as an acceptable minimum. A copy of your Spanish bank statement or evidence that you receive a pension from abroad would be acceptable.

One *comisaría* requires that you have €1,800 in a Spanish bank to grant the 90-day extension. Ask locally, as practice varies. With these papers in hand, the *permanencia* is routinely granted, and you can stay another 90 days as a tourist.

Benefits of tourist status

With Spain's full entry into the European Union, most advantages of remaining on tourist status have disappeared.

Formerly, only a non-resident could hold bank accounts in freely convertible pesetas or other currencies. With the introduction of the euro, currency exchange restrictions no longer exist, for Spaniards or residents.

Formerly, only a non-resident could own an automobile on tax-free tourist plates. Now, as European Union citizens, no EU person can do this, as he is not a "tourist" in the EU. Non-EU citizens, however, continue to enjoy the right to the tourist registration, without paying Spanish taxes.

So there aren't really many advantages to remaining on tourist status when in truth you are a resident.

People sometimes think that a person on tourist status does not become liable for Spanish income tax. It is simply not true. A person who lives in Spain more than 183 days in one calendar year — whether or not he holds a residence permit — becomes legally liable to pay Spanish income tax.

European Union citizens can continue to use their EU national driving licences after they take out a Spanish residence permit, so even that is not a problem (see chapter On the Road in Spain).

You as a resident

On balance, if you really reside in Spain, it seems wiser to take out a formal residence permit. If you are an EU citizen, we should not call it a "permit". It is a residence card.

If you intend to earn money in Spain, you will need a work permit. Many residents do not have work permits, their papers being stamped "not valid for working in Spain". Those who do have work permits also have residence permits.

It is illegal to work in Spain without a work permit, or an EU registration card — *Tarjeta comunitaria* — if you are a working EU citizen. The normal residence permit is renewed once every five years. Renewal is usually a simple matter. The EU card is issued for one year, and five years on renewal.

Tax advantages for residents

Foreigners often think that taking out an official residence permit in Spain will cost them money and expose them to Spanish taxes which non-residents can avoid.

The truth is often the reverse. The resident property owner has a number of tax advantages over the non-resident.

1. If you are a resident and more than 65 years of age, and you have lived in your home for three years, you will not be subject to Spanish capital gains tax when you sell it, no matter how great your profit.

2. If you are a resident, your maximum capital gains tax is 18 per cent, and it can be even less, whereas the non-resident pays 35 per cent. However, this is only true until January 1, 2007, when both resident and non-resident will pay 18 per cent (see Taxes on Property for details).

3. If you are a resident and you sell your property, you are not subject to having 5 per cent of the total purchase price withheld and deposited with Spain's Tax Agency as a guarantee against your tax liabilities.

4. If you are a resident and you bequeath your home to a spouse or child who is also a resident, you can probably avoid Spanish inheritance tax on 95 per cent of the valuation. The conditions are that you have owned and lived in your home for a minimum of three years. The inheritor must be a resident and must undertake not to sell the property for 10 years, while continuing to be a resident. Top limit on the 95 per cent reduction is €120,000. Over that, you must pay.

5. Spanish property owner's imputed income tax does not apply to the owner's principal residence. A resident of Spain also has

an exemption on the first €108,000 of valuation for Spanish capital assets tax, "wealth tax". The non-resident pays from the first euro of valuation.

If a husband and wife jointly own a property worth €120,000 and they are non-resident, they will pay a non-resident property-owner's income tax of €600 each year plus €240 of Spanish wealth tax, a total of €840 per year. The resident is exempt from these taxes. For wealth tax, the exemption is €108,000 each for husband and wife (see section on Taxes for more details).

6. If you really live most of the year in Spain, you are violating the law if you do not obtain a residence card. The law says that your tourist stay, even as a European Union citizen, is limited to 180 days per year. You can be fined €300 if you over-stay this limit.

Applying for a residence card becomes easier for EU citizens

Spain's revised Foreigner's Law, which went into effect March 1, 2003, has made it easier for EU citizens to apply for a residence card and even exempted some of them for the need to renew their card. Early enthusiasm for the new law started people saying that no EU citizen needs a residence card, but it simply isn't true. The only persons exempt are those who are living and working in Spain and paying into the Spanish Social Security system. EU pensioners still need a card.

The residence law is Royal Decree 178/2003 of 14/02/2003. It applies to EU member states and to Norway, Iceland, Liechtenstein and Switzerland, as members of the European Economic Area.

Two groups of people are exempt. These are workers who presently pay Spanish Social Security and those retired workers entitled to a Spanish state pension who have lived in Spain more than three years and have worked in the 12 months before retirement. All others need a card.

In any case, it seems that even those who are exempt will do better to renew their present cards. If you want a resident mortgage at the bank instead of a non-resident mortgage or if you want to exchange your UK driving licence for a Spanish one, the card will be easy proof of your status.

Non-EU Citizen

Now you will need that *Visado de residencia* which you obtained from the Spanish consulate in your home country before you came to Spain to settle. Obtaining the visa gave the Spanish authorities a chance to check you out, along with your financial means, even before you arrived.

In addition, you will need:

1. Proof of financial means. European citizens can be accepted to live in Spain without working on minimum financial means but non-EU persons will be required to show higher incomes. No specific figure is set but you ought to have more than €700 per month coming in or you will never get the visa.

2. *Certificado de Antecedentes Penales* (Certificate of Criminal Record). This certificate shows that you have no criminal record. You can request this from your local police authorities. Ask the consulate in your home country for the proper form.

3. Medical certificate.

4. Consular inscription. This a letter from your own nation's consulate in Spain showing that you are registered with them.

5. Medical Insurance. Your private medical coverage must be contracted with a company which has an office in Spain.

6. Passport and photocopy.

7. Marriage certificate and official translation.

8. Three passport-size photos.

9. Payment of fee in differing amounts, depending on your country of origin. The fee is not high.

10. Statement from your Spanish bank showing that your income is arriving from abroad and being deposited in Spain.

11. Title deeds to Spanish property or a rental contract, with photocopy.

12. Birth certificates of children under 18 if they are included in the residence application. Translations.

13. The filled-up form requesting the residence permit.

BE ADVISED: To pay the small administrative fee, you must first obtain Form 750, then take it to the bank and make the payment. All European Union citizens pay the same six euros. Other nationalities pay differing amounts. The bank returns to you the form stamped as paid. If you can obtain the form from your police station beforehand and pay it in advance, you will save yourself waiting time. If you can't, ask for the form as soon as you arrive, take it to the bank, and then join the queue.

Try to find out in advance just what you will have to present. We try to keep this book up to date, but some offices may want four photos instead of three, for example. Well-organised offices will actually give you a list when you make your first enquiry.

If you are not an EU citizen and are requesting the unified work permit/residence permit, you will have a number of other documents to present, relating to your employer in Spain, or the money you are bringing in to start a business, if that is the case. See the section on "Working and Starting A Business" for more details.

Tax identification number (NIE)

Your residence permit will include your *Número de Identificación de Extranjero* (NIE), which identifies you to the Spanish tax authorities. The number is necessary for practically any transaction in Spain, such as paying your taxes. Even a non-resident who has any relation with the Spanish tax system, either by owning property or by drawing interest from a bank, also needs this NIE.

All this sounds complicated but if you speak just a little Spanish and want to have some direct contact with official procedures in your new country, you can handle your request for a *residencia* yourself. Assembling the necessary documents and dealing with the different people and offices involved is an education in Spanish ways of doing things.

You can also use the services of a *gestoría* to lead you through the process. The *gestor* is licensed by the government as an official middleman between you and the state and provides, for a reasonable fee, many useful services. It is his business to know which little window to go to at what time, and a good one can save you much time and trouble. This Spanish institution is more fully described in the section on "You and Your Legal Advisers".

EU citizens can vote

Finally, if you are an EU citizen, you will be able to vote in Spain's municipal elections even if you are non-resident. Not only can you vote, you can be elected to office. If this prospect appeals to you, be sure to present yourself at your town hall immediately to be registered in the *padrón*, the list of municipal inhabitants, which is the basis of the voter list. Obtain a *Certificado de Empadronamiento* proving that you have registered. (See section on voting in You and the Spanish Authorities)

Some months before the elections check to make sure that you appear on the voting list, or you will not be permitted to cast your ballot. Perhaps the Popular Party (equivalent of the Conservatives) or the Socialist Party will ask you to stand for office.

GLOSSARY

Autorización de Residencia – residence permit
Certificado de Antecedentes Penales – certificate of criminal record
Certificado de Empadronamiento – certificate of registration in municipality.
Formulario – form
Gestoría – professional administrative agency
Número de Identificación de Extranjero (NIE) – tax identification number
Padrón – registry of inhabitants in municipality
Permanencia – 90-day extension of tourist visit

BUYING PROPERTY

REAL ESTATE AGENTS	37
COMMISSIONS IN COASTAL AREAS	39
YOUR SPANISH LAWYER	40
WHAT TO WATCH OUT FOR	41
NEW PROPERTIES	41
PGOU – TOWN URBAN PLAN	42
BEFORE SIGNING ANYTHING	42
ESCRITURA PUBLICA	43
IBI RECEIPT	44
REFERENCIA CATASTRAL	45
COMMUNITY FEES, STATUTES AND MINUTES	46
UTILITIES BILLS	47
TRANSFER COSTS	47
WHO PAYS WHAT?	48
HOW MUCH TO DECLARE?	49
THE CONTRACT	50
ESCRITURA DE COMPRAVENTA	51
POWER OF ATTORNEY	52
FREE OF CHARGES AND LIENS	54
FINAL TITLE AND REGISTRATION	55
METHOD OF PAYMENT	57
CERTIFICATE OF NON-RESIDENCE	58
FIVE PER CENT TAX DEPOSIT	58
BUYING OFF-PLAN	59

BUYING NEW PROPERTY — 60
PROPERTY PURCHASE CHECK LIST — 61
BUYING WITHOUT ESCRITURA — 62
205 PROCEDURE — 63
EXPEDIENTE DE DOMINIO — 63
OFF-SHORE COMPANY — 64
BANK REPOSSESSIONS AND AUCTIONS — 65
CAPITAL GAINS TAX — 66
FINANCING BY DEVELOPER — 67
BANK LOANS AND MORTGAGES — 67
SUBSIDISED HOUSING — 70
INSURING YOUR HOME — 71
TIMESHARE LAW — 72
EXPROPRIATION OF PROPERTY — 74

YOU're right. You should have bought a holiday home or a retirement residence in Spain three or four years ago. Depending on the area, you would have seen an average 30 per cent rise in the value of your property, and even more in some areas.

The Spanish property market has definitely cooled for 2006, with price increases of under 15 per cent in most areas, but do not despair. Experts predict that prices will continue to rise for the immediate future, and that they certainly will not drop. This means that you are still in time to make a sensible purchase that will bring you pleasure and keep your investment safe.

You have a wide choice of sunshine property available to you now. New construction of high quality is booming all over Spain and particularly in the Mediterranean areas as well as in the major cities of Madrid and Barcelona. Spanish property sellers are also giving prospective purchasers good terms and more professional service.

FACT: *The Economist* reports that house prices in the last 20 years have risen faster in Spain than anywhere else in the world.

Mortgage rates in the euro zone are beginning to rise from their record lows of the past few years. The base rate, called the Euribor, is set to rise past 3 per cent. This will slow the housing market, but mortgage rates of under 6 per cent are still attractive. See section on Mortgages for more details

Nevertheless, the foreign buyer needs to take care. Too many purchasers seem to leave their common sense at the airport when they enter Spain.

You need sound legal advice from a Spanish professional who may be a lawyer, a registered estate agent, a specialised *gestor,* or an *administrador de fincas,* any of whom is qualified to act in your interests and make sure you are protected and well-advised in the transaction. It's foolish to depend entirely on the seller of the property to make sure you are treated fairly.

Real estate agents

Let's start at the beginning. Your first contact when you decide to buy property in Spain will almost certainly be the estate agent. In many countries, an estate agent is a registered professional who can be held financially responsible if he acts as intermediary in a sale and the terms later turn out to be falsely based.

In Spain there is no law regulating real estate agents. Anyone may act as intermediary. This means it is difficult to hold an estate agent responsible when a purchase goes wrong. Citizens of Scandinavian countries, or the UK, for example, where consumers are more carefully protected, even from their own mistakes, should be warier in Spain.

There are, however, two professional associations which require examinations and set standards for their members. One of these offers the title of *Agente de la Propiedad Inmobiliaria,* or API for short. The other is the *Gestor Intermediario de Propiedades y Edificios* (the GIPE). You will do well to deal with an estate agent who holds one of these titles.

Even so, if your Spanish estate agent causes you to suffer loss, either through negligence or honest error, you will have a hard time obtaining any recompense. Ask your agent if he carries professional indemnity insurance, and, if so, how much. You may again be surprised to find that most estate agents have either no insurance at all or a minimum amount required by the official Spanish agents' association. Ask your agent if he operates a Bonded

Clients' Account, into which any deposits will be placed, and which is untouchable except for the stated purpose of the deposit.

Example: sellers make off with deposit

Here is what can happen if you pay your deposit directly to the seller.

A British couple found a villa they liked on the Costa del Sol. They agreed a price of €180,000, and they transferred a deposit of €18,000, 10 per cent of the price, to its German owners to reserve the villa.

The British couple used a Spanish lawyer plus the advice of a British property agent working in Spain and they felt all was well. They sold their home in the UK, shipped their furniture to Spain, wound up their business, and came to Spain for the closing of the sale, when they would pay the rest of the price and sign the deed.

Just before the date with the Notary, their lawyer received a message from the German sellers, saying they could not make it that day and that they would be in touch later. This set off alarm bells with everybody involved. It turned out that the owners had in fact sold the property a month earlier for €210,000 to another buyer, had kept the €18,000 deposited with them, and had left Spain for parts unknown.

Of course the unfortunate British buyers have a clear case against the German sellers for breach of contract, with the right to recover their deposit, plus damages and loss, but how are they going to find them? In fact, they have the right to a sum twice the amount of the deposit if the seller backs out of the deal.

In many European countries, the buyers would also have a case against the estate agent and perhaps the lawyer as well for negligence in performing their services. In Spain they also have a case, but here standards are less strict and the lawyer and estate agent may declare that they simply followed accepted practice and were just as dismayed as their clients, and a Spanish court may well accept their arguments.

So, be sure to take care that any deposit you make goes into that escrow account, a blocked account, where neither party can get at it until the sale is closed.

Unscrupulous agent can take advantage

In a few cases, unscrupulous estate agents have taken advantage of distressed or innocent sellers, telling them that they can obtain only a very low price for their property. This might be a widow who has returned to her home country and wants to sell her Spanish property because she needs the money. The agent tells her he can get only €90,000 for the property.

She had the idea it must be worth €120,000 or more in today's brisk market, but she lets herself be convinced. The agent also convinces her to sign an agreement which authorises him to keep anything he can get over that price. The agent then sells the property for €125,000, just as he knew he could, making himself a "commission" of €35,000.

The buyer makes out the cheque to the estate agent, who puts €35,000 in his own account and €90,000 to the owner. All legal and in order. He never tells the seller what he sold it for, and since the buyer and seller never come into contact, the truth is never discovered. Even if it was, the agent has done nothing illegal. After all, the seller signed the agreement, didn't she? This sort of sharp practice becomes a great temptation for agents where owners are often absentee and ignorant.

Even the final figure of the purchase price on the sales contract may be the under-declared amount of €90,000. In any case, since the agent is acting with a power of attorney to sign the contract for the absentee seller, nothing can be done about it after the fact.

These cases and others like them make a powerful argument for using a Spanish lawyer when you buy property. I will say it again and again: you should use a Spanish lawyer when you buy property in Spain. You should use a lawyer in your own country when you buy property. Why should it be different in Spain?

Having stated this warning, we find that most Spanish estate agents and foreigners selling property in Spain, are both registered and honest. They only want to make a fair commission by selling good properties which will make their buyers and sellers both happy. Be careful anyway.

Commissions high in coastal areas

Most Europeans will be surprised to find that estate agents dealing with Spanish holiday property take commissions starting at 5 per cent and going up to 10 per cent. These high commissions, say the agents, are justified because they have to deal with many unusual factors in a market where a buyer comes from one country and the seller from another and the transaction takes place in Spain, a third country. They also cite high marketing expenses from international advertising.

Let's just say that, when you are in the final stages of negotiating your purchase price, even the amount of the estate agent's commission might come on the table for a little reduction. Keep in mind that the API, for example, recommends 3 per cent commission for its agents in most areas of Spain.

Spain has all sorts of estate agents, ranging from the small office in the High Street, who has been in the town for many years and knows everybody personally, to the most modern international real estate offices, filled with computers. Some of the major agencies can contact their offices in Frankfurt or London by Internet, and screen you five views of their offerings right there on the computer. In addition, there are many "Euro agents" of all nationalities who quite legally operate in Spain, although their credentials may not be as well established.

One of these agents should be able to find the property you are looking for. Very few agents in Spain are exclusive, so you could find two agents showing you the same property.

The estate agent is working for the seller, so his presentation of the property will be the most favourable one, and you should check the facts carefully through your own representative. A reputable estate agent will be very happy to have you verify any of his information through your own lawyer, for example.

Your Spanish lawyer

Many Spanish lawyers working in areas with many foreigners speak excellent English or other languages. They are accustomed to dealing with foreign residents and their special problems, including property purchases.

How to find a good Spanish lawyer? Good question. Here is perhaps one of the few areas in which you can ask advice from people you know. Ask around until you find some satisfied clients. You can try walking into a bar and asking the people if anyone knows a good lawyer. Everybody in the place will have a story about either a good one or a bad one.

Consulates also maintain lists of lawyers who speak the language of their nationality, English, German, and so on. These lists do not mean that the lawyers are the most highly regarded.

How much will it cost? Figure the lawyer to charge you around one per cent of the value of the transaction, unless there are some unusual complications. Settle this with him before you start.

What to watch out for

Let's give the basic "Buyer Beware" warning first. It goes like this: Believe Nothing, Check Everything.

When they say there is no outstanding mortgage, check the Property Registry. When they say it measures 145 square metres, measure it. When they say the terrace is included, check the plans. Any reputable seller will be perfectly happy to have his offers checked. Spoken words do not count. Only pieces of paper count.

Both the European Union and the Spanish government have investigated fraud reports in holiday property, revealing the presence of illegal urbanisations where unwary buyers end up having problems of unpaid taxes, unregistered title deeds, and difficulty in obtaining municipal services or building permission. Spaniards have also been defrauded and problems with house purchase make up a principal area of complaint for the Spanish consumer associations.

To make sure your urbanisation is legal and registered, ask to see the *Plan Parcial* approved by your *ayuntamiento,* the town hall. The *Plan Parcial* is not a partial plan, as it sounds, but the plan of *parcelas,* or building plots, which must be approved. This assures you that your urbanisation is legal. If the developer cannot show you this approved plan, you may have a problem.

If the development is on the beach, make sure it is approved by the *Jefatura de Costas* as well as the town hall. Spain's 1988 *Ley de Costas,* or Law of Coasts, empowers the authorities to restrict building and to control height and density within 100 metres of the high-water mark.

New properties

In the case of a new property, you want to make sure that the property has been declared to *Hacienda* for IBI *(Impuesto sobre Bienes Inmuebles* or annual real estate tax), as you can incur more fines for not registering it. Make sure that your developer has made a *Declaración de obra nueva,* a declaration of new building, and has paid the small tax associated with this, as well. Make sure that your *escritura* mentions the house you have purchased as well as the plot of land on which it stands. Sometimes the deed only refers to the land.

This makes you the owner of anything standing on the land, of course, but you may find yourself subject to taxes and fines relating to an undeclared building. Even worse, you may have bought an illegally constructed house which can never be registered because of zoning regulations. Check this at your town hall's *urbanismo* department (see below).

Sometimes, the purchase of an undeclared building can even work in your favour, but you will need expert advice to make sure you stay within the law. Once you are sure that the building can in fact be registered, you make a contract to purchase only the land from the seller. That's all he has title to, anyway.

The price for the land alone is much lower than the price for the land and house together, for a considerable saving on the property transfer tax of 6 per cent. You purchase the house separately by a private contract.

Then the new buyer makes the *Declaración de obra nueva,* just as if he himself has built the house. Building permits and other papers are necessary for this, but it can all be arranged, and the buyer will pay only one half of one per cent, compared to the transfer tax of 6 per cent. It has been done but sound legal advice should be taken because the plan will not work in all areas and situations.

PGOU – town plan

It is also important to have a look at the town planning maps of the area around you. A newly prosperous Spain is improving the road system all around the country. What if one of those highways is planned for the bottom of your garden? You can find out from the town's urban plan. This plan is called the *Plan General de Ordenación Urbana,* the PGOU for short. If you yourself cannot read plans, and few of us can, have your lawyer do it.

Before you sign anything

Before you sign anything in Spain, even a small reservation deposit agreement, there are some pieces of paper you should see. These include:

1. The seller's own title, known as the *escritura pública,* and a report from the Property Registry called a *nota simple.*
2. The paid-up receipt for his annual property tax, the IBI.

3. The *Catastral* certificate giving the exact boundaries and square metres of area.

4. Paid-up receipts for the annual fees of the community of property owners, the statutes of the community, and the minutes of the last AGM.

5. Paid-up receipts for all utility bills.

Escritura pública

The *Escritura Pública* is the registered title deed of the property. It is inscribed in the *Registro de la Propiedad,* the Property Registry, and it is the only iron-clad guarantee of title in Spain. If your seller cannot produce an *escritura pública*, something is wrong. In this title deed you will find a description of the property, the details of the owner. If any mortgages or court embargoes exist against the property, they will be registered here as marginal notes. You want to see the seller's title deed, if only to make sure that he really is the owner of the property being sold to you.

Your lawyer can obtain a *nota simple* from the Registry, containing the pertinent details and notes of any mortgages against the property. As of 2002, you can obtain a *nota simple* very rapidly on the Internet if you are entered in the Registry programme. However, it would be best if you could see a copy of the complete deed.

Strange things can happen with deeds. In one recent case, a widow was selling her property in Spain. However, living in another country, it had never occurred to her to declare the death of her husband in Spain, and his name was still entered on the title deed as half owner of the property. This was done in perfect innocence, because she simply considered herself the full owner of the property when her husband died.

By Spanish law a property held jointly in two names cannot be sold without the signatures of both parties. Because no one had seen the full *escritura* before the scheduled closing and final payment, the fact did not come to light until both parties were ready to sign at the Spanish Notary.

The signing had to be postponed for months until the widow could declare her husband's death, which had happened 10 years before, prove that she was the heir, formally accept the inheritance, re-register the property in her own name, and finally sign to sell it.

One fortunate consequence of her error was that she did not have to pay any Spanish inheritance tax, because the demand for the tax lapses after five years. Some people do this deliberately, but her lack of action was inadvertent.

All this inheritance settlement could have taken place early in the negotiations if the title deed had been available for examination. You will do well to insist on seeing the complete *escritura*. After all, it's important to know that the seller is really the owner of the property.

Check IBI receipt

One very important paper you must see before purchasing any second-hand Spanish property is the *Impuesto sobre Bienes Inmuebles* (IBI), the municipal real estate tax. When purchasing from the second or third owner, you must always ask to see the latest paid-up receipt for the IBI before you sign any contract with the seller. If not available, something is amiss. Really, you want to see the IBI receipts for the last five years, not just the current one, because you can be liable for five years of back tax.

Here again your lawyer or property consultant will have valuable advice. A new property bought from a developer will not have an IBI receipt yet and it will be your responsibility to register the property for this tax.

The IBI receipt will show the property's catastral reference number and also your *valor catastral,* the official assessed value of the property. This is a very important figure because various taxes are based on it (see section on Taxes). The assessed value is almost always considerably less than the real market value, but it has been steadily raised over the last few years.

Your annual real estate tax is charged by the municipality, It can be as low as €120 if you own a small cottage in a village, or as much as €2,000 a year if you own a new luxury villa on acres of land near Marbella.

A surcharge of 20 per cent will be added to the bill if it is not paid on time. You can arrange to have this bill paid directly through your bank, in order to avoid forgetting it. Fill out the forms authorising the bank to pay it and the tax people will send the bill directly to the bank. In many municipalities those who pay their IBI tax early get discounts of 10 per cent, and a standing order at the bank will ensure that this is done.

The current IBI receipt must be presented to the Notary at the signing of the contract, because it contains the *catastral* reference number, but you as the buyer want to see it well before that.

Referencia Catastral

Every property sale must include a mention of the *Referencia Catastral*. As noted above, this reference number appears on your IBI receipt.

The *Catastro* is a second system of property registration, concentrating on the exact location, physical description and boundaries of property, unlike the Property Registry, which focuses on ownership and title. The *Catastro* is also concerned with the valuation of property and is the source of the famous *valor catastral,* the assessed value of property for tax purposes.

These two systems, strangely enough, have never even communicated with each other, and we find that the *catastral* description of a property sometimes differs greatly from the one in the Property Registry.

As a first step in trying to bring the physical reality into line with statements people sometimes make in contracts, the Spanish authorities have begun to require that all property transactions now include at least a mention of the *Catastro* reference number in addition to the *escritura.*

It is a very good idea for the buyer to request the actual certification from the *Catastro* with a full description of the property. If it matches the data given in your contract, you are all right. If there are large differences, perhaps something is wrong.

The certification itself comes in two parts, one being a description in words of the property and the other being a graphic representation, either a plan or an aerial photo. Get both of them. It costs only a few euros, although it can take up to two months for the *Catastro* to deliver the certificates, so you had better start early.

It is astonishing how often the boundaries and square metres of a property can differ so much. This is because people through the years have simply accepted the vague descriptions made in the title deed, and do not check any further. Be warned that, when you ask the seller or the estate agent for this *catastral* certificate, they will pooh-pooh the idea, saying it is not legally necessary yet, although it will be in the future. Do not pay much attention to them. Insist on getting it, so you can be sure of your real boundaries and the real size of the property.

The Notary is also empowered to call attention to the fact that discrepancies exist between the *Catastro* and Property Registry descriptions. The buyer and seller can go ahead with their transaction, but they have been advised of the discrepancy.

Community fees, statutes and minutes of AGM

If you are buying a flat, a townhouse, or a villa on an urbanisation, ask also to see the latest paid-up receipt for community fees. These are the fees charged by your *Comunidad de Propietarios,* the Community of Property Owners, which is the Spanish term for "condominium", meaning the legal body that controls all the elements held in common. In a building this would be the lift, gardens and pool for example.

In an urbanisation, the community as a whole jointly owns the roads, gardens, pool, lighting system and other elements as well. Each owner is assigned a quota, or percentage of the expenses, which he must pay, by law. See the section on Communities for full details. Just remember that you become a member of the community, with legal rights and obligations, just by purchasing your property. Only those who buy a country property or a house on a normal street in a town will not have to deal with community problems.

The receipt for community fees assures you that the fees are paid and gives you a good idea of your monthly charges in the future.

Read the statutes, the regulations of the community, too, as they will be binding on you once you have signed the purchase contract. If the basic statutes that rule the community prohibit the keeping of pets in the building or on the estate, you will have real problems if you want to keep your dogs, for example. Get a copy of these statutes in a language you can read, even if the Spanish regulations are the only valid ones.

Then you want to see the minutes book, the official record, of the last annual general meeting of the community. Decisions are taken by majority vote of the owners at each year's AGM, and these actions are recorded in the minutes book, which is an official document. If you find that the principal point at last year's meeting was how to solve the community's chronic water shortage, then you will know you are going to have problems in your new house. Talk to the community president if this is possible. A well-run community can add thousands of euros to a property's value, and a community with problems is a source of endless aggravation.

Utilities bills

You want to see paid-up receipts for the owner's electricity, water, rubbish collection and even telephone. These assure you that the bills are paid and also give you an idea of what it will cost to run the place.

If you should get stuck with unpaid bills by the previous owner, be aware that these are personal bills from private companies. They do not attach to the property, only to the person who signed the electric or water company contract.

The company will insist that they will cut off the service if the bills are not paid. Let them cut it off. For a reasonable fee, you simply go into the company office and sign a new contract, starting fresh without the previous owner's bills. This fee is exactly the same as the charge for changing the electricity contract into your own name in any case.

Once you and your lawyer or adviser are satisfied with these checks into the situation of the property, and you and the seller have arrived at a price, you can factor into your calculations the amount of taxes and fees that will be paid on the transaction.

Transfer costs

What are the taxes and fees going to cost you? They will probably be less than 10 per cent of the purchase price if the breaks are with you, but can go as high as 15 per cent if certain taxes turn out to be higher than usual in your individual case.

You have two taxes and two fees to pay on the transfer of property. The two fees are for the notarisation of the deed and for its registry in the Property Registry. The two taxes are the transfer tax and a sort of capital gains tax on the increase in value of the land, usually called the *Plus valía* tax. This tax is a municipal tax.

Notary: You pay the *Notario* a fee fixed by an official scale. The fee varies according to the amount of land, the size of the dwelling and its price, but let's say between ¤350 and ¤600.

Property Registry: Then there is a fee for the inscription of the property in your name in the official *Registro de la Propiedad*. This will be a similar amount. Your lawyer or property consultant can tell you exactly how much these fees will be before you buy.

Transfer tax: The transfer tax, called *Impuesto de Trans-*

misiones Patrimoniales (ITP) in Spanish, is 6 per cent of the value declared in the contract for private sales. If you purchase new property from a developer, this tax will be IVA (value added tax) at 7 per cent because the sale is a business operation, not a private deal between two individuals. In addition to this, you pay a documents fee, or stamp duty, of one half of one per cent, so buying a new property will draw tax of 7.5 per cent.

In Andalusia the ITP is charged at 7 per cent and the documents fee has been raised from one-half of one per cent to one full per cent. This means total tax charged on a new property is 8 per cent and a re-sale will also be 8 per cent.

Plus valía: The other tax on property sales is the *Arbitrio sobre el Incremento del Valor de los Terrenos,* the municipal tax on the increase in the value of the land since its last sale. This is usually called the *Plus valía* for short, and it can vary widely. In the case of an apartment or a townhouse in a new urbanisation, where little land is involved and where there has been no real increase in value because such a short time has passed since it was developed, the tax can be very low. It will be much higher if you buy a house with several thousand square metres of land, which has not changed hands for 20 years and which has been recently re-zoned from rural to urban land, thus jumping greatly in value.

This tax is based on the official value of the land, which is always lower than the market value, and it varies from 10 per cent up to 40 per cent of the annual increase, depending on the length of time between sales and the town where it is located. The land is officially re-valued periodically for this purpose.

Do not confuse this *Plus valía* tax with the non-resident's 35 per cent capital gains tax on profits from the sale (see Tax section).

You can find out exactly how much your *Plus valía* will be simply by going into the municipal tax office in your town and asking. They keep the records there for each property and will be glad to tell you the assessed value, so you can find out in advance. Or have your lawyer or property consultant do it.

The *Plus valía* tax can be charged directly against the property itself, meaning that an unscrupulous seller might promise to pay it and "forget", leaving the new owner to pay it.

Who pays what?

In deciding who pays what, the buyer and seller are free to contract whatever terms they choose. There is no Spanish law which requires that one of the parties must pay any particular tax.

Traditionally, the seller has paid the Notary's fees and the *Plus valía* tax, as he is the one making the profit on the increase in the land's value, while the buyer pays the *Impuesto de Transmisiones* and the registry fee, as he is the one who is interested in making sure the property is truly registered in his name. Spanish consumer regulations state that this should be the normal division of costs.

It is a frequent practice, however, for the contract to state that the buyer will pay *todos los gastos,* all the expenses arising. There is nothing illegal about this. Remember that the two parties are free to make any contract they choose.

This practice, which may seem unfair to the buyer, has come about because tax bills, especially the *Plus valía,* have often gone unpaid, especially by non-resident sellers. By the time the new purchaser realised this, the seller was gone and the buyer stuck with the taxes anyway, as they were billed to the owner of the property if the seller did not pay. Charging the new owner with all the taxes is at least straightforward and avoids complications.

Nevertheless, you can use this point in negotiating your final price. If the contract you are offered states that you as the purchaser must pay all taxes and fees, you could suggest that the seller take something off the price.

How much to declare?

Formerly it was the practice to declare a ridiculously low amount for the value of the house, in order to minimise the transfer tax, but now Spanish lawyers advise sellers and buyers to declare the approximate market value, normally the real value of the sale. Spanish tax inspectors will make their own assessment if they feel the declaration is too low.

Spain's Tax Agency, *Hacienda,* maintains its own tables of values on property, and they are empowered to set a higher value on a sale if they judge the declaration to be under market value. More than one property purchaser has been disconcerted to discover that he has to pay extra taxes when he gets a new tax bill six months after the sale.

If in doubt, you can ask the tax office what value they will accept on any particular property. Inquire at the *Oficina Liquidadora,* the payment office at your nearest Tax Agency office, and they will tell you exactly what value they assign to your purchase. They base their valuation on a careful study of various factors, such as location, size, quality, age, and others. Or just do as more and more people are doing today and declare the actual amount of the sale.

Buyer beware: When you go to resell your property, you will be charged Spanish capital gains tax on any profit you make. If you are a resident, you pay it as part of your income tax with a maximum of 15 per cent. This rises to 18 per cent for 2007. If you are a non-resident, you face the 35 per cent capital gains tax on the profits you have made. The good news is that this tax drops to 18 per cent for 2007, the same as for residents. If you declare a low value now, you will be liable for tax on a much bigger profit when you sell later. It is in your own best interests, as the buyer, to declare the full amount of the sale (see section on taxes for more details).

The contract

Let's suppose that you have found a property that suits you, that all of the pre-purchase checks have satisfied you, and you have negotiated the price down to what you can pay. Keep in mind that very few sellers will not come down on the price. Make an offer and see what happens.

Terms of the sales contract will be your next concern.

Because most buyers take some time to assemble the cash needed for the purchase, it is usual for the buyer and seller to make a "private contract " first, with the buyer putting down a non-returnable deposit of, say, 10 per cent. This reserves the property while the buyer brings his money into Spain or perhaps obtains a Spanish mortgage. If the buyer fails to complete the sale, he loses the amount of his deposit.

If the seller finds another buyer in the meantime, willing to pay more, and sells the property, the first buyer can claim twice the amount of the deposit back.

Remember never to pay the deposit directly to the seller. Make sure that it goes into an escrow account, a blocked account called a Bonded Client Account, from which it will not be released until the sale is final. Insist on this.

The seller, through the estate agent, will certainly have a prepared private contract all ready for you to sign. The contract they offer may suit you perfectly, but it is quite likely that it will contain some clauses more favourable to the seller than to you, the buyer.

This is when you want your lawyer to read the contract and make suggestions.

It is a very good idea to have the contract made in Spanish, with a translation into English or German or your native language, so you can be absolutely sure about what you are signing.

Although most property sales between individuals follow this system of private contract and deposit, followed by closing and final payment, there is nothing binding about it. If you like the property and have the price ready, you can proceed directly to the Notary, pay over the full price, and get your title deed.

Escritura de compraventa

This private contract, although it sets out all the details of the agreement, such as payment terms and who pays what share of the taxes, is not the final document for the sale.

This final document is the *escritura de compraventa* and it must be signed by you and the seller in the presence of a *Notario* in order to make it legally binding. You can make a *poder* — a power of attorney — allowing another person to sign for you if you cannot be present (see section below for more on Power of Attorney). The Notary keeps the original document in his files in case any question arises later. The *Notario* is an official of the state, not a private lawyer, who makes sure that contracts are legal. His duty is to certify that the contract has been properly signed, the money paid, and that the purchaser and seller have been advised of their tax obligations.

He does not verify or guarantee the accuracy of the statements made in the contract. Too many people think that the *Notario* assures them that all statements made in the contract are true. This is not so. The Notary can, however, give useful advice to both parties.

Contracts can be quite simple or very complicated. If you are paying one lump sum and the property is to be delivered at once, there remains only the question of who is to pay the taxes and fees.

If you are paying in stages, there will be a number of further provisions in your contract, relating to the timing and amount of the payments. The buyer may find that the seller offers him a contract which states that he loses all sums paid out if he fails to keep up the payments, as well as having to vacate the property immediately. In fact, this is always negotiable. If a buyer who cannot keep up the payments takes his case to court, the court will almost certainly allow him to receive some of his money back in exchange for vacating the property, which he loses.

This will depend on how many payments the buyer has already made, for example. If he has already paid more than half of the full price, the court will not allow the seller to keep it all.

The buyer really needs a Spanish lawyer to make sure this sort of complicated contract is fair to him.

Power of attorney

A "general power of attorney" or *poder general,* is frequently used in Spain. The power comes in a standard form, which lists all of the actions that can be carried out by the holder. These include buying and selling property, handling bank accounts, spending and receiving money, taking out a mortgage or other loan, and just about anything that the granter of the power can himself, or herself, do with their assets.

The form contains a clause declaring that all of these actions shall be taken for the benefit of the granter of the power. This means that, if you decide to take the money and run, the granter has a case against you for defrauding him, if he can find you.

There are also other forms of power of attorney, limited to carrying out certain specific actions in the name of the granter, such as signing a contract for the sale of a specified property at a given price, during a given time period, after which the power lapses.

But the general power is the one most used, simply because situations change and unforeseen complexities arise in any transaction. This can mean that the holder of the power is unable to act because the power does not mention the specific circumstance which has arisen, such as signing at the bank to obtain the money transfer from abroad.

The wide powers of the general power of attorney avoid these problems. In an international property market, we often find that a seller or a buyer cannot be physically present at the moment of signing a purchase deed at the Spanish Notary, so he gives his lawyer or some other trusted person a general power of attorney to sign for him.

Once the deed is accomplished, the granter then revokes the power of attorney, again at the Notary, and all goes on as before.

A power of attorney can also be very useful for persons who have aged parents in Spain because it allows the child to manage the property and finances of the granter of the power. The only possible hitch is whether your aged parent wishes to grant you all of these powers. In the usual circumstances, however, the aged parent is only too glad to have all these matters taken off his hands.

You make the *poder general* at the Notary. Although it is always a good idea to consult a lawyer before taking any important legal step, it is not necessary. The Notary has the power of attorney forms, probably in his computer, which will print copies for you while the Notary himself retains the original authorisation. A reminder: you need copies authorised by the Notary in order to use the power of attorney at a bank or in a property sale. The simple copies you can also obtain are for information only.

The only documents necessary are the national identity document or the passport of the maker of the power. He will need the name and identity document or passport details of the holder.

The entire operation should not cost much more than €60. Yes, it all seems too simple and too cheap for such a wide-ranging document, but there you are.

The recipient of the power of attorney does not need to appear at the Notary. The document requires his signature, but he can do this at his own convenience. So the maker of the power can simply post it to the recipient.

Contract must describe property accurately

The contract must accurately describe the property being sold. This is one area where the *catastral* certificate is important. Too many buyers have discovered too late that their boundaries are not what they thought, and the hedgerow at the bottom of their garden, an obvious division, is not the legal line at all, but belongs to their neighbour. This sort of error does not necessarily imply bad faith on the part of the seller. He may have happily accepted the boundaries and square metres set out in his title deed, and never checked them.

Remember that we mentioned the *Registro de la Propiedad* is concerned mainly with ownership of property, while the *Catastro* is concerned mainly with the physical measurements and characteristics. The Property Registry is quite often wrong, so get the *catastral* certificate and be sure.

If you really have problems with boundaries, you should have an official surveyor, a *topógrafo,* come and survey the plot. On a transaction of €200,000, the €500 or so that he charges is very little.

Even those buying apartments will do well to measure their square metres of enclosed space and terraces, to make sure they match the description offered. It is astonishing how often the flat actually has fewer square metres than stated. If you discover this, it may make a bargaining point for getting the price down.

Buyers of rural land will certainly need a property surveyor to measure the land and identify its boundaries. In these cases, even the *Catastral* department may not have the correct data. The titles to many rural properties state only that the *finca* borders on the north with Juan García's farm, and that is simply not good enough.

Contract must identify buyer and seller

The contract must also fully identify the seller and buyer. Remember that the seller is the owner of the property, not the estate agent handling the deal. It is always a bad practice to make your cheque out to an agency. You should know exactly who the seller is and make your cheque directly to him. If the seller insists on anonymity, meaning a bearer cheque, make sure that no money changes hands until you are actually at the Notary, where you will sign the final contract.

Make your cheques out only to the name of the seller. In the case of reserve deposits before the sale is completed, and where you may never have met the absentee seller, insist that your cheque be deposited in an escrow account, a Bonded Client Account. Then the money can be paid out only to the seller and only when the specified time limit has elapsed.

Free of charges and liens

One extremely important item in your contract is the clause stating the property is sold free of all charges, liens and mortgages. Fine, you say, but how do you really know this is true? This is where your lawyer comes in. He can make a check at the property registry, the *Registro de la Propiedad,* where any such mortgages or liens must be registered against the *escritura.* The *Registro de la Propiedad* is an extremely important office for the property purchaser.

Any mortgage on the property must be registered there, and the true owner of the property is listed. For a small fee, the *Registro* will give you a *nota simple* for any property. This is a summary of the property's entry into the registry books, which would include a reference to any mortgages pending on the property.

Such a check-up can avoid problems. One horrible case occurred when a British owner returned to Spain to find that the house he had just bought had been seized by court order and auctioned off to pay an outstanding mortgage left by the seller. The locks had been changed and the house was no longer his. His only remedy was to sue the fraudulent seller for breach of contract and fraud. That is, if he could find him.

He could also have solved the problem if he had been aware that his property was under threat. If he himself had been present in Spain to receive legal notice of the coming seizure and auction, he could have arranged with the court to pay the mortgage, which attaches to the property itself, not to the previous owner.

Paying the mortgage would have been an unpleasant experience but much cheaper than losing the entire property.

Notices of such legal actions appear by law in the *Boletín Oficial,* the official legal gazette, and often in the local newspapers as well. If the new owner cannot be located by the court, these published notices constitute sufficient legal notice to make the seizure of the property correct in law. Overworked Spanish courts have been severely criticised for failure to make sufficient attempt to locate the absentee owners, but the practice continues.

A lawyer will also check to make sure that no back taxes are owed on the property and that its original registration is in order. Back taxes must be checked with *Hacienda* or the town hall. They are just about the only debts not listed at the Property Registry.

Final title and registration

In fact, even the *escritura de compraventa* contract does not fully assure your title until it is registered with the Spanish Property Registry, thus making it an *escritura pública,* a public document. It is, in fact, the same document, now registered and with the stamps of the *Registro de la Propiedad* on it.

Notice of the contract signed can be sent by fax directly from the Notary's office, at the time of signing, to the *Registro de la Propiedad.* This notification will ensure that no one else can register the property, until the full contract is presented at the Registry. Or you can have someone deliver the signed contract directly to the

Registry. Normally, this will be someone from the Notary's office.

You yourself will never have the original of your *escritura pública*. The original document is stamped at the Property Registry, which converts it from a sales contract into a public document, the famous *escritura pública,* which is your final and definite title, proof against all comers.

The document is then returned to the Notary, where it is kept safely on file. If you, or any official body, needs a copy of it, you request it from the Notary, who produces an authorised copy. The copy is what you take home.

In fact, you no longer sign the contract itself. In these modern times of easy and foolproof copying, the parties to the contract sign a blank sheet of paper, and the Notary keeps these samples in his files for later authentication when necessary. So, nobody can copy your signature from a copy of your title deed because it isn't there.

In cases where the same piece of property has been fraudulently sold two or three times, the purchaser who first has it registered will be the owner, regardless of the dates of the other sales.

Slow as the administrative bureaucracy may be, your deed should be registered within a few months. Usually your lawyer or whoever is handling the matter will ask you for a deposit of money in advance to cover the estimated taxes and fees, and will either bill you for the remainder or refund to you the overpayment when the deed is registered. This is normal and acceptable practice.

If the matter seems to drag on for months, you had better look into what is happening. There was a case a few years ago where one property consultant took people's money, put the cash into his own bank account and the *compraventa* deed into a drawer. He used his clients' money for a year or so, enabling him to make down payments on Costa del Sol property, and then, at last, presented the deeds for registry. The registry came through in due course and he notified his clients, who often got a small refund, which made them happy. Everyone mistakenly assumed that it took a year and a half for the registry to process the papers.

What can go wrong: unpaid mortgage

The reason for haste in delivering the sales contract to the Property Registry is simple. As long as the property continues to be registered in the name of the seller, he can use it to take out a mortgage, for example. The bank checks the Registry, finds the property correctly listed, and grants the seller a mortgage of, say, €120,000 on the villa valued at €180,000. He then disappears to some other country with the €120,000.

Our criminally-minded seller has prepared this operation well in advance with the innocent bank, but he does not execute it until after the sale has taken place, in the time between signing the *compraventa* contract and the new owner's registration of it as an *escritura pública*. Otherwise, the buyer would have found the mortgage listed against the property in the Property Registry when he got the *nota simple*. This is also why it is a good idea to get the *nota simple* immediately before signing the contract.

The unknowing buyer is perfectly happy with his new property, convinced that pre-purchase checks have assured that the title had no charges against it (which was true at the time).

Happy, that is, for a few years, until he suddenly discovers that the property has been sold at a court auction — *subasta* — without his having been informed, and the police are coming with a court order to put him in the street.

How can this be? The bank foreclosing the unpaid mortgage of €120,000 and repossessing the property will inform only the person registered as owner when the mortgage was taken out. The court has no reason to inform the new owner because he does not exist as far as they are concerned. They are repossessing the house of the person who failed to pay the mortgage. These cases have happened.

The buyer may find out about the mortgage because the bank in fact checks at the house and finds him there instead of the mortgage-holder. No matter how he protests, legally, the new owner has no case. The bank acted in good faith and their mortgage claim has preference. The only choice is whether to pay €120,000 more or to abandon the property. It's possible, of course, to bring suit against the seller to recover the money. If he can be found.

Such cases are rare, but they happen.

Method of payment

Give some thought to your method of payment. One point to consider is whether you are buying from a resident or a non-resident. In the old days before the European Union, property buyers had to pay Spaniards or residents in pesetas, and had to prove importation of foreign currency if they later wanted to export the money from Spain. With the lifting of exchange controls, this is no longer necessary, although a report must be made to the bank.

You can pay for your Spanish property in euros, through a bank cheque, from your Spanish bank, along with a bank certificate that you have imported foreign currency for this purpose. You can also pay by a cheque in foreign currency. Or you can pay by direct transfer from your foreign bank to the seller's foreign bank, so that no money enters Spain.

Certificate of non-Residence

If you wish to keep the money transfer completely undocumented inside Spain, you can do this, but you must then obtain a certificate of non-residence from the Spanish authorities. Be warned that this can take up to two months to obtain, and the Notary will not authorise the completion of the sale without it. If you file your bank certificate and use a normal cheque, this certificate is not necessary.

Five per cent tax deposit if you buy from non-resident

If you buy from a non-resident, you must deposit 5 per cent of the total purchase price with *Hacienda* in the seller's name, as a guarantee on his taxes.

You pay the seller only 95 per cent of the price. You pay the other 5 per cent directly to *Hacienda,* presenting Form 211 to justify your payment. The Notary will want to see your copy of Form 211, showing that you have made the payment and filed the form with the Tax Agency.

This amount serves as a guarantee against the non-resident seller's Spanish capital gains tax liability and for his payment of the annual Spanish wealth tax and non-resident property owner's imputed income tax. Non-resident owners of Spanish property are required to declare 2 per cent of the official rated value, the *valor catastral,* of their property as if it were income. They then must pay income tax on this imaginary income at a flat rate of 25 per cent (see section on Taxes for more details).

If *Hacienda* discovers that the non-resident seller has failed to keep up his yearly imputed income tax payments, they can retain this amount from the deposit of 5 per cent.

The deposit is mainly designed, however, to cover the non-resident's liability for Spain's non-resident capital gains tax of 35 per cent on his profit. This tax drops to 18 per cent in 2007. See Taxes on Property for details.

Buying off-plan

In theory, buying Spanish property off-plan sounds like a very attractive proposition. It means that you start to pay for the property when you have only seen the plans, even before construction begins.

Because you are paying up front, you can save a good deal of money at the end. The builder gives you favourable terms because you are financing his project, and the flat is worth perhaps 25 per cent more when it is finished, a year or more later.

When prices are rising rapidly, off-plan purchase also becomes an attractive investment. Investors make the first payments with the intention of selling on the contract, even before the flat is finished, for a quick profit of 15 or 20 per cent. Perhaps they should be called speculators in this case. Thousands of buyers, both Spanish and foreigners have taken advantage of the plan, sometimes in fast-growing cities and sometimes in the coastal areas.

However, a thousand things can go wrong with off-plan buying, so it is best to be cautious.

A recent study shows that more than 80 per cent of all new properties in Spain are delivered late, sometimes very late, like six months or even a year. Further, more than half of all new properties have defects when they are occupied by their new owners.

So, what should you watch out for and what are your options if you find yourself in this situation?

First, you want to make sure that the builder actually has a building permit. This is so basic that buyers can be forgiven for not thinking of it. There have been cases where the project never started because the developer had begun selling properties before he was able to obtain the permit.

Your purchase contract must state a delivery date, meaning that you can take occupation of the premises, with all work finished and all legal documents in order.

Spanish law specifies that a purchase contract must contain a date of delivery. What you as the buyer want is a specific date, such as January 3, 2008, with a penalty clause obligating the seller to pay a certain amount of money for each day he is late.

In practice, sellers often ignore this completely or fudge it by putting in a clause which says the property will be delivered within 90 days after the issuance of an extremely important document called the First Occupation Licence, the *Licencia de Primera Ocupación*. This is issued by the municipal building department when they verify that all requirements are met for inhabiting the building.

This licence can be delayed for a number of reasons. In one recent case, the new building was located in a recently developed zone where the town had failed to complete some of the necessary services, such as access roads. This meant that the first occupation licence was not forthcoming from the town hall, which gave the builders their excuse for late delivery.

There is little you can do about late delivery if you do not have this clause. Of course you have the final protection of the money-back guarantee. This clause states that, if the property is not delivered to you under the conditions of the contract, you have the right to your money back. The builder is obliged by law to hold bank guarantees for this amount.

This sounds fair enough but you don't want your money back. You want the property, because you have paid, say, €200,000 over the preceding two years but the property today is worth €250,000 or more. The builder will be only too happy to refund your money and re-sell the property at today's price.

Under these circumstances, all you can do is grit your teeth and wait, with the consolation that your flat is rising in value every moment.

Another option might be to strike a deal with the developer to occupy the flat without the first occupation licence. In cases where the property was complete and ready to live in, but the licence was delayed for some outside reason, thousands of flat-buyers have talked with the promoter and simply moved in. Some of them have continued to use the builder's electric and water supply for up to a year before the paperwork was complete.

Watch these points for any new property

1. When you first look at a new property, the developer must show you the plan of the apartment, the plan of the building and gardens, and the construction specifications, the *memoria de calidades*. These specifications will form part of your purchase contract, and you have recourse if they are not met.

2. By law, the information offered in any advertising material for the flat forms part of the contract. That is, if the photo shows a pool and gardens and these are not provided, you have action against the seller.

3. All amounts paid to the developer must be guaranteed by a bank. The developer must show you the document for this. He may not charge you a fee for it.

4. At the very beginning, the developer must provide a copy of the contract you will sign so that you can study it.

5. Make sure the contract includes a provision that the developer pays his own *Plus valía,* a municipal tax on the increase in value of the property.

6. The developer or builder will probably offer you a mortgage which he has already constituted on the property. You may choose to accept this or handle your own arrangements. You may not be charged a cancellation fee if you do not accept the builder's mortgage.

7. Under Spain's recent building laws, the developer is responsible for any finishing defects for one year, any minor defects in the apartment for three years and for structural defects during 10 years.

Finally, it is always wise to use a Spanish lawyer, if only to vet your contract.

Property purchase check-list

1. Advice from a Spanish lawyer or property consultant.

2. The seller's *escritura pública,* or title deed, as registered in the *Registro de la Propiedad.*

3. A *nota simple* from the Property Registry, showing that no mortgages are registered against the property.

4. *Referencia Catastral.* The number itself appears on the IBI receipt, but you want the full certification document, the *Certificado Catastral,* that describes the property in detail.

5. A check on the legality and *Plan Parcial* if you buy in an urbanisation, and assurance of a building permit if you buy a plot.

6. A paid-up receipt for the *Impuesto sobre Bienes Inmuebles,* or the *Declaración de obra nueva.*

7. Receipt for paid-up community charges and a copy of the statutes if you buy in a condominium.

8. Copies of owner's bills for electricity, water, rubbish collection

and even the telephone.

9. A contract, in Spanish, and a translation into your own language, with terms you understand.

10. A decision about your form of payment, whether in euros or other currency, and be sure to insist on declaring the full amount.

11. An *escritura de compraventa* signed before a *Notario*.

12. Payment of fees and taxes, and the 5 per cent deposit to *Hacienda* if you buy from a non-resident, using Form 211.

13. An idea of how and when you will get your final *escritura pública,* which makes you the real owner.

Buying without *escritura*

Sometimes the seller does not have an *escritura pública,* for perfectly legitimate reasons, or at least for reasons which will not affect you, the purchaser. Perhaps he has not completed his own purchase yet, or it has taken a longer time than usual.

One reason for owning property on a private contract only, without a public title deed, is that the property cannot be seized by the court in order to pay a debt of the owner. Only registered property can be attached by a court. Another reason is simply to avoid the payment of the transfer taxes and fees, which can total 10 per cent or even more of the value. A third reason is, of course, to conceal assets, either from a creditor or the tax man, or an ex-wife, for example. When the Property Register is checked, there is nothing listed under that name.

On the Spanish Costas, where there was a freewheeling property market for some years, many properties changed hands so quickly as buyers sought quick profits that they simply did not register them. They just waited for the next buyer to carry out all the formalities, thus avoiding transfer taxes.

It is possible that a house you fancy has had two or three owners in the last five or six years and that not one of them ever got his final *escritura pública*. It might be that the house does not legally exist, as it has never been declared to the tax authorities in a *Declaración de obra nueva*. The only legal document for the property simply refers to the plot of land and does not even mention the house.

Or you might buy a tract of land in the *campo,* the owners of which are seven brothers whose family has owned the land for a hundred years but never had a written document.

There are perfectly legal ways of solving all these problems.

Maybe you can have the piece of land made over to you by the original seller, three owners back. You yourself can make the *Declaración de obra nueva,* even though you did not build the house.

But be careful. If you want to establish the title through a series of private contracts, you may find that you are liable for quite a lot of back taxes, perhaps two or three *Plus valías* which have never been paid by the previous owners. This tax may be charged to the present owner of the property.

205 Procedure

One completely legal and frequently used solution for property which has no registered title at all is called a 205 procedure, after the number of the regulation which controls it. In this process, you obtain from the Property Registry what is called a "negative certification". This means that the Registry has searched its files and finds no registered owner for the property. Here again you will find the *Certificado Catastral* useful, because it will have an accurate physical description.

You then request that the property be registered in your name because you have bought it from whoever is the seller, who, in turn, justifies his title by whatever document or evidence he presents. This transaction must be published and posted publicly in case anyone wishes to protest. If no protest is made against your claim, at the end of about a year's time you will get a solid title.

If you are going to buy under these conditions, be sure to hold back a percentage of the price until the property is registered in your name. No matter how simple the procedure appears when you start, there is always the possibility of some unknown person coming forward with a claim to the title. There is an element of risk.

Expediente de Dominio

This process, roughly translated as an ownership proceeding, requires more time and expense than the 205 procedure, because it involves more investigation and court action. The *Expediente de Dominio* can also be used to establish title when the property is in fact registered, but in the name of a person who no longer claims it either because he has sold it to someone on a private contract, who has never registered the sale, or perhaps because the original owner has died. This will take about two years.

The claim must be published in the official bulletin and evidence taken in court. Finally, the court will rule on the title and it will be solid. There is always the chance of some nephew who should have inherited the property making a claim of his own against the present purchaser, and the court will decide where the best claim lies.

In any of these procedures to establish title and register the property, be warned that you will be unable to obtain any mortgage funding, and you cannot borrow against the property for two years after its registration.

In any of these cases, you need sound legal advice. Ask around among older residents for an *abogado* or an *administrador de fincas* or a *gestor* whom they trust.

Property owned by offshore company

You might be offered property already owned by an offshore company registered in one of the many "tax havens" around the world.

This means that the property is not registered in the name of the owner. It is registered in the name of a company located in Gibraltar or Panama or the Caiman Islands. The owner of the company owns the property.

These "tax havens" earn their name because they are legal jurisdictions where taxes on locally registered companies are nil or very small, and secrecy is assured from the owner's own tax jurisdiction.

The advantages are clear. When you sell your Spanish property, it is only the company that is transferred. The same company continues to own the same Spanish property, so no Spanish transfer taxes are charged. Only the offshore company has a new owner. The same applies for inheritance tax when the company is bequeathed to an inheritor. The offshore location charges no tax on this.

The disadvantages are that Spain, keenly aware of the tax loss, has placed a flat tax of 3 per cent per year on any property held by an offshore company. They have a list of tax havens. European Union authorities are also preparing to place restrictions on these companies, so it is becoming a doubtful proposition.

In the Spanish property boom of the 1980s, these companies became very popular, but they don't look so good now, in most cases, even though they remain perfectly legal.

As a buyer, you have a choice between purchasing the off-shore company itself or buying as an individual and paying the transfer taxes.

See section on Taxes for advantages and disadvantages of offshore companies.

Bank repossessions and auctions

After the 1989 crash of the Spanish property market, the sunshine coasts were littered with real bargains. Some of these bargains were on sale by people who could not keep up the payments on their property, some of them were offered at cut-rate prices by developers who were stuck with stock they couldn't sell, and some of them were villas and apartments that had been repossessed by banks.

Bank foreclosure of mortgages is one of the few Spanish legal procedures that works quickly and effectively. A few of the properties were even those seized by courts and sold at auction to satisfy a debt against the owner, as in several of the frightening examples we have seen earlier in this section.

The standard wisdom today is that all of these bargain properties have been sold, and the few remaining are those which are so undesirable that nobody wants them at any price. This is mainly true, but there are still some bargains available if you look for them.

One of the easiest ways to make a stab at buying a cut-price property is simply to walk into the offices of bank managers in an area where you would like to live. Go into the bank, say that you would like to speak with the manager about a business matter. He will probably speak English and he will probably receive you after a short wait. Say to him: "I am interested in buying a repossessed property. *Reposesión.* Do you have any on your books?"

You may be as astonished as I have been when he points to a stack of *escrituras* on his desk and says: "How about one of these?" If the bank is a bit more modern, he may punch up a list on his computer terminal and inquire about the price range that interests you. So, you look at the list and pick a villa or an apartment that seems promising. You view it, like it, and buy it from the bank for maybe half what it would fetch on the market. It can be that easy. Or you might find that banks in your area do not have anything that interests you.

So why aren't these properties already sold, you ask. Good question. The answer seems to be that banks simply don't know how to sell real estate. A few of them have established their own departments for selling their repossessed properties, but most of them just sit in the files until the court gets around to auctioning them off at official proceedings.

So, although the conventional wisdom is largely correct, more than a few decent properties still remain with the banks. If you are willing to make an effort to search them out, some great bargains are waiting for you.

Be prepared to haggle with the bank and be sure to have your lawyer help you. If the bank says they will take €120,000 for the property you are told is worth €150,000, offer them €90,000. Keep in mind that the next bank will also have some repossessions available.

If you really feel like getting into the system, you could even try the court-ordered auctions of property being sold to satisfy debts. These auctions, called *subastas,* can offer some incredible buys to those who get into the inside on how they work. Properties have been sold at one-tenth their real value, for example. Yes, in northern European countries this simply cannot take place, but under the Spanish system the court is obliged to take the highest offer, no matter how low, after the property has been offered several times.

You are right if you think that this system attracts abuses. In many courts, there are professional *subasteros* who work together, sometimes in collusion with corrupt court officials, to offer low bids. Later, these professionals split the take among themselves. They often assign the properties to third parties, who are not real buyers, but who also get their share of the profits once the property is sold on again.

Capital gains tax

Prices are rising more slowly and demand is lessening, but there are still profits to be made in Spanish property. Today's buyers need to be warned, however, that Spain has already removed an important deduction from its system of capital gains tax.

As of January 20, 2006, the reduction factor of 11.11 per cent per year for each year you owned your property up to 1996 has been removed. All other reduction factors on any asset at all have also been cancelled, retroactively, as it were.

This is bad news for long-term property owners. It means that all sellers of property can now apply only a coefficient of reduction that more or less matches the inflation rate, meaning that your

Spanish property purchase will certainly attract capital gains tax when you sell it, no matter how long you have owned it (see section on Taxes on Property for more complete information).

Financing your Spanish property

There are a number of ways in which you can finance your Spanish property, as you probably did when you first purchased a house in your own country. Mortgages of 20 and 30 years, along with mortgages of 100 per cent of the value of the property, are now available in Spain. For a non-resident buyer, the mortgage is usually limited to around 70 per cent of the valuation of the property.

Financing by the developer: Let's look first at financing which may be offered you by the developer of the project where you purchase. There are dozens of different schemes here and you should be wary.

The contract must stipulate the down payment, enumerate the following payments and state when such payments end. It will be clear from the total of these payments just how much the developer's financing will cost you in comparison to paying cash. If the difference is acceptable to you, you have a deal.

Make sure you know what happens if you miss a payment. There should be some provision which is not too harmful to you, allowing you to make a certain number of late payments for only a small penalty.

Another essential provision will allow you to pay off the remainder of the contract in a lump sum at any time you choose, without having to pay the total remaining interest. You might at a future date come into money, enabling you to make such a payment. Or you may wish to pay off your terms with the developer in order to resell the property.

Developers often offer excellent terms to purchasers who begin their payments before the building is finished. This can be favourable to the buyer, but he must be sure that the developer is reliable and solvent, and can bring the project to completion.

Yes, we recommend that you use a Spanish lawyer, under *all* circumstances. Follow the old legal axiom: the seller may not need a lawyer, but the buyer always does.

Bank loans and mortgages

You as a non-resident can qualify for a Spanish mortgage to purchase your sunshine holiday home, but you will find interest rates in Spain and the euro zone rising steadily from their rock-bottom rates.

The Central Bank of Europe raised the base lending rate, the Euribor, in March of 2006 to 2.75 per cent and all predictions pointed to continuing small rises for the immediate future. This means mortgage rates in Spain must rise.

Until recently, Bankinter, one of the banks concentrating on Internet operations, offered a variable-rate mortgage locked into 3.5 per cent for the first five years. After that the rate is Euribor plus 0.35 per cent. The Euribor is the base interest rate set by the European Central Bank, as the Libor is the London rate set by the Bank of England, used as a base for lending in the UK.

That bargain rate is no longer available, but rates under 5 per cent are normal and banks are competing for mortgage customers. You will still find your Spanish property rising in value. If your property appreciates at, say, 10 per cent in today's market, and your mortgage rate is 5 per cent, you are making money. Even more satisfying, you are making money on the bank's money.

Fixed, variable, or mixed? This can be confusing. Should you take a mortgage with an interest rate that is fixed for, say, 20 years? Or should you choose a mortgage which has an interest rate that varies along with the central bank base rate? Perhaps you should pick one of the mixed products, like the first one offered by Bankinter, where the rate is fixed for the first few years and then changes each year as the central bank adjusts the base rate.

Most Spanish banks will mortgage no more than 70 per cent of assessed value for a non-resident buyer. Some will go to 80 per cent. This means you will need a substantial down payment for your Spanish property.

Two magic words: In addition to all this financial strategy, you will need to examine a Spanish mortgage contract carefully to determine the opening commission, the closing commission, the survey fee, whether you are required to take a life insurance policy for the value of the mortgage, study charges and other fees. If these charges are high, they can spoil the effects of a low interest rate.

This is when you need to learn the two magic words that will help you and your financial advisers sort it out. These words are "oferta vinculante", a binding offer. Spanish consumer regulations oblige the bank to present you with such an offer, which lists every term in the mortgage contract. The offer is binding on the bank and is valid for 10 days. This gives you time to study the offer. If you get two or three of these offers from different banks, you can compare them.

The offers will list such items as:

Tipo nominal – This is the listed interest rate.

Tipo anual efectivo - This TAE is the real effective interest rate, taking into account that your charges and fees reduce the real amount of money available to pay for your property.

Opening commission – This is often charged at one per cent of the amount of the mortgage, though some of the new offers charge half of one per cent or even less.

Evaluation charge – This is for the property surveyor's report by which the bank decides the value of the property for mortgage purposes. Figure around €300-€500.

Redemption penalty – This is the cancellation charge for early repayment of the mortgage in its entirety. This commission is usually about one per cent but it varies. It is based on the amount remaining.

Home insurance: You may be required to take out home insurance through the bank.

Cancellation fee, too: Even when you have paid off your mortgage, you have one final responsibility. You must make sure that the mortgage entry in the Property Registry is cancelled. If you do not, your inscription will continue to show that a mortgage is outstanding. The bank will handle this but you must remind them, and pay the fee.

Life insurance: It is quite common for the bank to insist on your taking a life insurance policy through them to cover the amount of the loan.

Mortgage insurance: This is a new development in Spain, with only some of the new offers incorporating a scheme which insures the mortgage repayment if the holder loses his job or falls ill. You can also insure your mortgage against sharp rises in the interest rate. It costs extra, of course.

Spanish banks and building societies make no formal distinction between mortgages and re-mortgages, and the idea of a buy-to-let mortgage does not exist. If you wish to re-mortgage a property you already own, the bank will study your ability to re-pay the loan just the same as mortgage to purchase. You are always free to change your mortgage from one bank to another, and Spanish law has recently lowered the charges for this change.

In addition to the costs noted above, you will have a notary fee and a Property Registry fee. The mortgage is a legal document and must be signed by you and the bank's representative before the Notary. The mortgage is also a property document and must be registered in the Property Registry against your property.

This list of charges sounds quite daunting and many property purchasers have been upset to discover that they actually receive €8,000 or €10,000 less than the amount. Prepare yourself and do the numbers.

Subsidised housing

In Spain, as in most countries, the government subsidises some types of housing. Ordinarily, this housing is destined for the poor and is offered to them on favourable terms.

Such housing is known in Spain as VPO, or *Vivienda de Protección Oficial*. You may think that this housing is not meant to help well-to-do foreigners purchase vacation homes, and you would be right. But there are several classes of VPO projects. One class, operated by the Spanish government, is available only to the poor, who must make a declaration of poverty in order to obtain it.

The other class, more frequently seen, is based on the provision of cheap government financing to the project developer, and these apartments are available to foreigners, although controls are becoming stricter. Purchasers now must be residents and they cannot have incomes of more than about €1,500 a month.

Nevertheless, especially if you are an EU citizen and an official resident of Spain, earning a living here, with a modest income, you may qualify for government assistance in buying your home, just as Spaniards do.

Remember, when purchasing VPO flats, the offer will stipulate that you make a very small down-payment, but if you can make a larger payment of €20,000 or so, and thus totally clear the constructor's own financial contribution to the project, this will be very advantageous. The balance, payable over 15 years or more on favourable terms, will then repay only the cheap government loan and not contribute further to the constructor's profit.

There are, of course, controls on the resale of such flats, which block speculators profiting at the expense of the government.

Insuring your home

As in any country, it is sound practice to carry homeowner's insurance protecting you against damage to the building itself, damage or theft of its contents, and against claims from others who may suffer injury or damage resulting from your ownership.

This is especially important when you are absent from your Spanish property for long periods, but be alert to clauses in your contract which render your insurance invalid if you are away from the property for more than a stated period of time. Often, by paying an extra premium, you can be covered even though you are absent much of the time.

Both Spanish and international insurers offer various policies at various prices. Make enquiries among older residents to find a company which has given good service.

You fill out a form in which you state a value for your house and its contents. Remember that, should you choose to insure your property for only half its real value, the insurance company, which makes its own evaluation, will pay you only half the value of any individual items which are stolen or damaged. People sometimes think they can insure half and then get full value when only two or three items are stolen or damaged, but this is not so.

The company will also ask you to report on whether your property will be unoccupied for lengthy periods, how old the building is, how many doors and windows there are, whether they are guarded by *rejas* (iron bars), if there is a burglar alarm system, and so on. If you do not respond truthfully to these questions, there can be grounds for a later denial of any claim you make. Your premiums will vary according to your situation.

Be sure to read the fine print in your policy. Often, insurance against theft of the contents of your property will not pay unless entrance has been forced and there is evidence for this. If a "guest" at one of your parties makes off with your wife's jewels, you will not be paid. If there is no copy of the contract available in your language, have someone translate for you.

What will insurance cost you? Policies and conditions vary, but you can estimate that about one euro per year per thousand euros of value will cover the building itself against damage by natural causes or fire or explosions if the building is in a town. An older house in the country, far from fire-fighting services, would cost more.

Insurance of your furniture and household effects will be somewhere around €2.50 per thousand euros of value if you live in an apartment; up to €3.50 per thousand if you live in a detached villa. This covers fire and theft.

If one of your steps collapses and the postman breaks his leg, or you leave the bathtub water running until your downstairs neighbour's apartment is flooded, they can claim compensation from you as the owner. You can cover yourself for claims up to €50,000 for less than €20 a year.

Most Spanish companies offer a comprehensive policy covering the building, the contents and third party claims. One company quoted a figure of €1,200 per year for comprehensive coverage of a villa and contents valued at €240,000. An apartment or townhouse would be less costly.

Timeshare law

A comprehensive Spanish law regulates important legal aspects of timeshare itself and provides consumer protection that brings the country into line with European timeshare regulations.

Putting a crimp into the high-pressure selling techniques of the timeshare touts around bus stations and tourist spots, the law provides a 10-day cooling-off period during which no deposit may be taken and the buyer can withdraw from the contract he has signed without any penalty.

Furthermore, the law requires that the timeshare operator provide full information and a contract in the buyer's own language. If any element of the purchase does not meet the brochure or written description or match the contract terms, the buyer has a further three months to rescind the contract unilaterally with no penalty.

The law also provides that any loan which the buyer may have taken out to purchase the timeshare will also be cancelled. This has been one tricky aspect of hard sales, in which the timeshare seller offers a low-interest loan to the prospective buyer. All well and good, but if the buyer later wants out of his contract, he finds that he still owes the loan to the bank, a third party, and it must be paid off. This practice is ended by the new law.

The law also provides that all contracts will be subject to Spanish law. That is, even if the buyer's contract states that its terms are subject to the laws of some distant offshore jurisdiction, where the timeshare company's headquarters is located, this provision is not valid and the contract will be subject to interpretation in Spanish courts.

This has been a thorny point in many timeshare contracts because the buyers found it difficult to dispute any point when the court was thousands of miles away.

Even the service companies which maintain the resorts have, until now, often been registered in offshore tax havens. This made it difficult for timeshare buyers to bring action against the companies when they failed to keep the resorts in good condition.

Under terms of Spain's new law, the service companies must have a permanent establishment registered inside Spain, where they can be held legally responsible.

Furthermore, the new law makes the resort owner finally responsible for proper maintenance of the resort, and action can be taken against the resort owner if the service company fails to perform.

On the other hand, the resort operator can repossess an owner's holiday weeks if the owner fails to pay one year's maintenance charges. The operator must give 30 days' certified notice before he can do this, and, unless this right is specifically renounced in your contract, he must pay back the owner the value of his remaining weeks in the scheme.

That is, a timeshare plan may run from a minimum of three years to a maximum of 50 years. If an owner has used his weeks for 25 years in a 50-year plan, and then defaults, the operator must pay him back half of his original price, as well as assuming the debt owed by the owner to the service company.

However, it is also possible for the timeshare contract to contain a penalty clause which will let the company keep the entire amount originally paid. Watch out for this clause in your timeshare contract.

The law also provides that timeshare contracts can be registered in Spain's Property Registry as a special right, although the law is also very careful to note that timeshare is not a property right as such, that it is a service contract not a property sale.

The full name of the law in fact is The Law Regulating the Rights of Rotational Enjoyment of Real Estate for Touristic Use, and it forbids any mention of property rights in timeshare publicity.

Unfortunately, the law does not mean that all timeshare sales are now regulated and controlled to protect the consumer. Timeshare companies have already come up with new schemes relating to "vacation plans" and "point systems" to move their products out of the area controlled by the law.

Expropriation of property

For most people, any improvement of the road system or flyovers and bypasses to increase safety is good news.

It may not be such good news if your property borders a projected highway or is affected by a new bypass, because the authorities — represented by a public works department such as the *Ministerio de Obras Públicas y Transportes* (MOPT) — can expropriate your property and put you off it.

They must pay you, of course. The doctrine of *justiprecio* applies, meaning they must pay you a fair price. You may have to fight them to get it, however.

There are legal avenues open to you to protect your rights in the matter.

First, the authorities must officially inform you that expropriation proceedings are about to begin against you. They will send you an official letter inviting you to attend the *acta previa a la ocupación*. This is a hearing, usually held in your town hall, at which you may present any protest you have about the extent of your property being expropriated.

Money is not discussed at this first hearing, only the amount of land being taken. You should take skilled legal counsel with you when you go to this hearing.

If the authorities are only interested in a few square metres of your vast *finca*, then you have no real problem. If, however, they want to put the road through the kitchen and reception area of your popular restaurant, or if the amount of land they take will leave you with too few square metres to be buildable, then there must be some negotiating.

In such a case, some lawyers advise that you attempt to make the authorities expropriate your *entire* property and not just part of it. This obviously is because the property, once divided, becomes all but worthless and such a situation is manifestly unfair to the person involved.

In these negotiations, the authorities are usually reasonable and fair, but they will be even more fair and reasonable when confronted by skilled counsel.

Your chances of resisting expropriation altogether are very poor indeed. The entire concept of expropriation or Eminent Domain exists because sometimes the public good takes precedence over private ownership. They are going to build the highway and your chance of moving the route away from your private property is very small.

Once the amount of land being expropriated is agreed, the authorities take the situation under analysis and then communicate their offer of payment to each owner. If the offer is acceptable, you inform them and the deal is done.

If, however, as is more frequent, you are not satisfied with their offer, you negotiate again. The doctrine of *justiprecio* is not just a word and it can be enforced. You will need to prepare a case for a higher price on your property, including sales prices of land around you, improvements you have made, and so on. You will need expert advice for this.

If you are unable to come to an agreement with the authorities by negotiation, you have recourse to the *Jurado de Expropiaciones,* which is a special court set up for this purpose only. The presiding members of this tribunal are not only judges; real estate experts are also included, and decisions it has rendered have ensured that fair market value is paid to many owners.

Beyond that, you can appeal this tribunal's ruling to the normal courts all the way up to the Supreme Court.

To sum up, in any expropriation proceedings, you have little chance of resisting entirely the order. But you do have two opportunities to protest both the amount of land being taken and the payment offered. Skilled counsel can make sure your interests are protected.

GLOSSARY

Abogado – lawyer, solicitor
Administrador de fincas – licensed professional property administrator
API – Agente de la Propiedad Inmobiliaria – real estate agent, member of long-established association.
Arbitrio sobre el Incremento del Valor de los Terrenos – municipal tax on property sales, see *Plus valía.*
Boletín Oficial – Official state gazette, where laws are published
Catastro – Land Office, concerned with measurements and physical description

Certificado Catastral – *catastral* certificate describing land and buildings

Comunidad de Propietarios – Community of Property Owners

Contrato – contract

Declaración de Obra Nueva – declaration of new construction

Escritura de Compraventa – sales contract

Escritura Pública – registered title deed

Expediente de Dominio – ownership proceeding, to establish title

Factura – bill

Finca – any plot of land or property

Gestor – licensed administrative expert in Spanish procedures

GIPE – *Gestor y Intermediario de Propiedades y Edificios,* title awarded by association of estate agents and property administrators.

Hipoteca – mortgage

Impuesto sobre Bienes Inmuebles (IBI) – annual real estate tax

Impuesto de Transmisiones Patrimoniales (ITP) – Property Transfer Tax

IVA (Impuesto sobre el Valor Añadido) – Spanish value added tax, charged when developer sells new property to first buyer

Jurado de Expropiaciones – special tribunal for expropriations

Justiprecio – doctrine of fair price by the state in forcible purchase

Ley de Costas – law protecting coastline

Ley de Tasas – law of public fees

Ministerio de Obras Públicas y Transportes (MOPT) – Ministry of Public Works and Transport

Nota Simple – certificate of registration from Property Registry

Notario – Notary

Plan General de Ordenación Urbana (PGOU) – town development plan

Plan Parcial – plan of building plots on urbanisation

Plus valía – municipal tax on property sale

Poder – power of attorney

Registro de la Propiedad – Property Registry

Reja – iron grillwork protecting windows and doors

Reposesión – repossessed property

Subasta – auction

Subasteros – professional auction buyers
Tasación – evaluation of property
Tasador – property surveyor, evaluator
Topógrafo – property surveyor
Urbanismo – town planning department
Valor catastral – assessed value of property for tax purposes

SELLING YOUR PROPERTY

4

TAX WARNING   *79*

PROPERTY SELLER'S CHECK LIST   *80*

1. YOUR REAL ESTATE AGENT   *80*

2. YOUR SPANISH LAWYER   *81*

3. THE SALES CONTRACT   *83*

4. HOW MUCH YOU DECLARE   *84*

5. ASSEMBLE YOUR DOCUMENTS   *84*

ESCRITURA PÚBLICA   *85*

IBI RECEIPT   *85*

CATASTRAL CERTIFICATE   *86*

INCOME TAX DECLARATION   *86*

NON-RESIDENCE CERTIFICATE   *87*

TAXES AND FEES   *87*

COMMUNITY CHARGES AND FEES   *88*

UTILITY BILLS   *88*

Tax warning

Sellers of Spanish property should be aware that they are subject to Spanish capital gains tax on the profits from their sale, whether they are resident or non-resident.

Furthermore, a sale of Spanish property attracts transfer costs that can total as much as 20 per cent of the price, in addition to that capital gains tax.

In some areas, real estate agents charge commissions of 10 per cent, although the Spanish estate agents' association recommends

3 per cent. Add to this taxes and costs that total about 10 per cent and you are looking at some very high transfer costs.

Non-residents pay capital gains tax at a flat rate of 35 per cent on their profit from the sale. This will drop to 18 per cent in 2007. The Spanish Tax Agency requires that a buyer from a non-resident withhold 5 per cent of the price and pay it directly to the Tax Agency. Residents pay a maximum of 15 per cent, with the tax calculated as part of their income tax. Resident tax will rise to 18 per cent in 2007, the same as the non-resident. Residents are not subject to the withholding of 5 per cent.

You may be exempt from capital gains in two cases:

1. You are 65 years old, a resident, and you have lived in your home for a minimum of three years.

2. You are resident and you use the full purchase price to buy another principal residence in Spain.

For full details on taxes involved in selling property, see the following section, Taxes on Property.

PROPERTY SELLER'S CHECKLIST

1. Your real estate agent

First, read the section on Estate Agent in the previous chapter, Buying Property.

One rule often cited by those who have sold their homes in Spain is: Don't try to do it yourself. Get an estate agent, or several, and let them handle the showing of the place and dealing with prospects. Otherwise, you go crazy. There may be exceptions to this rule, but most sellers are in agreement.

Very seldom do Spanish estate agents demand the exclusive right to market your property, so you will probably list your sale with several agents in your area. Each agent will have his own form of agreement with you, in which his commission is stated if he brings the client who eventually buys your property. This agreement will contain the commission charged. Some agents charge as high as 10 per cent. Five per cent is more frequent. You make your own deal on this.

An agent can help you get your price right. He will know what the market is in your area. You can then decide if you want to put a higher price and wait longer to sell, or a lower price in order to attract an immediate buyer. Be warned that an agent will not work very hard to market your property if he thinks it is overpriced and unlikely to sell.

A good estate agent will see you through the entire process of finding a buyer, negotiating the price, making the contract, securing the payment, signing before the Notary, paying the necessary taxes, and all the other details that arise.

The usual sequence is:

1. Seller and buyer to agree all the details of the purchase on what is called a "private contract", at which time the buyer makes a substantial deposit, usually 10 per cent.

2. This deposit takes your property off the market and holds it while the buyer assembles the full amount of the purchase price, either from his own resources or by obtaining a mortgage. If the buyer does not complete the sale, he loses his deposit. If you, the seller, accept a higher offer in the meantime, you have to return double the amount of the deposit. Be warned. It is astonishing how often an apparently serious purchaser is unable to come up with the cash. Don't count your chickens before they have hatched. Be warned also that many buyers will try to make stage payments and get possession. If they do not complete the payments, you will have plenty of trouble getting them out and recovering your property. (See section below on on Lawyers).

3. When the two parties are ready to complete the sale, they go to the Spanish *Notario* and sign the sales contract at his office. The contract can also be signed by proxy. This often happens with an absentee seller. He gives his lawyer a power of attorney, called a *poder* in Spanish. This *poder* empowers the attorney to sign in the name of his client. A seller who does not wish to return to Spain can even make this proxy at the Spanish consulate in his own country (see Power of Attorney section in Buying Property chapter).

4. This sales contract is stamped by the *Notario* and it should be immediately taken to the Property Registry office, where it is converted into the famous *escritura* — the title deed. The contract is called an *escritura de compraventa,* a purchase contract, and the title deed is called an *escritura pública,* because it is a registered document of public record. They are exactly the same document, before and after its registration. The original deed is then kept at

the Notary's office. You yourself never have it. You have only an official copy.

It is only this public deed that makes the buyer the new owner, with a title proof against all comers. Discuss the entire procedure step by step with your agent, so you know what is going on at each stage.

The steps listed above are the most usual form of property transactions, but there are many possible variations. If your buyer has the cash ready and you have your title deed clear, there is no reason why you cannot go directly to the Notary and complete the sale immediately, for example.

Don't forget that you want a proper bill — a *factura* — from your estate agent, listing the amount of the commission and adding 16 per cent IVA to this sum. Make this clear at the beginning of the transaction. The entire amount is deductible from your profit as a legitimate expense when you go to calculate your capital gains tax.

2. Your Spanish lawyer

Conventional wisdom says that the buyer always needs a lawyer but the seller may not. We say that the seller, in the complex world of international property transfer, really ought to have a lawyer, too. Your estate agent may be perfectly competent, but complications can arise outside his area of expertise. It is always good to have two people working for you as well so you can compare and contrast their views.

For example, some "buyers" will make you an offer of renting with option to buy but their sole intention is getting a cheap rental. They pay you a low rent, and then they stop paying the rent altogether, and then they leave. They never had any intention of buying the place. And it isn't worth the expense for you to try to collect the last three or four months of rent that they didn't pay, even if you could find them. Furthermore, your property has been off the market for six months or a year.

So, when the term of option to buy is mentioned, you or your lawyer or your estate agent should be aware that it ought to mean that the buyer pays you €10,000 or €15,000 for this option, which will be deducted from the total price when they purchase. If they let the time limit of the option expire, which might be two or three months, they forfeit what they have paid for it.

For all our dire warnings throughout this book, the majority of property transfers are quite clear-cut and no problems arise. Very few turn into nightmares.

Lawyer's fees vary widely. You can take one per cent of the purchase price as a guideline for a standard property transfer. Get this clear with your lawyer before you even start. Ask him how much he will charge you. Your legal fees are also deductible from your profits as a necessary expense in realising your capital gain. Again, you need a bill with Spanish IVA charged at 16 per cent.

3. The sales contract

Your lawyer will also explain to you some things not expressed specifically in the contract.

For example, your contract may state that your buyer pays €50,000 now and takes possession of the property, paying another €30,000 after three months and another €30,000 after an additional three months to complete a total price of €110,000. If he fails to meet any payment, he forfeits the amount already paid and the property returns to you. He promises to vacate immediately. You don't like the idea of the stage payments, but you feel safe because of this clause in your contract.

Your lawyer will warn you that this clause is not strictly enforceable and matters will not turn out so easily if the buyer fails to complete payment. If the buyer can't pay and refuses to leave, you will have to go to court to resolve your contract and get your property back. It will not happen automatically.

The court will probably rule that you indeed get your property back, but that you can't keep all of the money the buyer has already paid you. After the court makes its own calculation of how long the buyer has been in the house, plus inconvenience to you, and a series of other factors, it will decide that you can keep, say, half of the money already paid. Then, after this procedure has dragged out for months, you can again take possession of the property and start again on the process of selling it. This is only one of the many complications that come up in property transactions.

Some other points you want to study beforehand will be the division of payment of the transfer taxes and fees. Will you follow Spanish tradition and charge the Notary and the *Plus valía* tax to the seller and the transfer tax and the registration fee to the buyer? Or will you try to make the buyer responsible for all charges in the transfer? What price will you declare, the real price or a lower figure? (See below for more details on these questions.)

A good contract will help you foresee and avoid some of these complications but even the best contract cannot protect you against every eventuality. The standard contract used by your estate agent is probably as good as any, but your lawyer may have suggestions to make in your own particular case.

4. How much you declare

It was formerly a common practice in Spain to declare a property sale at much lower than its real price, in order to save money on transfer tax and wealth tax later. The Tax Agency is now watching property sales much more closely, however. If they believe that your sale is undervalued — and they have their own tables of market values — they may send you a notice that your sale has been re-assessed by them, along with a bill for how much extra tax you owe.

Today, more and more contracts are declared at their real value. Furthermore, as buyers become more sophisticated, they have realised that a low declaration now means that they will show a larger profit on paper when they go to sell later, making them subject to a higher Spanish capital gains tax.

If you want to know exactly how much *Hacienda* thinks your property is worth, you can find out by asking at your regional *Oficina Liquidadora*. They will give you the amount listed in their own tables. Any attempt to declare a value under that figure will probably bring you a notice to pay more.

5. Assemble your documents

It will help your sale to go smoothly if you have all your documents in order before you even begin to advertise. It builds confidence in the possible buyer — and his own lawyer — to see all the right papers in order when they consider purchasing.

DOCUMENTS YOU NEED

Escritura pública: The most basic paper of all is your title deed, which shows that you are the registered owner of record with an incontestable title. In fact, you have probably never seen your real title deed. What you have is an authorised copy. Unlike some systems of property registration, in Spain it is not the piece of paper itself which counts; it is the inscription in the *Registro de la Propiedad,* the property registry office.

If you lose your deed, you can always get another copy from the Notary, where it is on file permanently. Listed on the inscription in the property registry are any liens, charges or mortgages against the property. Back taxes, however, are not listed.

Your prospective purchaser will get for himself a *nota simple* from the registry, which is an extract showing the basic information and any charges against the property, but he will want to look at your copy of the full deed in any case.

In a few cases, owners have their property only on a private contract and the house may not even be registered. If this includes you, don't panic. This can be solved in various ways, depending on the individual circumstances.

You can offer your buyer the possibility of a Regulation 205 procedure or a full-scale *Expediente de Dominio,* (see reference in previous chapter) in which a court will study the case, publish the proceedings, and finally issue a clear title to the property. You might even find a new buyer willing to run the same risks as you in order to avoid taxes, who will simply purchase the property on a new private contract.

Or you can register the property and pay the taxes.

IBI receipt: Your receipt for the paid-up *Impuesto sobre Bienes Inmuebles,* the Real Estate Tax, is an important item. The IBI receipt shows first that the estate tax is paid for this year. It would be a good idea to have the receipts for the last five years, to show good faith.

The IBI receipt also shows the amount of the *valor catastral,* the official assessed value of the property for tax purposes. This value is almost always less than the real market value, but they are gradually being raised. The IBI receipt also confirms that the house exists and is registered for taxes, which can be an important point when no *escritura pública* exists and the owner holds the property only by virtue of a private contract. Finally, the IBI must be presented when you sign the contract at the Notary because it also displays the number of the *referencia catastral,* which, since 1997, is a required part of the documentation in property transfers.

Referencia catastral: The Catastral Reference is the file number of the property's registration in the Land Registry, which in Spanish is called the *Catastro,* a word that exists but is rarely used in English.

Property is registered here by its measurements and boundaries and physical characteristics. The Property Registry is concerned with ownership and mortgages.

You are right if you think that it doesn't make sense to have two separate bodies — which don't even talk to each other — dealing with land and property registration. Now, even the Spanish authorities begin to agree with you and, as a first step, they require that the *catastral* reference number accompany any property transfer.

Furthermore, the Notary and the Property Registry office are now authorised to make note of the fact if there is any great difference in the physical description of the property given in the *Catastro* and the legal description given in the sales contract and title deed.

This difference might include the fact that the *Catastro* shows a four-bedroom villa and a swimming pool while the sales contract mentions only a plot of land at a very low price. It is yet to be seen just how effectively the Notary and the Registrar of Property will inform the tax office, but the way is now clear, so be warned.

It is a good idea for the seller to obtain the completely detailed *Certificado Catastral* and include it in his documentation. This will add to the prospective purchaser's confidence, and will make it absolutely clear what he is buying.

Land descriptions on title deeds are often quite vague, even misleading. The *Catastro* is usually more accurate, because they have been updating their information for some years now, sending inspectors to check the physical reality of land and houses, and using aerial photographs as well.

It can take several months to obtain the certificate. There is a small fee.

Income tax declaration: If you are resident, and so not subject to the retention of 5 per cent of the price, you may be required to present your most recent income tax declaration when you sign the contract at the Notary. The income tax declaration is as important as the residence permit in proving your tax status in Spain.

If you are a non-resident, the buyer may want to see your current Form 214, on which you declare each year for the same property owner's income tax as well as Spanish wealth tax. Non-residents must pay wealth tax because they do not have the exemption of ¤108,000 that residents have. Non-residents should be warned that any unpaid property owner's income tax or wealth tax can be taken by the tax man from the 5 per cent retention.

Consult the chapter on Taxes on Property for discussion on how to calculate your capital gains tax on the sale, and the annual taxes on property that you pay every year.

Non-residence certificate: This belongs to the buyer, not to the seller, but be warned that, if the buyer is a non-resident and the form of payment is not through a bank cheque which identifies the buyer as the issuer, along with his bank, the buyer must obtain beforehand a certificate of non-residence from the Spanish Ministry of the Interior, and it can take as long as two months for this certificate to be issued.

If payment takes place abroad, for example, by transfer from the buyer's account in London to your own account in London, this is perfectly legal, but it offers the Spanish tax man no control over the transaction for documentation purposes. So, they require this certificate.

If the buyer works through a Spanish bank, he will have a certificate of changing the foreign money into euros for property purchase, and Spain can document the transaction. If the sale takes place in pounds or another currency outside Spain, this is perfectly legal, and acceptable as long as the cheque is presented when the deal is completed at the Spanish Notary.

It is only when the buyer himself wishes to keep the details anonymous and confidential that he must present the certificate of non-residence. Spain wants to know where the money comes from, or at least that someone has made a deal without telling them.

Taxes and fees

We have discussed in the chapter on Buying Property the two taxes and two fees on property sales.

The two taxes are the ITP — the property transfer tax of 6 per cent or 7 per cent in Andalusia — and the *Plus valía,* a sort of artificial capital gains tax charged by the town hall on the increase in an official set of values for the property.

The *Plus valía* varies widely, depending on the amount of time that has passed between sales, as we mentioned earlier. You can find out exactly how much it will be by asking at your town hall. They have a *Plus valía* office which will tell you the exact amount of the tax beforehand.

The two fees are for the Notary and the Property Registry. They will be in the neighbourhood of €500 but can be higher on large transactions. You can find out exactly how much by asking in advance.

If you determine the amount of these taxes and fees on your sale price in advance, you can include them in your sales presentation kit, which will impress the buyer and his lawyer with your professional approach.

Community charges and statutes

If you are selling a flat or townhouse that belongs to a community of property owners, you will want to include your last bill for the *cuota* — the community yearly charge, along with a copy of the statutes that regulate your community. The buyer will want to know what the yearly charge is and he will want to see the statutes of the community he is joining. It would be a good idea to have a copy of the minutes of the last annual general meeting as well, to prove to your prospective purchaser that your community is well run and a nice place to live.

Utility bills

Copies of your bills for rubbish, water, electricity and even telephone are necessary parts of your sales presentation. Any buyer will want to know how much these charges are on the property, and he will also want to be sure that they are paid up.

Once you have assembled all this paperwork, it would be a good idea to prepare a folder with photocopies of each relevant document, so that you or your lawyer or your estate agent will be prepared to answer any question that a prospective buyer might have.

GLOSSARY

Abogado – lawyer, solicitor
Administrador de fincas – licensed professional property administrator
API – **Agente de la Propiedad Inmobiliaria** – real estate agent, member of long-established association.
Arbitrio sobre el Incremento del Valor de los Terrenos – municipal tax on property sales, see *Plus Valía.*
Boletín Oficial – Official state gazette, where laws are published
Catastro – Land Office, concerned with measurements and physical description
Certificado Catastral – *catastral* certificate describing land and buildings
Comunidad de Propietarios – Community of Property Owners
Contrato – contract
Declaración de Obra Nueva – declaration of new construction
Escritura de Compraventa – sales contract
Escritura Pública – registered title deed
Expediente de Dominio – ownership proceeding, to establish title
Factura – bill
Finca – any plot of land or property
Gestor – licensed administrative expert in Spanish procedures
GIPE – *Gestor y Intermediario de Propiedades y Edificios,* title awarded by association of estate agents and property administrators.
Hipoteca – mortgage
Impuesto sobre Bienes Inmuebles (IBI) – annual real estate tax
Impuesto de Transmisiones Patrimoniales (ITP) – Property Transfer Tax
IVA (Impuesto sobre el Valor Añadido) – Spanish value added tax, charged when developer sells new property to first buyer
Jurado de Expropiaciones – special tribunal for expropriations
Justiprecio – doctrine of fair price by the state in forcible purchase
Ley de Costas – law protecting coastline
Ley de Tasas – law of public fees

Ministerio de Obras Públicas y Transportes (MOPT) –
Ministry of Public Works and Transport
Nota Simple – certificate of registration from Property Registry
Notario – Notary
Plan General de Ordenación Urbana (PGOU) –
town development plan
Plan Parcial – plan of building plots on urbanisation
Plus valía – municipal tax on property sale
Poder – power of attorney
Registro de la Propiedad – Property Registry
Reja – iron grillwork protecting windows and doors
Reposesión – repossessed property
Subasta – auction
Subasteros – professional auction buyers
Tasación – evaluation of property
Tasador – property surveyor, evaluator
Topógrafo – property surveyor
Urbanismo – town planning department
Valor catastral – assessed value of property for tax purposes

BUILDING YOUR OWN HOUSE

5

BUILDING PERMIT   93
URBAN LAND   93
PGOU   93
BUILDING COSTS   94
COUNTRY LAND   95
LAND MEASUREMENT   96
CHECK *CATASTRO*   97
BUILDING EXPENSES   98
VALENCIA LAND LAW   99
ARCHITECT   99
MEMORIA DE CALIDADES   100
PAYMENT SCHEDULES   101
CONSTRUCTION LAW LOE   102
DECLARACIÓN DE OBRA NUEVA   102

IF you intend to build your own castle in Spain, the first item on your list should be finding a good lawyer.

This may sound a backwards approach, but when you check out the list below of all the things that can go wrong with buying property, getting a building permit, and contracting the construction, perhaps you will agree.

The second item on your list should be a promise to yourself that you are prepared to put a lot of your own time into overseeing the entire project, from beginning to end. Getting what you want depends on your own personal supervision.

Most building projects go up just as planned, with only minor setbacks, but it is best to be prepared and take care before you start.

So, let's suppose that you are determined to buy land and build your dream house. More foreigners than ever are doing this because of the shortage of quality ready-made villas, and more builders and architects than ever are ready to help you realise your dream.

The rewards are great. But be prepared for plenty of exasperation and, above all, don't leap in with your eyes shut.

Too often, the aspiring house-builder thinks that all he has to do is pick one model of villa from a selection that the developer or builder shows him, and that it will appear as if by magic a few months later.

Sometimes this method works out perfectly well, but not all of us can read a plan and visualise the final result with accuracy.

Too many people tell their builder that House Type B suits them very well, pay a fat deposit, and go back to their native country. When they return six or eight months later, they find: that House Type B doesn't look anything like they thought it would; that the builder hasn't placed it in the spot they had agreed on; and, furthermore, they absolutely hate the yellow tiles in the bathroom.

It will take your personal supervision to get it done the way you want it. With forethought and patient attention to detail, you can indeed have your dream house. But let me repeat that first warning. You simply cannot walk away and expect to return finding that your house has been built just the way you want it. You will have to be there every day. Let me repeat. Every day.

Finding the land

First, however, you have to find a plot where you can build. Everything mentioned in the previous chapter about buying property applies here, and there is more besides.

Building land is available already divided into plots with all services on many urbanisations. Country land is also much easier to find than before because thousands of foreigners are moving inland from the coastal areas. This means that estate agents with local knowledge are making greater efforts to have on hand the sort of country plots that these foreigners want.

These plots of land are still there but new restrictions on country building have complicated the picture all around Spain. For years it was a common practice to build a country house on rural land that was not zoned for residence, pay a fine, and have the property made legal.

So many foreigners and Spaniards did this that development officials have now cracked down on rural building and it has become almost impossible. In most parts of the country small towns and inland villages are now preparing new urban plans which will open up land for building again, but on a legal basis.

Once these plans have final approval, it should be easier to realise your dream of a cottage in the country. Until then, you must take extra care.

Building permit

The first thing you have to know is, can you get permission from the town hall to build on it? The permit is called a *Licencia de obra* or *Permiso de obra*. Be advised that building permits cost around 4 per cent of the estimated construction cost. This can vary from town to town.

Urban land

If your land is in a registered urbanisation, or housing estate, with its papers in order, you will probably have no problem. Sometimes the land comes with the building permit already arranged. This land, of course, is more expensive because it has been prepared for development. But, even on a registered urbanisation, some problems can arise.

There are zoning changes from time to time, and you may find your beautiful property is in the middle of a green zone where no building can take place.

Do not take the seller's word as gospel. Your town hall's *urbanismo* department is a very important stop for you. Go yourself and take someone who speaks Spanish. Your lawyer, for example.

PGOU

You want to see the PGOU, the *Plan General de Ordenación Urbana*. This is the Town Plan. These plans generally are approved every four years. Any interim changes in them must be publicly posted and approved, with a chance for affected property owners to protest or make claims.

In many municipalities, you may find that many changes have been made in the building codes and town plans, which though sometimes approved by the town hall still need the final go-ahead from the regional government, which must vet and clear the municipal plans.

In some cases, there are special building codes set up for specific zones. The PGOU analysis is not for amateurs. You need a specialist to make sure you understand it.

If your land is located in an existing and approved urbanisation, the permit will probably be forthcoming, but you must still check on it. You must also be sure that the urbanisation is an approved one.

There are some developments that never received official approval and where building is stopped today because they never met the legal requirements for the services they must provide, such as roads of a certain width, or water supply. You can find out by asking to see the *Proyecto de urbanización* and the *Plan Parcial,* or the plan of parcels, building plots, at the town hall.

In many autonomous regions, such as Andalusia, the building permit issued by the town hall must also be vetted and approved by the regional building department. These departments exercise this control over the municipal departments to ensure that regulations are followed.

BUILDING COSTS

These costs are very approximate. So many variations come into building costs that it is extremely difficult to calculate an average price that means anything. Nevertheless, the table should give you some idea of what to expect.

Basic Construction: figure 600 –700 euros a square metre.

Good Construction: 700-900 euros a square metre

Quality Construction: 1,000 euros a square metre and up, way up.

BASIC CONSTRUCTION means walls using large solid building blocks with no cavities and the use of basic flooring and finishing materials.

GOOD CONSTRUCTION at the top end of the price will include cavity walls and some higher quality finishing materials. No air-conditioning or central heating, however, and no marble.

QUALITY CONSTRUCTION: The sky is the limit here. Remember that the area of location is also an influence. Labour costs are higher in Marbella than in the interior, for example.

Be sure to check also the building regulations for plots and areas around your chosen spot. One of the worst, and most frequent, horror stories on the fast-growing coasts of Spain is the nightmare of the cut-off view. That is, you return to your pleasant villa on a hillside overlooking the Mediterranean to discover that a four-storey apartment building now blocks your view, and your new neighbours look right into your bedroom window. Make sure that you know what type of building permits will be issued around you before you buy.

In today's building climate, this check-up may be more complicated than it sounds.

In some municipalities the urban planning authorities even make special deals with developers, whereby land is rezoned to permit greater building in exchange for part of the builder's profits going into the town's coffers. This is neither illegal nor corrupt, as the profits help all residents of the town, but it can harm the interests of those who already have purchased.

These special arrangements are called *convenios,* meaning simply "agreements". In Marbella, for example, municipal authorities issued so many building permits and made so many deals that the Andalusian regional development department has acted to take building control out of local hands entirely.

Regional officials charge that, in complete defiance of the law, some building permits have been granted for land zoned for parks and schools.

Country land - *rústico*

If your land is deep in the country, you will need to check on other factors at the town hall, such as whether you need to buy, say, 10,000 square metres of land, or 30,000 square metres of land, in order to build.

Most country land is zoned as *rústico,* which means land not programmed for development. It might be farmland or pasture or forest. Under the recent changes in land laws now coming into force all over Spain, the land is now usually zoned as *No urbanizable,* which means you cannot build on it.

Furthermore, where the regional authorities formerly allowed local town halls to authorise building in the country, they are now cracking down on the practice, so you will find country land hard to find.

If building is permitted at all on this type of land, it will be restricted. Regulations vary around Spain, but a frequent requirement is that a minimum building plot must be 10,000 square metres if the land has a source of water, and 30,000 square metres if it is zoned as "dry".

Do not believe a seller who tells you that you can build on 6,000 square metres illegally and later have the house registered, paying only a small fine. This has been true in some cases, but most municipalities are now cracking down on such practices. They can order the structure demolished. Make sure you buy enough land.

You can find this out at the local town hall. The *urbanismo*, or development, department can tell you exactly what will be permitted or prohibited within any area of the municipality.

Visit the town hall yourself, taking someone who speaks Spanish, or send your lawyer, to make absolutely sure that a permit will be forthcoming.

The land may also have a *camino real* or a *servidumbre de paso*, an old pathway that crosses the land. It is a right of way and you can't cut it by building. People can pass over your land and it might even be transformed into a road some day.

Or an irrigation ditch might exist, which again is a legal right of way you cannot block, nor can you deny access to it for those who use it. Country land may have water problems, too. Where does the water come from? Can it be cut off? If you intend to drill your own well, you will need a special permission for this.

Have an expert check the town planning maps to see if any new highways are planned for the zone. It can come as a nasty surprise two years later when you see the bulldozers starting work next door, or you are called to a hearing where proceedings are launched to expropriate the bottom of your garden.

Once you have determined that a building permit will be forthcoming and that no special encumbrances exist on the land, you can start to find out just what land you are buying.

Land measurement

The seller must have an *escritura*, a title deed, for the land, just as for a flat or land with an existing house. Sometimes there is no registered title for the land, only a private document. See the preceding chapter for various ways of getting the land officially registered.

But, in the more usual case where official title exists, this *escritura pública* will describe the land, but sometimes the description isn't exact enough to suit you.

Descriptions in the Property Registry often use vague terms like the bare statement that the land borders on the east with the land of Pepe García. Well, Pepe has a big farm. Just what part of it constitutes the border? It could be where the fence is or where the ditch is or where the path is.

Then you need an official survey. Remember that the Property Registry is concerned with ownership, not with exact description. A surveyor is called a *topógrafo* and he will measure your plot exactly.

You can have this done independently but you should also check the *Catastral* registry.

Check the *Catastro*

Here again, just as with buying a house, you want to check with the *Catastro* as well as the Property Registry. The *Catastral* office lists the boundaries and measurements and physical characteristics of the land. You want to be sure that this description squares with the description in the *escritura*.

If not, you may be able to get the *catastral* reference to square with the reality of the land, and this in turn with the title deed.

The *Catastro* will have a map, a plan of the land, so that you can see that the boundary with Pepe García's farm runs along the fence, just as you thought. Or you may see that your plot includes a piece of land which Pepe García thinks belongs to him. Especially in old country properties, there is often some confusion.

You want to have exact, officially recognised boundaries, and the number of square metres that match the survey and the *escritura*. They probably will not agree, but you can correct this when you purchase, so that your own title and the physical description are in agreement. This clarity will be greatly to your benefit should you later wish to sell your land and house.

Ask for the official surveyor at the town hall. The survey will form part of your *escritura* when you buy the land. If your land is on an approved urbanisation, there will likely be an up-to-date survey already existing. The survey and the *Plan Parcial* will also show your access and where your water and electricity come from.

Once you have determined that you can indeed build and you

know the exact borders of your land, you had better find out if the seller is in fact the owner of the land.

Are you buying from the developers of the urbanisation, or from an individual? If the land is in the *campo,* does Juan really own it? He may share it with his two brothers, one of whom does not want to sell. Or there may be a mortgage on it. The same rules apply as for any property purchase. Check the *Registro de la Propiedad.*

Finally, you sign the *escritura de compraventa* at the *Notario,* and you are ready to proceed with building. When you checked restrictions at the town hall, you should also have discovered what building code problems you may have. Do you have to leave three metres between your boundary and any building? Can you put a wall closer to the road than one metre? Is two storeys the absolute limit? If you are in an established urbanisation, does the association of property owners require you to submit your building plans for approval?

BUILDING EXPENSES

Architect fee: 8 to 9 per cent (official college says 6 per cent, you can try to negotiate)
Aparejador **(building engineer):** 1.5 per cent
(he supervises building construction)
Building licence: 4 to 5 per cent (varies from town to town)
Topographic land survey: 0.66 per cent.
Safety study: 0.8 percent
Geological report: 0.94 per cent
First occupation licence: 0.5 per cent
Declaration of new construction: 0.5 per cent (you pay this when you register the house for taxes)
Total: 16 to 19 per cent

We repeat that checking the building code sounds simple but in practice it is often complicated. Many municipalities have old building codes in place, with new ones written and approved by the town council, but not yet ratified by their regional governments, which must give final approval.

This means that even official *permisos de obra*, or building permits, are sometimes granted on the basis of shaky legality.

Valencia, Andalusia laws may complicate matters

Land laws in the Valencia community and in Andalusia may complicate your land purchase even further.

In Valencia, the LRAU has outraged country property owners. The initials stand for the *Ley Reguladora de Actividades Urbanísticas,* the Law Regulating Urbanisation Activities. It has come to be known as the "land-grab law". The law provides that town halls may designate private developers as "urbanising agents", with the power to compel private owners either to sell parts of their land at low prices, or to pay high charges for infrastructure.

The law is clearly open to abuse and even the British ambassador has questioned the Valencia government about the protection of citizens' basic rights. Investigators sent by the European Union issued a devastating report on the abuse of citizens' basic rights.

The Valencia government has enacted a modification of the LRAU, called the LUV, the *Ley Urbanística Valenciana,* but affected owners charge it is simply more of the same high-handedness. Now the protesters are taking their case to the European Court of Human Rights.

If you buy in an established urbanisation on the Costa Blanca, you should be all right. If you buy country land or property, make sure you check on any possible urbanisation plans in the area.

In Andalusia, the revised *Ley del Suelo,* the Land Law, has some similar provisions, but authorities affirm that more protections are in place to guarantee the rights of private owners.

The revised law also cracks down on the practice of illegal construction on *suelo rústico,* or country land. Its principal first effect has been virtually to halt the sale of country plots, as we mentioned above.

Architect

At last you need an architect. You have your rough sketches but you need someone who can turn them into real blueprints. In fact, you will need architect's drawings in order to get your building permit in any case.

The only way to find a good architect is to ask around. If you prefer to use a foreign architect for your design, you may do so. Since Spain's entry into Europe, EU architects can now practise and sign plans for approval by the official *Colegio de Arquitectos*.

Architects' fees, at least as a minimum, are standard and are set by the *Colegio*. They are about 6 per cent of the estimated cost of construction.

To this you must add another 1.5 per cent for the *aparejador* (see below), so your design and supervision will cost you about 7.5 per cent of your estimated construction cost. This construction cost, by the way, will be less than either your real cost or the real market value of the house when finished.

The price includes final plans that must suit you, and the six copies necessary for approval by the College of Architects and for your building permit. The fees stated here are only suggested minimum charges, as the College no longer has the legal power to enforce the rates. Hence, you may be able to get a cheaper fee by a little negotiating.

Memoria is binding agreement for building specifications

The price also includes preparation of the *memoria de calidades,* or building specifications, which includes items like the size of pipes, the formula for the concrete, and the type of materials to be used.

You yourself want to have a personal hand in this. You can choose here just what sort of electrical fittings and bathroom fixtures and kitchen tiles you want. This is the time to think of details about shelves and about whether you want wood window frames or aluminium, and so on.

It is important to give this a great deal of thought because the *memoria* is what you will give your builder in order to get his bid on the job. He will set his price according to the materials stated in the *memoria,* and any changes you may make later, or any additions, will cost you extra. These extras can add up to a lot of money, so the *memoria* is a very important document.

If the builder fails to install any items as set out in these building specifications, he can be held responsible.

The architect's fee includes overall supervision of the construction, but you are not likely to see your architect on the building site once he has finished the design.

The actual supervision usually falls to the *aparejador*, a professional architectural engineer who sees that the building is carried out to the specifications required. He will visit the site from time to time to check on things and he will take his own fee, about half what the architect charges you. He signs the documents certifying that the house is properly constructed, which you will need in order to occupy your house legally and to get your electricity connected. Your architect will be able to recommend an *aparejador*. Often they work out of the same office.

Finally, you are ready to find a builder. It is only reasonable to get several bids on your job, remembering that the lowest bid is not always the best deal and that the highest bid does not ensure high quality. Ask around.

Your contract with the builder should include the *memoria*. It should state the total price; whether or not the site grading and preparation and final clean-up are included; the manner of payment; and give a definite completion date, with a penalty clause for late delivery. You ought to have your lawyer vet this contract.

Be advised that many building projects are not finished on time. If your contract contains a penalty clause, well and good. Often, however, the only guarantee is that you can get your money back if the project is not delivered on time.

In real life, you don't want your money back. The apartment or house is already worth 10 or 20 per cent more than you paid for it a year ago, when construction started, so you would suffer this loss. In this case, you simply wait.

Payment schedules

Payment terms are not standard, but a typical schedule might be:
1. A deposit of 20 per cent when the contract is signed.
2. Another 20 per cent when the walls and roof are completed. (At this point, it is customary to have the *bandera* party, when a flag is placed on the roof, and the owner invites the workers and his own friends to a *fiesta* at the site.)
3. Another 20 per cent when the door and window frames are installed and the inside is more or less complete.
4. Another 20 per cent when the house is painted and ready to inhabit, with plumbing and electricity installed and functioning.
5. A payment of 10 per cent when all the outside work included in the contract is finished, such as patios, walls, pool.

6. The final payment of 10 per cent should be held back for six months to a year, if you can swing the deal, to cover any defects in construction which don't show up until the rains start, for example. There is always something.

Construction law - LOE

Spain's building law makes builders legally responsible for 10 years for any damage resulting from the foundations, load-bearing walls and other structural elements. The builder is responsible for three years for damages caused by construction material defects, and for one year for the state of finishing elements. The law is called the LOE, the *Ley de Ordenación de Edificación*.

Declaración de obra nueva

Before you can register your new house for real estate taxes, you must make a *Declaración de la obra nueva,* a declaration of new work, in order to have the structure appear on your *escritura.* So far, your deed mentions only the piece of land, not the house you have just built.

The declaration of new construction will cost you one half of one per cent of the declared value of the construction. Again, if the Tax Agency does not agree with your declared value, they can raise it.

Your lawyer or property consultant will show you how to register the new house. If you do not register *(dar de alta)* with the tax people, you can be fined, so take care of it as soon as possible. Two per cent of the value of your house is also calculated as income when you go to file for your Spanish income tax if you are a non-resident (see Taxes on Property).

When you go to make your declaration of new work and register the house, you will need the *Certificado final de obra* issued by the architect, the *Licencia de obra,* building permit, issued by the town hall, and the *Licencia de Primera Ocupación,* the permit to inhabit the dwelling, from the town hall.

Then you will be the completely legal and registered owner of your dream house and you can begin to pay both property owner's income tax and Spanish wealth tax on your new property.

That is, if you are a non-resident. Since 1999, the resident is exempt from property owner's imputed income tax on his principal dwelling, as well as having the exemption of 108,182 euros on his wealth tax.

GLOSSARY

Aparejador – building engineer
Arquitecto – licenced architect,
Bandera – flag, here referring to "flag party" when house is roofed
Camino Real – royal road, meaning right of way across land
Catastro – Land Registry, distinct from Property Registry
Escritura de Compraventa – conveyance deed
Escritura Pública – registered title to land
Certificado de final de obra – construction completion certificate
Declaración de obra nueva – declaration of new construction
Licencia (or Permiso) de obra – building licence
Licencia de Primera Ocupación – licence to occupy the dwelling
Memoria de calidades – detailed building specifications
Plan General de Ordenación Urbana (PGOU) –
  municipal building plan
Plan Parcial – plan of building plots in housing estate
Proyecto de Urbanización – housing estate development plan
Rústico – country land, not zoned for building
Servidumbre de paso – legal right of way
Topógrafo – land surveyor
Urbanismo – urban development office

LETTING AND RENTING

6

BUYING TO LET	*105*
TENANTS IDENTIFY LANDLORDS	*106*
LETTING LAW	*106*
THREE RENTAL SITUATIONS	
(1964-1985, 1985-1995, 1995-PRESENT)	*107*
RENEW CONTRACT UP TO FIVE YEARS	*109*
DEPOSIT	*109*
EVICTION	*109*
NECESSARY NOTIFICATION	*110*
HOLIDAY RENTALS HAVE DIFFERENT RULES	*110*
LANDLORDS, BE WARY	*110*
LETTING AGENCIES	*111*
NON-RESIDENT RENTAL TAX	*113*
RENTING IN SPAIN	*113*
FOREIGN CONTRACT	*114*
SPANISH CONTRACT	*114*
ONE-YEAR CONTRACT	*115*
NO CONTRACT	*115*
REGISTERED CONTRACT	*116*
RIGHT OF FIRST REFUSAL	*116*
COMMUNITY FEES	*117*
FORMAL NOTIFICATION	*117*
HOW TO COMPLAIN	*118*
BUSINESS PREMISES	*118*
LEASING	*118*
WATCH OUT FOR	*118*

Buying to let

There has been a genuine boom in buying to let in Spain for the past few years. Even in today's slowing property market, it remains an attractive investment option.

With the present low interest rates and high rentals, you can buy a flat on the Costa del Sol, mortgage 70 per cent of the purchase price, and sit back while your rental income pays off the mortgage.

If you are paying mortgage interest at 5 or 6 per cent effective annual rate and your rentals are bringing in a return on capital of 7 or 8 per cent, you are making a profit of 2 or 3 per cent.

This doesn't seem like much, but you are doing it with the bank's money, not your own, and you are paying for your property.

Plus you have the use of the property for several months of the year because few holiday lets attract tenants for 12 months of the year.

Plus you have capital appreciation as your property grows in value. Many Spanish properties have doubled in value in the past five years, for example.

Tenants identify landlords

This sounds like a tough deal to beat, and the Spanish tax man has further sweetened the package by introducing a reduction of 50 per cent in rental income for tax purposes. This unfortunately applies only to official residents of Spain, and is designed to stimulate the rental market.

Resident landlords can also deduct just about every expense imaginable from their rental income, meaning that most landlords will pay little or nothing in income tax.

Residents benefit from this Spanish income tax reduction, but non-residents declare their rental income on a special form 210, which is not affected by the measure (see page ????).

Landlords, be warned. Tenants who make tax declarations in Spain are now required to list their landlord's name and tax identification number on their income tax declaration. We all know that many owners rent out their flats and say nothing to the tax man. This measure will help the Tax Agency identify undeclared income.

Letting law

Spain's current Law of Urban Lettings, the *Ley de Arrendamientos Urbanos,* went into effect on January 1, 1995, but many renters and letters, especially foreigners, are still unaware of its provisions.

The law brought some good news for those Spanish property owners who were still stuck with sitting tenants under the pre-1985 law, and it also brought good news for tenants who were victims of arbitrary rent rises under the law in force from 1985 to 1995.

The 1995 law ended a maze of contradictory Spanish legislation which made life difficult for tenants and landlords alike and all but ruined the rental property market in Spain.

Two of its main provisions make life easier for both landlords and tenants.

1. The current law ends the forcible extension provision of the 1964 law, which made rental contracts indefinitely renewable by the tenant. The present law allows landlords gradually to raise the old controlled and ridiculously low rents of the 1964 law to market prices today, and, eventually, to recover their own property.

2. The law also provides tenants with more security than the 1985 law stipulated, now obliging landlords to renew residential rental contracts each year for up to five years.

Three rental situations

We must distinguish three possible situations for rentals existing in Spain today, depending on when the original contract was made.

1964-1985: Under the terms of the rental laws in effect from 1964 to 1985 tenants were so protected that landlords gave up in despair and stopped building rental apartments, which led to a critical housing shortage. Almost half a million apartments in Spain are still occupied under this old law, which protected a tenant so strongly that he could pass on his rights to his children and even his grandchildren. Further, his rent could never be raised, or raised only by a small percentage related to the inflation rate.

Incredibly, there are still almost 500,000 apartments in Spain whose tenants pay less than 50 euros a month There are buildings in Madrid where the grandchildren of the original tenants are living in spacious flats in prestigious areas, paying rents of five euros a month. Until 1985, the landlord was helpless to do anything about it, even though his real estate tax is 1,500 euros a year and his community fees are another 1,000 euros. Next door, another tenant may be paying 1,200 euros a month for the same type of apartment, having signed his contract after 1985.

Some foreign property owners on the Spanish Mediterranean

coast fell into this trap before 1985. Thinking to make a little money on their holiday flat or eventual retirement home, they rented it out, with a contract for some specific time period.

Later they were horrified to discover that their tenants refused to vacate and had become entitled to the forcible extension of their contracts, regardless of the landlord's desire to end the letting and recover his property.

Many landlords chose to leave their apartments empty rather than risk the dangers of a sitting tenant. Landlords refused to repair the crumbling buildings which brought them no profit, and nobody would even think of constructing new rental property.

1985 - 1995: Revised rental laws passed in 1985 by the Socialist government aimed to remedy this situation in the best capitalist way, by making rental properties good business. The revised law provided that all contracts ended when they said they ended, without provision for forcible extension. The law also ended any restrictions on rent increases. Landlords immediately began to raise rents sharply and to offer short-term contracts with little protection for the tenant. Now it was the tenants who suffered, because they were unwilling to settle into a flat from which they might be evicted in one year's time, or be forced to pay sharp increases.

1995: The 1995 rental law now in force is designed to provide a better balance between the rights and needs of tenants and landlords and to bring at last a final solution to the generations of sitting tenants.

If you are one of the foreign property owners stuck with a sitting tenant, you are now able to recover your property. Don't cheer too loudly, however, because it can take you the tenant's lifetime, plus two years. However, you will be able to raise the rent to a normal level over either five years or 10 years, depending on the tenant's income.

If the tenant earns less than 28,000 euros a year, his rent can be gradually raised to market levels over 10 years. If he earns more than that, his rent can be raised in five years to a market figure.

The old-law tenant still has the right to pass on the apartment to his spouse or children. After that, the landlord will at last be able to take possession of his own property. In the meantime, of course, he will have been able to raise the rent to the price levels of today.

Landlords in this position should take legal advice from property specialists in order to make sure they are effectively exercising their rights.

There are a number of legal steps that each landlord must take before he can begin raising his rents, such as citing the tenant to declare his income. If the tenant does not respond, the landlord can then begin raising the rent to bring it to a market level within five years, the faster option.

Contract renewable up to five years

The present law provides that residential contracts, as distinct from short-term holiday lets, are subject to yearly renewals up to five years. Rental contracts are usually made for one year but the law requires that the contract is renewable for a total five-year period of tenancy.

A landlord can offer a contract of two years or three years, but, if the tenant decides that he wants to stay on, this contract is renewable for a total period of five years. If the tenant himself wishes a contract of only two or three years, this is all right.

The rent can be revised upward by an inflation factor each year.

At the end of the five years, the landlord can raise the rent as much as he chooses, either for his new tenant or for his existing tenant, if he decides to stay on at the new and higher rent.

Deposit

The current letting law also establishes the landlord's right to a deposit as a guarantee against damages. The deposit can be held by an agency independent of both landlord and tenant. This agency will not release the deposit until both parties agree.

The deposit consists of one month's rent for a residential unit and two months' rent for commercial premises.

The deposit, called a *fianza,* can be held by the housing department of the regional government. In Andalusia, for example, it is deposited with the *Consejería de la Vivienda* of the Andalusian autonomous government, which has offices in major cities.

Eviction is difficult

When can an owner evict a tenant and recover his property?

Some justifications for eviction are: failure to pay the rent (although courts have often ruled that these arrears must exceed six months before any action will be taken); damage to the property; use of the property for immoral purposes; subletting unless agreed in the contract; and causing a serious nuisance to the neighbours.

In any of these cases, a court order must be obtained against the tenant and many months could pass before you get the tenant out.

Necessary notification: If you have let your property on a five-year *vivienda* contract (see above) and you wish to take possession yourself at the end of that time, remember that you must officially notify the tenant well before the end of the contract that you do not intend to renew it. If you do not do this correctly, the contract can be regarded as renewed for two years and at the same rent.

Holiday rentals have separate rules

This law does not affect short-term holiday rental contracts, called *arrienda de temporada*. These holiday contracts do not grant the tenant any right to automatic extension and they require that the tenant vacate when the contract ends.

So, foreign property owners can be assured of this legal protection when they let their holiday homes for periods of several months. However, they should still take some care with vetting tenants because the legal procedures for eviction of a tenant who refuses to leave can take more than six months, even when the law is on the landlord's side.

There have been a number of recent cases in which unscrupulous tenants have signed up for holiday rentals, say, for two months, and then simply remained in the apartment without paying any further rent. Four to six months later, the landlord is able to obtain an eviction order, but the tenants have lived rent-free for that period. A court may enter a judgement against them for the amount of rent owed, but they simply move to another town and repeat the scheme.

Landlords must be wary

If you are a property owner and you wish to let your own flat or villa in Spain, or go into the tourist accommodation business, you must be very careful about the terms of your contracts and the quality of your tenants.

The opportunity to pay off your property by letting it looks tempting on paper. It can work out to your entire satisfaction, and in fact it usually does. Nevertheless, many problems arise and you need to be wary.

Tenants may damage your furniture or harm your plumbing and electrical installations. Letting agents may keep your money and allow your apartment to fall into ruin while you are absent.

Or you might fall into the short-term contract trap, when your tenant tries to turn his brief holiday rental into a protected five-year residential let (see below for more details).

In good faith you rent to a young Spanish man who says he has a six-month work contract in your town, and needs a short-term let. Then he moves in his wife and children, who were not mentioned when he signed the contract, and then he brings in his own furniture,

Then he goes to court to accuse you of coercing him into signing the short-term contract when he really wanted a place to live. As he lives and works in the town, the court will probably rule in his favour, and you will have to wait five years to recover your property.

The safest way is to let only to people you know and trust. Even then it is a good idea to get the rent in advance and a deposit against possible damages as well. Electric bills always arrive late, so it is best to include an estimated charge in the rent.

If you have a telephone, you will find that having it discon-nected and reconnected is an irritating exercise. But it's worth it. You can get a lock for it, but that is never quite sufficient. Perhaps the best idea is to have the sort of phone which you can unplug from the wall and remove. There have been many, many problems with telephones.

A property owner interested in long-term letting should be aware that the residential tenant has the right to first refusal if the property is put up for sale. See Right of First Refusal below.

Letting agencies

If you want to let your property on a casual basis and for only a few short periods each year, you will most likely let by word of mouth to people you know or to people recommended by friends.

If you want to let on a more regular basis, you will probably use an agency or holiday company. You may find that your garden apartment development or your urbanisation office includes a letting service which, for a commission, will handle all the details for you. This could be your solution, but read the agreement carefully and talk to others who have used this service to make sure they are satisfied.

There are also holiday companies which bring people to Spain for two or three-week self-catering holidays. These are becoming more and more popular, especially for young families who prefer to stay away from hotels. These companies are always looking for new properties to let. Because they charge their clients high prices for short stays, they can afford to pay you, the owner, a good price for the use of your property.

Again, be sure to read their agreement very carefully. Remember that a series of holiday tenants can do a lot of damage to your property.

Also make sure that this company is legally registered and that it is paying all the proper taxes. Because, when you provide linens and other hotel-type services, and deal with many tourist visitors on a short-term basis, you move into a new area legally. You are now a business yourself and you should legally declare your property as a tourist letting accommodation. This means that inspectors will come to check the standards and the tax man will be informed.

It also means that you or your holiday rental company must declare the income, and set aside 25 per cent of the rent as a withholding tax to the Spanish government. You declare for this tax on Form 210, just as the individual letter does. You or your holiday company must also add an extra 16 per cent IVA, value added tax, to the rent, which must be paid to the Tax Agency as well.

On the other hand, you can now deduct maintenance expenses from your Spanish income tax. You cannot do this when you inhabit the property yourself, but maintenance becomes a business expense when you let out your property regularly.

You may also employ a real estate agency in Spain to handle your letting, but be sure you are dealing with people who are competent and whom you trust. All too often one finds that extra fees and charges from the agency soon add up, or they do not properly see to the maintenance of the place. Figure about 15 per cent fees for property management of this sort.

There have been cases where the agency has rented out the property and told the owner that it was not rented. The agency kept all of the money and the absentee owner assumed that his flat was empty.

The risk of being stuck with a sitting tenant was much greater under the previous laws, but it can still happen, as we mentioned above. A tenant, after a short stay, wants to renew his contract, or stay a few more months. The owner, or his agent, agrees and takes the tenant's cheque.

Then the owner wants to come to Spain and enjoy his home for a few months. The tenant refuses to vacate. He says that he has become an official resident of Spain and declares that the house is his only home. If the courts uphold him, the landlord is stuck.

Make sure that your letting agent is not empowered to sign extensions of contracts or make new contracts without your knowledge and consent.

Non-resident rental tax

It is quite legal and proper for you, as either a resident or non-resident property owner in Spain, to rent out your property. Be advised, however, that you must declare your rental income for Spanish income tax.

Even if your tenant pays you in Danish kronor before he leaves for Spain, legally this income arises in Spain because the property is in Spain. It is almost certainly true that most owners who let their property occasionally say nothing about it to the tax authorities and the chances of their getting caught are slim. Nevertheless, Spanish income tax is due on any profits arising in Spain.

If you are a non-resident, you are liable for Spanish non-resident income tax of 25 per cent from the very first euro of rental income, declared on form 210. You may not take advantage of the reduction of 50 per cent for resident landlords.

If you are a resident, you should add your rental income to your other income when you make your annual Spanish income tax declaration. If you register your property as a tourist letting operation, you can put down the maintenance expenses of your property as a business expense and deduct this from your tax.

Renting in Spain

If you decide to rent in Spain, you will find thousands of apartments and villas at prices to suit almost every pocket.

Some are basically equipped small flats designed for self-catering holidays and often rented through agents in Britain, Holland or Germany. Others are real homes being let by their owners in the hope of making a little money from their property until they can retire to enjoy it full time.

For those who intend to live in Spain, it is a good idea to rent a place in the area where they hope to live permanently.

When you have found a property that suits your needs, you will be asked to sign a rental contract.

Foreign contract

If you are renting a holiday flat for a self-catering visit to Spain, you will probably find this contract in your own language, to be signed in your own country before you leave with the rental company handling the property.

This is perfectly all right. Just make sure the rental company has a sound reputation. Sometimes the accommodation promised you does not measure up to your expectations, so be alert (see below for How to Complain in Spain).

The contract forms are usually quite standard, including a list of all the equipment and furnishings, and requiring a deposit to cover any damages the tenant may cause. There is not normally any dispute about the return of this deposit if you have left the flat in good condition.

If you have seen the way some holidaymakers leave their rented flats, you would understand why the companies insist on this deposit.

Spanish contract:

If you are already in Spain when you rent, you will also be asked to sign a contract. It will specify the amount of the rent, the manner of payment, any deposit and the time period.

The contract will be headed *por temporada,* which means short-term. This is to distinguish it from a long-term rental, called *vivienda,* or residence, because long-term tenants have rights which short-term tenants do not.

A *temporada* contract might even be as long as one year. There is no specific time limit past which a contract becomes long-term.

However, unless otherwise specified in your short-term rental contract, the landlord may put you out at the end of the period stated, or he may offer you a new contract increasing the rent as much as he likes.

These short-term contracts are designed for holiday rentals, not as long-term or permanent residence. Such a *temporada* contract running for one year would be pushing it a little, but the idea is to show the intention of impermanence, so the tenant does not establish full rights. This does not always work as planned, which we have seen in the example above. Even short-term tenants can sometimes try to claim a longer contract.

The *vivienda* contract, on the other hand, is meant for those long-term lets when the tenant truly makes the apartment his home. The tenant is much more protected and Spanish law requires that a *vivienda* contract be renewable for a minimum period of five years.

This gives the tenant some stability, as he knows that he has at least this period, and he must be officially notified well in advance of the end of the period if the landlord does not intend to renew the contract.

One-year contract

Let's suppose you want to rent a villa in Spain for a year, or even more, and you find that a rental agency in your home country, or even in Spain, has the perfect house at the right price. They offer you a one-year contract, in German or English, with option to renew. This contract, in your own language, will not say that it is either a *temporada* or a *vivienda* contract. The agency does not think in terms of Spanish law, and they don't expect that you will, either.

This foreign-language contract is perfectly legal, although it would have to be translated into Spanish for any court proceedings, and it is a perfectly good offer, which, in fact gives you as the tenant more protection than it gives the landlord.

You can renew the contract if you want. If the landlord wants you to leave, you can threaten to go to court, claiming that the villa has become your retirement home. You can say that you will ask the court to have the contract extended to the full five years of the long-term let.

The landlord and the agency will be reluctant to become involved in any legal dispute in Spanish courts first, because they will probably lose their case, and perhaps they are not declaring all the rental income for Spanish taxes.

Even if the tenant pays in pounds in another country, the income derived from property in Spain is still subject to Spanish tax.

No Contract

Some owners do not want to make any contracts. This can be perfectly all right, too. Just make sure you have clearly written receipts for the rent you pay, which will constitute an implicit contract. Such an implicit rental contract exists even if you don't have the receipts, as soon as the owner cashes your cheque, but it's better to have some piece of paper as evidence.

If you are paying month to month in such a situation, the implicit contract ends at the end of each month you pay, or on the date stated on your receipt.

Registered contract

For full security in your rental, you also want your rental contract registered with the housing department. This means that you will have full legal protection in the event of any court case about your rental.

Let's face it: most rental contracts, especially with foreigners, are simply not registered and the landlords are probably not declaring the rental income for tax purposes. Your contract is still valid in court, but only the registered contract, where the landlord is completely legal in his operations, has the full protection of the law.

As we noted earlier, the landlord can require a deposit, usually a month's rent, which can be held by an agency independent of the landlord and tenant. Though it is a common practice, it is never a good idea to pay the deposit directly into the landlord's account, as he then is in complete control over whether to release the deposit or not at the end of the let.

Right of first refusal

In today's fast-moving Spanish real estate market, one of the important rights acquired by a long-term residential tenant is the right of first refusal when the property is put up for sale.

If the landlord sells the property, he is required by law to offer it first to the long-term tenant. He should do this in writing, stating the price and conditions of the sale. If the tenant does not reply or if he refuses the offer, the landlord is then free to sell the property to anyone he chooses.

If the landlord sells the property without informing the tenant in advance, the tenant even has the right to have this sale annulled and to purchase the property himself at the price declared on the sale contract.

As the price of a property sale is often under-declared on Spanish contracts, this means the tenant would buy the property at the lower price which was officially declared. This provision acts as a further deterrent to the landlord.

In Spanish this right is called *tanteo y retracto*.

Community fees

Long-term, or *vivienda*, contracts often contain provisions requiring the tenant to pay community fees, that is, the dues charged each year by the property owners' collective for that block of flats, and even the real estate taxes, known as the IBI.

An owner is within his rights to make such a contract, but you should be wary and know what you are getting into. Such extra charges can add up. Furthermore, clauses obliging the tenant to pay the community fees and real estate taxes are considered abusive under Spanish law, and you can protest if you choose, even after you have signed the contract.

If these charges are not mentioned in your contract, they are the owner's responsibility and you can refuse any attempt by him to make you pay for them.

To sum up, in strictly legal terms, the taxes and fees are for the property owner's account. However, it is not illegal for the landlord and tenant to agree in the contract that the tenant will pay them. As long as you know what you are getting into, and the amounts of these charges are clear, and you as the tenant are disposed to accept the price, then it is okay.

If, however, you feel that you have been deceived by the landlord into signing the contract, you can protest the clause and you will surely win your case.

Formal notification necessary

Be advised that, if you have a five-year *vivienda* contract and your landlord wishes to terminate your rental at the end of the period, he is obliged to notify you officially, for example, by a notarised letter, well before the end of the period. If he does not notify you officially, the contract can be regarded as renewed for two years and for the same rent.

In any of these situations, most Europeans will find the tenant to have more protection than is normal in many countries. That is, even though the law states that the rental period is finished, a landlord will have some trouble putting out anyone who chooses to stay. He cannot simply summon a policeman and order you out. He must get a court order for this and the procedure will take some time, even when the law is entirely on the landlord's side.

How to complain

Finally, if you feel that your holiday apartment does not meet the terms of your contract, or if your landlord has abused his side of the deal, you can complain. If you are a genuine tourist, the tourist office of the province or town where the property is located will hear your complaint. If you are a semi-permanent resident, you will do better at the OMIC, the *Oficina Municipal de Información al Consumidor*. This is the consumer information office, usually directed by the regional government. Its mission is to deal with consumer problems and these include rents.

Business premises

More and more foreigners are coming to Spain to start their own businesses. Not the least of their problems is the leasing, purchase or rental of the business premises. This is an area where you really need the best legal advice, apart from your normal good business sense.

Leasing

A Spanish leasehold, which used to be called a *traspaso* but is now known as a *cesión*, gives the lessee the right to re-sell it on to a third party, although he must first offer it to the property owner. If the property owner chooses not to buy back the leasehold at the price asked, the tenant can sell it to another person, with the landlord having the right to perhaps 10 per cent of the sale.

The new type of leasehold called *cesión* is less rigid than the old *traspaso* and there is no exact legal format required. A property owner and a business tenant can agree on any conditions they choose, which often means that the deal is much like a normal rental contract. These business rentals or leases are usually open-ended, with no final cut-off point as long as the tenant continues to pay the rent.

Watch out for:

Be particularly alert to the terms of any lease or rental contract you purchase from a presently operating business. Sometimes it is presented by the seller as a leasehold when it is simply a rental agreement which gives the tenant no rights to any of the profit from re-selling it.

When you are asked to pay a large sum of money for a "leasehold", you want to be very sure that you are buying something which you will later have the right to sell. If all that is being offered is a rental agreement, then you are paying for nothing.

This has happened to more than one business purchaser in Spain, who sees the term *traspaso* on the contract heading and believes he is buying a lease, when the contract, when carefully read, turns out to be just a rental.

Take legal advice before you get into a Spanish lease.

GLOSSARY

Alquiler – rental
Arrendamiento – rental, lease
Cesión – lease
Contrato de vivienda – long-term residential contract
Contrato por temporada – short-term holiday contract
Fianza – deposit
Inquilino – tenant
Ley de Arrendamiento Urbano – rental law
Propietario – owner, landlord
Tanteo y Retracto – right of first refusal to buy property
Traspaso – old form of leasehold

YOU AND YOUR CAR AND ON THE ROAD IN SPAIN

7

SECTION ONE – YOU AND YOUR CAR

CARS ON FOREIGN REGISTRATION	122
POLICE CHECK FOREIGN CARS	123
TAX-FREE IMPORTATION	125
TOURIST REGISTRATION	126
CARS ON SPANISH PLATES	127
MUNICIPAL VEHICLE TAX	129
BUYING USED CARS	130
TAKE CARE WITH TRANSFER	131
VEHICLE INSPECTION	132
JUNK YOUR OLD CAR	132
BUYING USED CAR IN EUROPE	133
BOATS, CARAVANS,MOTORCYCLES	133
INSURING YOUR CAR	135
IF YOU HAVE AN ACCIDENT	138

SECTION TWO - ON THE ROAD IN SPAIN

WHO NEEDS WHAT LICENCE?	140
EU CITIZEN NON-RESIDENT	140
EU CITIZEN RESIDENT	140
NON EU CITIZEN NON-RESIDENT	141
NON-EU CITIZEN RESIDENT	142
NEW LICENCE POINT SYSTEM	143
TRAFFIC CODE FOR 2006	145
VIOLATIONS AND PENALTIES	146
FINES PAYABLE ON THE SPOT	148
PROTEST TRAFFIC TICKET	148

SECTION ONE -
YOU AND YOUR CAR

WHEN you move to Spain, do you sell your old car and buy a Spanish one?

Can you take your present car with you and keep it in Spain on its UK or other European registration?

If you do, what happens after you've spent some time in Spain?

Can you import the car and register it in Spain?

Can you keep your foreign-plated car in Spain to use on your holiday visits?

If you become a resident, do you have to have a car on Spanish registration?

Let's look at these questions one by one.

Cars with foreign registration

Let's suppose that you already own a car with British or German registration. If you are a tourist in Spain, you can operate such a car for six months in a calendar year with no formalities beyond the presentation at the border of your driving licence, car registration and insurance certificate. That is, if anyone bothers to stop you at the frontier.

You can keep your foreign-registered car in Spain permanently, but you will have to garage it for six months of each year. You can only drive it on Spanish roads for six months.

With Spain's entry into the EU, the international insurance certificate, or so-called "green card", is no longer necessary, but you may find that your individual policy gives only minimum coverage when you are outside your country without it, so check to be sure.

Your driving licence from your home country will be acceptable for the first six months of your stay in Spain, though authorities recommend that you have either an international driving licence or an official translation of your licence, which you can get from the Spanish consulate in your home country.

Neither the translation nor the international licence is absolutely necessary if you are an EU citizen. For more on licences, see the next chapter.

If you own a vacation home in Spain which you visit at Christmas time and in the summer, you can freely operate your foreign-registered car, using your foreign driving licence, with no further problems, as long as your total visits to Spain don't pass six months in any calendar year. The six months need not be continuous. It could be three visits of two months each, for example.

Because this period lies in a calendar year, it has this peculiarity: if the visitor enters Spain after June 30, he can keep and operate his foreign-registered car for the last six months of that year, and the first six months of the following year.

The six-month period is based on the stay of the person himself in the country, rather than on the length of stay of the car. That is, a European who stays in Spain for four months without a car, then decides to return to his home country and bring his car back with him, can only operate the car in Spain for another two months. He can keep it in Spain but he can't legally drive it.

So how do they know whether or not you are driving the car? Good question. For European Union citizens, there really is no effective way to know whether the car is being driven or not. They formerly were required to have the car officially "sealed" for six months of each year, but EU citizens no longer have to do this.

If you go to the trouble of obtaining exit and entry stamps in your passport, you will have definite proof of the length of your stay.

Warning: Police are checking foreign-plate cars in Spain

We all know that many Europeans really live full-time in Spain without obtaining a residence card, perhaps working illegally as well, and continue to operate their cars on non-Spanish plates.

The Spanish traffic police have been very lenient about these cars but they are now starting to crack down. In some areas where many foreigners live, they have stopped the cars they see regularly on the road and politely asked the drivers to clarify their situation.

When the EU driver says that he comes and goes and that he is never in Spain for more than six months in one year, the police politely ask him for documentary evidence.

They understand that it is difficult to produce a passport stamp inside the EU these days, so they will accept practically any paper, such as a recently dated airline ticket or train ticket or any other evidence that the person has travelled within the last six months.

If you are coming to Spain by car, we advise you to take all the trouble necessary to obtain an exit stamp from your home country.

Even if you have to go and search for a border official, take the time and do it. This proof of your date of departure can be very handy later.

The police are also interested in whether the car is insured in its country of origin, or whether it is insured by one of the international companies. EU legislation requires that a car be insured in its country of registration. This means that no Spanish company can insure a vehicle registered in another country. This is a problem because your home country's insurance companies will not insure the car without a valid inspection certificate. And you cannot obtain this because your car is in Spain. The Spanish vehicle inspection is not legally valid in your home country, although some international insurance companies will accept it.

The police also observe the last date of the vehicle inspection. If it is a UK car, and its last MOT in Britain dates from 10 years ago, this would arouse suspicion. The law says that a foreign-registered car may stay in Spain as long as it is road-legal in its home country. This means that a UK car must have a current MOT. In practice the police do not usually insist on this but they can do so if they choose.

If the car has been inspected in Spain, in order to obtain the insurance, this is another piece of evidence. If the driver cannot produce any documents to prove his own absence from Spain, they have levied fines of €1,800 and more. They then require that the car be either imported into Spain and issued with Spanish registration, or immediately taken out of the country. You have been warned.

Non-EU Citizens subject to sealing

Non-EU citizens, such as Americans and Canadians, are still subject to the sealing requirement if they wish to keep their foreign-registered cars permanently in Spain. It works like this:

If you decide to stay in Spain after your six-month period is up, and you do not wish to drive your car out of the country, you can ask the Spanish customs officials to "seal" the car for you until you wish to remove it.

To have your car sealed, or *precintado*, you notify the customs officials, Aduana. They in turn notify the Guardia Civil, who will come, fill out the forms, and put some strips of tape across the steering wheel of the car, designed to ensure that you do not use it. The process is not expensive.

When you are ready to depart with the car, contact the customs office again; they will unseal the car.

You can then use the car six months, have it sealed until the end of the year, and use it again for the first six months of the following year. This sealing provision is useful for people who wish to keep their foreign-registered car in Spain all year round, but who only operate the car during their visits here.

Further, if you are not an EU citizen, you are required to have the car sealed if you leave it in Spain for more than two months while you yourself are absent. This sealing procedure applies only to non-EU citizens.

This is all very well, you say, for a tourist or a regular visitor, but I intend to take up full-time residence in Spain, and I want to know if I can keep my foreign-registered car with me and use it on Spanish roads.

No, you can't. An official resident of Spain must operate a car on full and normal Spanish registration. There is no way around this. After all, a Spaniard living and working in the UK would not be allowed to keep his Spanish-registered car forever, either.

Tax-free importation

Anyone, EU or non-EU, moving to Spain to take up official residence gets a break if they want to bring with them a car they already own.

This car will be exempt from import duties, from Spanish IVA of 16 per cent, and from Spain's own special registration tax of 12 per cent or 7 per cent, a noteworthy saving of 28 per cent.

If the engine size is less than 1600 cubic centimetres, the special tax is only 7 per cent. The 7 per cent also applies to diesel vehicles under 2000 cubic centimetres.

For Europeans, of course, there are no duties in any case, but for other nationalities the exemption from Spain's 10-per-cent import duty comes in handy.

The conditions for the exemption are that you must have owned the car for at least six months, you must have paid VAT in the country of origin and you must obtain a certificate of *baja de residencia*, a certificate of non-residence, from the country you are leaving.

Some nationalities can obtain this certificate from the town hall where they live. It can also consist of a declaration made to the

Spanish consulate in your home country, declaring your intention to leave your residence and reside officially in Spain. Or you can make the declaration to your own consulate inside Spain after you arrive, stating that you are taking up residence in Spain.

The consulate will then issue the certificate, allowing you to apply for tax-exempt importation of your car.

Warning: Procedures to import a car this way must be started within one month from the date of issue of the residence permit. Be careful here, because you may very well receive your actual residence permit, which you must present, several months after the issue date stamped on it

Really, it is best to apply for the car exemption at the same time you apply for your residence card. Because of this complication and the rest of the red tape involved in this application, you will need the services of an expert gestor — but it can be done.

Citizens of most countries must also report to their home country traffic department that their vehicle is being permanently exported. This will avoid your being charged road tax in your home country for a vehicle which is no longer registered there.

Even without paying any taxes, the procedure will cost you around €700 for the various papers involved.

Remember that any concession on the duty-free import of cars applies only to people who take out an official residence permit. Such persons have always been able to import their household effects and furniture into Spain free of duty (see section on "Importing Your Possessions"), but automobiles formerly were not included.

Cars on tourist plates

Real savings are available to non-EU persons who remain non-residents and purchase a new car on Spanish tourist plates.

This is the "export" registration provided by a number of countries. An American tourist, for example, can purchase his Mercedes-Benz directly from the factory in Germany, drive it around Europe for six months on the "Z" plates issued to him, without paying any of the normal German taxes. He will finally import the car into the United States, pay duty on a used car, and have it definitively registered.

This registration is designed, by its nature, to be temporary, lasting only until the car is taken to its new home, where taxes are paid.

An American who buys a €30,000 vehicle on Spanish tourist plates can save himself almost €10,000 by skipping Spain's total taxes of 28 per cent. He can have the car to use for a total of six months in any calendar year. These six months need not be continuous. He can make several visits as long as the total time does not exceed six months.

He is also required to have this tourist-plate car *precintado*, or sealed, if he is absent from Spain for more than two months (see above).

If he wishes to have the car available for use twelve months of the year, he can renew this tourist registration every year indefinitely. One *gestoría* cited a total cost, including their fees, of around €600 for each renewal. This means twice a year. If the tourist plate has expired, the renewal fee is much higher. If you keep the car permanently in one town, they will charge you annual municipal vehicle tax as well.

The only requirements are that the car must be purchased with foreign currency and it cannot be bought on hire purchase.

Meanwhile, official residents and Spaniards themselves are paying the full freight of 28 per cent on each car they buy on normal Spanish registration.

Buying a car on Spanish plates

Buying a car on Spanish plates, just the way Spaniards do, can save a lot of complications and has certain advantages. You do not have to pay in foreign currency and you can purchase on the instalment plan.

Britons in particular will find that new Spanish cars are priced lower than the same models in the UK.

A foreigner may buy a car on Spanish plates if he meets one of the following qualifications:

1. He holds an official residence permit.

2. He presents the *escritura* (title deed) to a home he owns in Spain. The deed must be for a dwelling, not a place of business, and it must be in the personal name of the foreigner, not in the name of a company, especially an offshore company;

3. He presents a *Certificado de Empadronamiento*, a certificate showing that he is a registered inhabitant of the municipality whose town hall issues the document. This is not a residence permit; it is only a registration certificate showing that the per-

son lives in that municipality. You get this certificate by presenting your passport, a title deed or rental contract at your town hall.

4. He presents a rental contract of one year's duration.

Note of caution: If you are a non-resident and you buy a car on Spanish registration, make sure that you obtain one of the following documents:

1. An International Driving Permit to carry in addition to your home country licence.

2. Or, you can obtain an official translation of your driving licence, often available through the Spanish Consulate in your home country.

3. Or, you can obtain a *Certificado de Equivalencia,* (a Certificate of Equivalence) which is prepared by Spain's Royal Automobile Club, the *RACE.*

This applies to both EU and non-EU citizens. The reason for the exercise is that Spanish traffic police want somebody who is regularly on Spanish roads and not merely a tourist visitor to carry a licence they can read and understand. You can be fined €300 if you do not comply. When you make the rounds of auto dealers in your part of Spain, collecting brochures and comparing prices, you will find many makes and models available, at prices in some cases a little lower than in the rest of Europe. Renaults, Fords, Opels, Seats, Citroëns, all manufactured in Spain, are among the best sellers. Dealers compete in offering guarantees, financing terms and special sales.

Besides these Spanish-manufactured cars, you can also find dealers specialising in imported cars on Spanish plates. Imported cars have actually captured 25 per cent of the Spanish market.

If you are a new arrival and don't own property, you may be asked to provide some financial certification that you can pay for the car, or even be required to find a Spanish co-signer to guarantee your payments.

You make a deposit on the car, which will vary from dealer to dealer, and agree terms from one to four years. Interest rates have come down on these plans as competition grows keener.

If you decide on a two-year scheme, for example, you will make your down payment and then sign a series of 24 *letras*, or bills of exchange, for the instalments. These *letras* oblige you to make the payments and are often addressed directly to your bank account for payment.

Government offers €721 off

If you are already a resident and running a Spanish car that is 10 years old, you can take advantage of a government offer that gives you a discount of up to €721 when buying a new Spanish car.

You must junk your old car to take advantage of this scheme, called the Prever plan, which is designed to encourage the scrapping of old cars circulating on Spanish roads.

You can even buy a used car up to five years old under the plan. The basic discount is €480 euros. If you scrap a car that burns regular gasoline to buy a new diesel, this discount rises to €721. The saving comes to the buyer as a discount against the special registration tax of 12 per cent.

You will usually find that the dealer can handle all the necessary paperwork for you, as well as sell you your car insurance. Full coverage is usually required if you buy your car on the instalment plan.

Municipal vehicle tax

You pay your vehicle tax each year at the town hall. If you are not paid up, you will not be able to sell or trade in the car later.

This is the *Impuesto Municipal Sobre Vehículos De Tracción Mecánica*, a municipal tax on vehicles registered in each town. Formerly this tax was charged at a single rate all over Spain, but now each municipality is free to charge whatever rate it sees fit, so the tax varies from town to town.

It is based on the *potencia fiscal* of the car, its horsepower as rated for tax purposes. Small cars pay around €50 and large cars €100 and even more. Motor cycles also pay this tax each year.

Your car will go on the books of the town where you live as soon as you are registered as the owner of the car with the traffic authorities in the provincial capital.

To pay the tax go into the town hall and ask for the appropriate window. April and May are the usual times to pay, but this varies from town to town. You will not necessarily receive an individual notification, but announcements will appear in banks, in the newspaper and on the municipal notice-board. It's best to ask when the tax is due. Late payment will draw a fine of 5 per cent during the first month and 20 per cent thereafter.

Many municipalities are now offering local taxpayers a carrot-and-stick programme, in which those who pay their taxes early get a discount. You can also arrange to have the tax paid by standing order at your bank.

This vehicle circulation tax receipt is one of the papers you should keep with you in your car, along with the car's official registration papers and insurance receipt, as the police may ask to see it at any time.

You cannot sell your car or trade it in for a new model without the paid-up vehicle tax receipt.

Be advised that you should take all your car papers into your *ayuntamiento* (town hall) when you purchase a new or used car to register for the tax. The Traffic Department is supposed to inform the town halls but it is best to be sure. The same applies when you sell or scrap your car. Make sure that you de-register your car at the town hall, or you will be charged tax for the following year.

Used cars

There is an active market in used cars in Spain, with many makes and models available. Used-car dealers can be found in all towns of any size and the new-car dealers have departments where they recondition and sell older cars taken as trade-ins for new ones. Dealers offer widely varying guarantees, prices and service, so be sure to shop around.

A resident can purchase a second-hand car on Spanish plates, just as if he were a Spaniard. You may be unpleasantly surprised at the high prices for second-hand cars, but that is the way the market is in Spain. As we have seen, taxes on automobiles are higher than in most other European countries, and in most parts of Spain the good weather ensures that cars deteriorate less rapidly than they do in many other parts of the world.

Many of the used cars available here are former rental cars. The Costa del Sol in fact may be the world's capital of hire cars, as those thousands of tourists who pick up their cars every week at Málaga airport attest.

Sometimes you can find a real bargain directly from a car hire company disposing of its two-year-old cars, and sometimes you find a real lemon being passed off by a dealer as a privately-owned car. Be alert.

The dealer who sells you your second-hand car will probably be quite happy to arrange the transfer of title to you for a small fee. In a private sale, you and the seller can go to a *gestoría* which handles automobile transfers.

You can also go directly to the *Jefatura de Tráfico*, the motor vehicle department in your province, and handle the whole thing yourself, thus saving any intermediary's fees.

Take care with transfer

To do this, you will need:

1. The application form which you obtain at the provincial Traffic Department.

2. The circulation permit of the vehicle, with the transfer of owners listed on the back, including the seller's signature.

3. The paid-up municipal vehicle tax receipt, along with a photocopy.

4. Receipt for the payment of the vehicle transfer tax, charged at 4 per cent on the sale of second-hand vehicles. This tax is paid to the Spanish Tax Agency on Form 620.

5. A current ITV report and photocopy. This is the *Inspección Técnica de Vehículos*, the vehicle inspection certificate.

6. Residence permit and photocopy.

7. Payment of €40 fee.

Present all your documentation at the Traffic Department, including a stamped, self-addressed envelope for them to send you the finished documents.

Be wary of handling the used-car transaction on your own, however. If you are selling your old car, make absolutely sure that the transfer is completed into the new owner's name. Do not deliver the vehicle until you see that the transfer has been registered with the Traffic Department.

Otherwise, you may find that the new owner conveniently forgets to register the car in his own name, which leaves you as the still-registered owner liable for any parking tickets or road taxes that come due on the car.

If you fear that this may be the case, you must then have the vehicle de-registered in your name. This is called a *baja de matrícula*.

Again, you obtain the form from the Traffic Department, and you must present the receipt for the current year's municipal vehicle tax. If you no longer have the circulation permit and the inspection certificate, because they are with the new owner, you can make a sworn declaration of this.

You must also make this application for *baja* when you scrap an old car. Sometimes you think that the car is off the road when it has in fact been repaired and someone totally unknown to you is illegally operating it.

Make the de-registration and you will be protected from later consequences.

Vehicle inspection required

Vehicle inspection is compulsory for Spanish-registered cars more than four years old. Be alert when purchasing an older car, and ask for the ITV (*Inspección Técnica de Vehículos*) certificate. If the car doesn't have one, you have to have the car tested yourself if you want to use it on public roads, and there's no guarantee it will pass the test. When you hear Spaniards say ITV, they mean MOT.

DOWNLOAD FORMS FROM TRAFFIC WEB SITE

The Spanish Traffic Department, the *Dirección General de Tráfico,* maintains a very useful web site that offers a great deal of information on all subjects having to do with cars, roads, and driving. You can even fill in and download many of the forms necessary for various transactions with them. The web site is www.dgt.es and the specific address for the forms is www.dgt.es/indices/dgthtm_impresos_es.html.

Junk your old car

Spain is now fulfilling the terms of a European Union directive that requires old cars to be scrapped with a minimum of waste and contamination to the environment.

Authorised centres for this disposal of scrapped vehicles are opening around the country. Generally you must go the centre with your car and its registration documents. They will scrap the vehicle in a proper manner and give you a certificate of its authorised destruction.

You should then take this certificate to your town hall and

de-register the vehicle to avoid their charging you further municipal vehicle tax.

(See "What to Do" section on junking your old car)

Buying used cars in Europe

Even though Spanish new car prices tend to be lower than new car prices in other EU countries, Spain's used cars tend to be rather more expensive, especially in the Mediterranean coastal areas. Perhaps they simply hold their value better in a sunny climate.-

This situation has given rise to a thriving market in used cars imported into Spain from Germany or Belgium. One estimate calculates that a mid-level BMW about two years old can be bought and imported from Germany at a savings of around 25 per cent. This includes the payment of that Spanish special vehicle registration tax of 12 per cent. Spain is the only EU country to maintain this tax.

Be warned, however, that there is plenty of paperwork and delay. Experienced *gestores* report that the process can take more than three months The various testing and registration fees can easily reach ¤600, in addition to the special tax.

They also advise the prospective importer to make sure the original factory invoice for the car is available and to have the vehicle inspected and certified roadworthy in its country of origin even before it enters Spain.

Boats, caravans and motor cycles

Yachts, caravans and motor cycles with engines of more than 49cc are treated basically the same as cars, but with a few differences.

Boats

You can enter a Spanish port with your foreign-registered yacht and keep it here and use it in Spanish waters for six months of a calendar year, just as with cars. The six-month period need not be continuous — an advantage for people who want to keep their yacht in a Spanish port but can only use it for a month or two at a time on extended visits. The customs authorities in the marina can seal the boat *(precintar)* while its owner is away, and unseal it when he wishes to use it. Thus, the non-resident can keep his boat in a Spanish port all year and use it for six months of that year.

Like cars, yachts are also available from dealers in Spain on a

Spanish tourist flag registration, under which they do not pay normal Spanish taxes. Such a yacht can be used six months of the year, and an extension of its tourist registration requested each year to permit its owner to use it all year.

One useful provision of the sealing process for the non-resident yacht owner is that he can have his boat sealed for the last six months of the year and continue to live aboard it. He may not sail it out of the harbour, but he can use it as his home.

Import duties on a used yacht still come to something more than half the value of the boat, depending on the evaluation the customs authorities make. In addition, you can only import the boat if you are taking up official residence in Spain.

A Spanish resident will also need to obtain Spanish marine certification to operate his yacht in Spanish waters.

Caravans

Caravans are treated almost exactly like cars. That is, if you enter Spain with your caravan pulled by your car, you have six months in the calendar year to circulate freely as a tourist. You can also have the caravan sealed by the customs officials should you wish to leave it behind and drive out with your car.

Motorcycles

Motorcycles (*motos*) with engines of more than 49 c.c. are treated exactly like cars, with the same six-month time limit.

The small 49cc machines are a different story. You do not need a *Certificado de Empadronamiento* or any other document to purchase one, and you can even import your foreign-registered bike duty-free as part of your personal possessions when you take up residence in Spain.

Initially your foreign licence and, later, your foreign licence with its translation, or an international permit, will be valid for these bikes. Your Spanish driving licence will also be valid.

If, like some people, you have no driving licence at all but want to operate one of these convenient little bikes for dashing around town, you can get a special licence to do so by taking a simple examination. Most driving schools can steer you through the process for a small fee.

Until recently even a youngster of 14 could ride a 49cc machine legally. No longer. Today the minimum age to get any *moto* licence is 16. At 18, your boy or girl can get a regular driving licence.

Don't forget to warn him/her that he/she must wear a helmet both in town and on the highway or risk a fine.

INSURING YOUR CAR

If you are visiting Spain, either for a short or extended stay, are still on tourist status and are driving your foreign-registered car, all the auto insurance you need is the coverage by your insurance company in your home country, extended to cover travel in Spain.

Your own company can issue you a "green card", as the international insurance certificate is popularly known. If you are from an EU country, you no longer need to present this to the Spanish border officials when you enter, but it is still a good idea to have it even if there are no longer any border guards. Because some insurance companies limit their coverage to the legal minimum outside their own national borders unless the policy holder has arranged for his green card.

Spanish cars:

Let's suppose that you have just purchased your Spanish car, on tourist plates or on normal Spanish registration, new or second-hand. The dealer who sells it to you will either have an insurance company representative as part of his organisation or will be happy to steer you to his brother-in-law who sells auto insurance. His brother-in-law's company may be fine, but it also pays to shop around, or at least ask among other foreign residents in your area to recommend a company.

If you are buying a new car on instalments, you may have little choice in what insurance you want. The dealer usually requires you to have full-coverage insurance on the car until it is paid off.

For a small car, this all-risk—*todo riesgo*— insurance will cost you between €1,200 and €1,800, depending on whether you are an excitable young man or a prudent woman of mature years (though you can find cheaper rates with companies offering their policies via the Internet).

These personal details are factored into your premium as insurance companies become more sophisticated. On the other hand, you can drive legally for as little as €400 a year, or even less, with a 50 per cent discount as a no-claims bonus. This price will cover the obligatory insurance, required by Spanish law. It now covers you for claims by third parties up to the amount of €360,000 for bodily harm and €100,000 for damages.

A "third party" is anyone who makes a claim against you for injury or damage suffered as a result of the use of your car. It includes driver and passengers in another car with which you may collide. It may include even passengers in your own car who are not members of your family. It includes pedestrians, and the owners of any property you may damage. If you drive your car into someone's wall and knock it down, the wall's owner can make a claim against you.

This minimum insurance does not cover you or your car at all. It covers only other persons and their property, and only up to the limits above. This coverage is the legal minimum.

If you are injured by a driver who has no insurance at all, the Spanish insurance consortium, which backs the entire industry, will pay out amounts up to these limits. The Spanish limits used to be even lower but they are gradually being raised. This of course means a corresponding rise in premiums.

If you want further coverage, you can take out additional insurance, and most people do. For a few hundred euros more, you can get the same third-party coverage, but up to much higher sums or even unlimited, which means no ceiling on what the company will pay in the case of a terrible accident with very high claims.

You can choose just what you need to insure. Such as yourself and your family, for example, who do not count as third parties, or your shiny new car. You can buy coverage against theft, fire, damage, death or injury, and even insurance to pay for legal costs involved in court proceedings brought against you or which you have to bring against another driver when claiming damages. You can get comprehensive insurance covering all these, or a policy covering only part.

Let's look at a few possibilities. Total coverage can cost you €1,000 or more, depending on the size and age of your car, but you can get quite a lot of protection by taking out a policy under which you yourself pay the first €200 or so of any small damage to your car. This exemption is called a *franquicia*. Because you promise to pay this much, the company saves expense in administration and paperwork, and you get your major coverage more cheaply.

A typical policy might be one in which you pay the first €300 of any claim against you and you are insured for:

1. The full value of the car in case of fire or accident.
2. Up to 80 per cent of its value in case of theft.
3. Coverage for you and your family in case of death or permanent injury.
4. Coverage of legal expenses.
5. Unlimited coverage for third-party claims against you.

This should cost around €700 a year for a mid-sized car. Over the years, if there are no claims against your policy, you will get a "no-claims bonus", i.e. a discount on your premiums.

Different companies offer different terms and premiums can vary widely. In my own case, I carry no insurance at all on my own car, as it is quite old, so I would have to pay any repair bills myself. This is a chance that I take. I also pay only €300 a year for my coverage because I have a discount of 50 per cent for many years without making a claim.

Finally, if your car is insured in Spain and you wish to drive it to an EU country, your Spanish insurance will cover you, but only for the legal minimum in each country, so it is a good idea to take out a green card for your trip out of Spain. Some companies charge extra for the green cards. Others offer it as a free service.

Foreign cars in Spain

Many foreigners stay for long periods in Spain as non-residents, keeping their foreign-plated cars with them.

Legally, a foreign-registered car can stay on Spanish roads for six months in a calendar year without any formalities at all. In fact, the car itself can remain in Spain permanently, although it can only be operated on the road for six months of that year and must be garaged for the other six months.

The new problem for these cars comes from European Union regulations which now require that all cars be insured in their country of registration. Formerly, the owners of these British or other cars simply insured them with Spanish companies. They can no longer do this.

Nor can they obtain insurance from the UK because the car has never been returned for its MOT and it is no longer a UK resident, as it were.

Some insurance companies have come up with a sort of off-shore insurance that will cover the car in any country except its original home. If you are in this situation, ask your insurance broker. With the European liberalisation of insurance companies, there are also Spanish branches of UK companies which will insure the car on UK plates.

These companies will require your car to pass the Spanish vehicle safety inspection, the ITV, to make sure it is in sound operating condition. You get your ITV sticker, which satisfies the insurance company but has no other legal force. Your car, if it is British-registered, remains illegal in the UK because it has no British MOT. Technically, the car is not legal in Spain either without its UK MOT, but police seldom ask. If you take it back to the UK, you will have to pass the MOT immediately.

What you really want to know is: what happens when you make a claim? Will the Spanish insurance company pay you? The short answer is, Spanish insurance companies are just as reluctant to pay out as most other companies, but they are also prepared to live up to their legal obligations.

If you have full coverage and someone dents your new car in the parking lot and departs without leaving his name, you will probably find that your insurance company pays up quickly and without a murmur for the repairs. But you may lose any credit you have been getting as a no-claims bonus. If the claim is not your fault, many companies will continue your credit.

On the other hand, if there is an accident and you feel the other driver is at fault, but he chooses to contest this, you may have to wait as long as three years for a court decision in back-logged Spanish courts.

If you have an accident

So some idiot has darted out of a side street without looking and pranged your new car. Or perhaps you yourself were careless, followed another vehicle too closely and banged into it.

In Spain procedures to follow after an accident are much the same as in any country. The police may appear and take all the details of both drivers. Or, in the case of smaller accidents, the two drivers can settle the matter between themselves. If there is no personal injury, it is not necessary to inform the police.

The two drivers can fill in the standard European Union form for a mutual agreement. This is called a *Declaración Amistosa*, a friendly declaration, in Spanish.

See "What To Do" section regarding an accident.

Keep in mind the two basic principles.

1. Do not admit any fault, even if your own actions are clearly the cause of the accident. Such admission can even give your insurance company a reason not to pay out.

2. Do not sign the mutual agreement form. Once signed, it is powerful evidence in court and can work against you if you have not understood it perfectly.

You must be sure to get the licence number, the name and the insurance company of the other driver. Do not be intimidated by any shouted threats. It is an upsetting situation, but try to keep your wits about you.

Remember that you have two months in order to bring a charge against the other driver. If you are sure that he is at fault, it is better to do this immediately, but it is not absolutely necessary.

If you live in Spain, the normal procedure will be to contact your insurance agent quickly. He will lead you through the process.

If you wish to make a charge, you go to the local police station, make a declaration and then let the insurance companies sort it out. Even if it seems clear that the fault is yours, do not be too quick to admit it. Again, let the insurance company handle it.

The Spanish courts do function, eventually. A friend of mine saw a car back into her own car in a parking lot, crumpling the door. The offending driver fled, but she was able to get the car's licence number. She traced the owner through this number, went to the police station and made a charge against him. Two years later she was summoned to a court hearing, where the other driver denied everything. The court ruled in her favour, however, and ordered the other driver to pay for all damages plus court costs, which his insurance company paid.

Two years was a long time to wait, but there is a satisfaction when justice is done.

SECTION TWO
ON THE ROAD IN SPAIN

A genuine tourist visiting Spain and driving either his own car from his own country or a Spanish rental car can do so on the licence issued to him in his home country. He needs no translation or official certification to do this, and the privilege is good for a visit up to six months.

After that it gets more complicated.

WHO NEEDS WHAT LICENCE?

EU citizen, non-resident
For the first six months of your stay in Spain, driving your car on European Union registration or a Spanish rental car, you can use your home country licence with no problem.

If you operate your UK or other foreign-registered vehicle for more than six months, however, you can be fined or even have the vehicle impounded.

If you are driving a vehicle which you own on normal Spanish registration, you must have one of the following extra documents:

1. An International Driving Permit in addition to your home country licence.

2. Or, you can obtain an official translation of your driving licence, often available through the Spanish Consulate in your home country.

3. Or, you can obtain a *Certificado de Equivalencia,* a "Certificate of Equivalence", which is prepared by Spain's Royal Automobile Club, the RACE.

This applies to both EU and non-EU citizens who own cars on normal Spanish registration. The reason for the exercise is that Spanish traffic police want somebody who is regularly on Spanish roads and not merely a tourist visitor to carry a licence they can read and understand.

If you do not have one of these extra documents, you can be fined €300 for improper licence.

EU citizen, resident
1. Spanish driving licence.

2. Your home country licence. It is no longer necessary to have this licence registered and stamped by the Spanish Traffic Department.

It is very easy now to exchange your EU driving licence for a Spanish permit. Go to your provincial traffic headquarters with your present licence and a photocopy, one photo, and your residence card and photocopy. If you are lucky and the line is short, you can get your Spanish licence within a few hours. Cost is only €15.80. This exchange procedure is called a *canje.*

If you later return to your home country, you can re-exchange your Spanish licence for a home country licence, just as you did here, only in reverse.

Spain allows EU citizens who take out a Spanish residence permit to continue using their original licences. Until the end of 2004, it was necessary to have this licence registered and stamped at the provincial traffic headquarters. After protests to the European Union, this registration is no longer necessary.

Non-EU, non-resident

For the first six months of your stay in Spain, driving your car on its home country registration, or driving a rental car, you can simply use your home country licence with no problem.

If you cannot document your absence from Spain in the past six months, you can be fined €300 for improper licence. Spanish traffic police know that many foreigners are staying in Spain over their legal time limit, and they are starting to crack down on this practice.

If you are driving a vehicle which you own, on Spanish registration, you must have:

1. An International Driving Permit to carry in addition to your home country licence.

2. Or, you can obtain an official translation of your driving licence, often available through the Spanish Consulate in your home country.

3. Or, you can obtain a *Certificado de Equivalencia,* a "Certificate of Equivalence", which is prepared by Spain's Royal Automobile Club, the *RACE.*

This applies to both EU and non-EU citizens. Spanish traffic police want somebody who is regularly on Spanish roads (and not merely a tourist visitor) to carry a licence they can read and understand.

Non-EU citizen, resident

Now things start to get tough for the non-European Union citizen. He absolutely must have a Spanish driving licence when he becomes a resident of Spain. There is no alternative.

Furthermore, he cannot exchange his home country licence for a Spanish one. Because the European Union is still working out its international agreements on driving licences, very few non- EU licences can be exchanged at this time, and for the immediate future.

This means that Americans, Australians, South Africans and so on must take the Spanish driving examination, both written and practical, just as beginning Spanish drivers do.

Furthermore, they must take the written exam in Spanish, except in some provinces, such as Málaga. Formerly the exam could be taken in several languages but now it is only in Spanish in most areas. Really, it is only logical. A person who does not know that *peligro* means "danger" could get into trouble.

Check driving schools in your area to see if you are among the lucky ones. The non-EU citizen must attend a Spanish driving school, and pay its fees, in order to take the exam. The Spanish *autoescuelas* have got a hammerlock on the system and have become semi-official bodies. You cannot go for the exam without the school.

A rock-bottom price for a few classes on the rules of the road, and a few driving classes, plus the exam cost, would be about €500.

And of course you must take the eye and reaction test as well.

The minimum age for a B licence, the most usual sort, is 18 and the maximum age is 65, if you have never held a licence before.

If you are 68 years old when you arrive in Spain, don't worry. The 65-year figure applies only to first-timers. You can continue to renew your existing permit as long as you are physically able to drive safely. If you are under 45, your licence will be issued for 10 years; between 45 and 70, for five years. Those over 70 will have to renew their licence every two years, which means a medical examination each time.

NEW FOR 2006: LICENCE POINTS

The big news for 2006 is that Spain has finally put into effect a point system for driving licences. This takes effect as of July 1, 2006.

Each driver starts with 12 points assigned to him. He can lose points for traffic infractions until he loses his driving privileges, and he can gain extra points for periods of safe driving.

Here is a summary of the new system, which is in addition to the existing system of fines, loss of licence and imprisonment in severe cases.

Two points off

- Exceeding posted speed limit 21-30 kph.
- Parking car in situation that causes risk to traffic or pedestrians or in bus lanes.
- Use of radar detection equipment.
- Driving without lights when required or incorrect use of lights.
- Carrying a child under 12 as passenger on motorbike.

Three points off

- Exceeding speed limit by 31-40 kph.
- Improper turn to change direction.
- Failure to maintain proper distance.
- Use of mobile phone, headset or other attention-distracting device while in movement.
- Failure to use seat belt, helmet or other required safety device.

Four points off

- Exceeding speed limit by more than 40 kph, unless the excess reaches more than 50 per cent of the legal limit.
- Alcohol content from .25 mg/l to .50mg/l in breath test. Half this amount for new drivers and professionals.
- Driving on motorway with unauthorised vehicle.
- Driving without proper licence.
- Throwing into the road or surroundings any object which could cause fire or accident.
- Negligent driving that causes risk to others.
- Running a stop sign or ignoring the rules of priority.
- Passing in a prohibited zone, causing danger or

hindering oncoming traffic, or passing under conditions of risk or in a zone of reduced visibility.
- Endangering or hindering bicyclists when passing.
- Backing on highways or motorways.
- Failure to heed indications of traffic officers.
- For professional drivers, carrying an excess of 50 per cent or more of the authorised passenger capacity, excluding the driver, except for buses.

Six points off

- Exceeding speed limit by 50 per cent when this is at least 30 kph above limit.
- Alcohol content in breath test exceeding .50 mg/l. For new drivers or professionals, exceeding .30 mg/l.
- Driving under the influence of mind-altering drugs, stimulants or other similar substance.
- Reckless driving, driving wrong way against traffic, unauthorised racing.
- For professional drivers, exceeding allotted driving time by 50 per cent or reducing allotted rest time by 50 per cent.

How the system works

Drivers are assigned 12 points. New drivers, with less than three years of experience, begin with only eight points. If the beginner drives for two years with no infractions, he gets four additional points to bring him up to twelve

Safe drivers are awarded two more points after three years without an infraction. After another three years they get one more extra point, making a total of 15 possible points.

CHECK YOUR POINTS

A driver can check on his number of points by going to the Traffic Department web site. The department is the Dirección General de Tráfico and the web site is www.dgt.es. The site also contains much more useful information.

When a driver loses points, he can recover up to four points by passing a course of driver safety education that consists of 15 hours of instruction. You can only do this once every two years. If a driver loses all his 12 points, he must wait six months until he can attend the safety course. He must also pass a theoretical exam. If a driver loses his licence for a second time, he must wait one year without a driving permit before he can attend the course.

TRAFFIC LAW AND FINES

Spain's revised traffic code cracks down harder on speeders and prohibits the use of mobile phones. It requires cars to carry reflective vests, regulates the use of child safety seats and stiffens penalties.

For the first time, police are empowered to retain the licence of a driver they estimate is not in condition to operate a vehicle. Drunk drivers face licence suspensions of one year and a possible six months in gaol.

Here are some of the principal new provisions:

Exceeding the speed limit by 50 per cent (and at least 30 kph) becomes a "very serious" infraction, with fines up to €602 and suspension of driving licence for three months.

This would include someone driving at 150 kph on a normal highway with a limit of 100 kph, for example. Or someone blasting his new BMW at 180 on the motorway, where the limit is 120 kph.

Speeding violations which do not exceed the limit by 50 per cent remain in the merely "serious" category.

Violations are divided into three categories, "minor", "serious" and "very serious" (see Box).

Further, the law provides that anyone who accumulates three "very serious" violations in a two-year period will have his driving privileges permanently revoked.

The new law specifically prohibits the use of mobile phones while driving. The only permitted use of either phones or radios is by a completely hands-off system. No headsets, microphones, helmets or similar rig may be used.

Radar detectors which warn drivers of the presence of police radar checks are also prohibited. You can be fined if you attempt to warn other drivers of police presence by flashing your headlights

VIOLATIONS AND PENALTIES

"Very serious" violations (*muy grave*)
(Fines from €302 to €602, suspension of licence up to three months)
· Exceeding limit of alcohol in the blood, or operating vehicle under the influence of drugs
· Refusal to take alcohol breath test
· Exceeding posted speed limit by 50 per cent, at least 30kph
· Reckless operation
· Driving against traffic
· Exceeding rated number of occupants of vehicle by 50 per cent
· For professional drivers, exceeding the permitted time at the wheel by 50 per cent, or not completing the programmed rest period by 50 per cent
· Racing

"Serious" violations (*grave*)
(Fines from €92 to €301, possible suspension of licence)
· Speeding in excess of 50 per cent
· Parking vehicle in dangerous position
· Negligent driving, driving without lights
· Throwing from car any object which could produce fire or accident

"Minor" violations (*menor*)
(Fines up to €91)
· Parking violations and a host of others.

Special cases
(Fines up to €1,503 and suspension of licence up to one year)
· Driving without proper licence
· Driving unregistered or improperly registered vehicle

Where a court finds reckless operation or other aggravating factors, drivers can be jailed for up to two years and have their licence suspended for up to six years, as well as awarding heavier fines and restitution payments to victims and families.

or making other signals.

Offenders can obtain a discount of 30 per cent for prompt payment of fines. If you choose, you can pay the policeman on the spot, or you can send a postal money order available at the post office.

The law places heavy emphasis on driver re-education in road safety. Drivers can reduce their fines by up to 30 per cent by attending consciousness-raising classes in special centres, including hospital visits to accident victims in some cases.

Even a driver who has lost his licence permanently may be able to recover it by attending these courses.

The traffic code puts stricter controls on infants and children in cars and on motorcycles. A child up to three years old cannot ride in the front seat under any circumstances. It must ride in the back, in a seat with restraints designed for its size.

A child from four to 12 years old who is shorter than 1.5 metres may ride in the front seat with a special seat or belt system. If none is available, the child must ride in the rear seat.

A child of 12 taller than 1.5 metres can use the adult seat belt in the front passenger seat. Any person shorter than 1.5 metres must be treated the same as the child.

The revised law makes parents of minor children responsible for paying fines incurred when these children operate motor-bikes, which they can do at 16 years of age, although they must wait until they are 18 to obtain a normal driving licence.

Children under 12 are not permitted to ride as passengers on motorbikes. In exceptional circumstances children seven years old may accompany a parent.

And, yes, in this nation of tailgaters a driver is required to maintain a safe distance behind the vehicle he is following, and he is obliged to leave enough space for another vehicle safely to pass him and pull in.

If you have ever thought of reporting a driver who follows too closely, you are perfectly within your rights. Any citizen may report a traffic violation. You must be prepared to testify in court, however, to make your accusation stick.

All Spanish cars must be fitted with seat-belts and they must be worn. You can be fined ¤90 for not wearing them, so be alert. It's a good habit anyway. All cars must be fitted with rear seat belts as well.

If the traffic police have reason to think a driver has been drinking they can require him to take a breath test to analyse the amount of alcohol in his blood. If it exceeds the minimum permitted, he can be heavily fined and have his licence revoked. It is your right to demand a blood test as well, if you feel the breath test is wrong.

Refusal to take the breath test can lead to a charge of disobeying a police officer, which can bring a penalty of six months in gaol.

Non-residents can be fined on the spot

If you are a non-resident tourist driving through Spain, you may be disturbed to discover that the Spanish police are authorised to demand payment on the spot for any traffic violation you commit.

The police can order your car impounded if you are unable to pay up. This is because their orders require them to take the steps necessary to ensure that the fine will be paid.

As a tourist has no property or other assets in Spain, which could be seized if he does not pay the fine, the agents can order that his vehicle be detained if he does not pay.

If you feel that you have been unfairly charged and wish to protest, you will have to pay the fine first, but you can fill in the space for contesting the ticket and mark *garantía* in the area where your payment is noted. This means that you consider your payment only a guarantee, necessary for the policeman to permit you to continue your trip, but that you intend to contest the ticket.

Just like the resident, you will be informed after a few months, when your court hearing is scheduled. You will have to list an address inside Spain for this purpose. You can then go to the Spanish court and make your case.

GLOSSARY

Aduana – customs
Baja de matrícula – de-registration of motor vehicle
Baja de residencia – non-residence certificate required for duty-free import
Canje – exchange of eu driving permit for spanish permit
Certificado de Equivalencia – certificate of equivalence of

foreign licence

Certificado de Empadronamiento – registration in municipality

Coche – car, automobile

Franquicia — automobile insurance policy excluding first part of claim

Impuesto Municipal Sobre Vehículos De Tracción Mecánica –
Municipal motor vehicle tax

Inspección Técnica de Vehículos – vehicle inspection, MOT

Jefatura de tráfico – Traffic Department headquarters

Letra – bill of exchange, signed for monthly car payments

Matrícula – registration

Matrícula turística – tax-free tourist registration

Multa – fine, traffic or otherwise

Permiso de circulación – permit for vehicle to circulate on public roads

Permiso de conducir – driving licence

Potencia fiscal – tax-rated horsepower

Precintar – to seal, as in automobile or yacht

Todo riesgo – comprehensive insurance covering all risks

YOU AND YOUR MONEY

8

IF YOU SELL YOUR PROPERTY   *152*
LOANS IN FOREIGN CURRENCY   *154*
TRANSFERS OF CASH, GOLD
  AND BEARER CHEQUES   *154*
OPERATIONS BETWEEN NON-RESIDENTS   *156*
TRANSACTIONS THROUGH BANKS   *155*
BANK ACCOUNTS IN SPAIN   *157*
NO COMMISSION ON PENSIONS   *158*
WRITING CHEQUES   *159*
TAKE CARE WITH *LETRAS*   *159*
DOMICILIACIÓN – STANDING ORDER   *160*
INVESTING IN SPAIN   *161*
INVESTING IN PROPERTY   *162*
TAX AVOIDANCE AND EVASION   *163*

FOR many European Union citizens in Spain, cross-border transactions have been greatly simplified by the introduction of the euro, with no more exchange rates and conversion tables to worry about. UK citizens, however, still have to deal with exchanging pounds for euros. So far, this is working in their favour. The strong pound has made Spanish property look so cheap that many Britons are buying in Spain.

The answer to your first question is: yes, you can take out of Spain all the money you bring in, and more. If you have made money by selling property at a profit or by working or investing, you are free to take your profits out of the country. There are forms to fill out and the normal Spanish taxes to pay, but you can do it.

Spain has free conversion of currency, but it also has a complex reporting system by which most transactions between residents and non-residents involving foreign exchange and a value in excess of ¤600 must be declared to the bank on Forms B-1, B-2 and B-3.

This declaration does not mean that the Spanish authorities can deny the exchange, only that it must be reported. Spanish banks have complained about the added paperwork, and it has been reflected in higher bank commissions for routine operations.

Both Spaniards and resident foreigners may hold bank accounts in foreign currencies, either inside Spain or abroad. If a resident opens such an account, he must inform the authorities within 30 days, however, and he must regularly present a form to the Bank of Spain detailing the movements in this account.

This measure makes it convenient for those expatriate residents who wish to retain bank accounts in their home countries, or who do business abroad, or who wish to keep their bank deposit certificates inside Spain but denominated in pounds or dollars. It also helps Spaniards who are doing business with other countries.

If you sell your property

Whether you are resident or non-resident, if you sell your property in Spain and receive payment in Spain, you have the right to take out the money and send it wherever you like.

If the amount is more than €600, however, you must have your bank fill in one of the "B" forms to report the transaction. These forms list full identification, details of the source of the funds and reason for the transaction. The forms are required in order to keep some control over laundering operations of black funds, where the source is not known.

The "B" form does not give Spanish authorities the power to refuse the transfer; it is only for information. In fact, our property seller does not need to present the form until 15 days after the transfer has taken place.

So, you can sell your property for €300,000, then change euros into pounds, and send them to your British bank account immediately. Or sell for euros. You can have a bank cheque made out in your name or you can have the bank transfer the funds to your British bank.

When a non-resident purchases Spanish property, he must also fill in the proper form. This is only to show that he originally imported the foreign currency into Spain and is not using black money — undeclared profits inside Spain — to make the purchase.

The non-resident buyer can also present a certified cheque in foreign currency if he is paying in another country's money. This is perfectly legal if the seller prefers to be paid in his own currency and avoids the need to fill in any forms at all.

The important element here is the identification. As long as the DGTE, the *Dirección General de Transacciones Exteriores*, the General Directorate of Foreign Transactions, knows who you are, which means that *Hacienda*, the taxation ministry, also knows who you are and what you have done, then they are satisfied.

If the taxes on the transactions are not paid, at least they know the name of the dodger and where to find him.

The Spanish Tax Agency has another control on non-resident property sellers. If you are a non-resident thinking you can take the money and run without paying your Spanish capital gains tax of 35 per cent on the profit, think again. The purchaser of your property must pay 5 per cent of the total purchase price directly to *Hacienda* in your name, as a guarantee that taxes will be paid (see tax section for details).

If you are tempted to obtain payment in some more portable and less traceable form, such as cash, bearer cheques, or gold coins, be warned that any such exportation over €30,000 is illegal unless the exporter obtains prior authorisation from the DGTE.

To do this legally, you must fill in form B-2, which contains all the pertinent information, and then await permission from the authorities to export the cash. This is routinely granted.

You then present the authorisation at the border to be stamped by the Spanish customs agents, if you can find one.

Falsification of any of the information on the form is an offence, as is attempting to take out of Spain more than €30,000 in cash or gold or bearer cheques.

Requiring this authorisation to export money does not square with European Council directives regarding free circulation of money and the European High Court has ruled that Spain may require notification but cannot limit the amount to be taken out.

Those caught taking out too much cash without authorisation can face prison sentences of up to 12 years. Spain so far has refused to change its legislation.

So Spain maintains a check on the amounts of foreign exchange passing across its borders, but you can transfer any amount of funds you choose in any form you choose. In practice, the government does not deny the authorisation, but you are warned that Spain is keeping an eye on you for your tax obligations. It seems fair enough.

Loans in foreign currency

A Spaniard or a resident can borrow freely from abroad in foreign currency for sums up to ¤1.5 million without any authorisation. Above that amount, permission is needed. The only condition is that the lender not be based in a "tax haven" on the Spanish government list.

This means that a home-buyer in Spain can obtain his mortgage from a lending institution in the UK or any other country, denominated in any currency he likes.

For some people, such loans or mortgages are the perfect solution. When your income is denominated in pounds, it is not a bad idea to have your loan in pounds as well, so you know that any currency fluctuations will not change your payment situation.

On the other hand, Spanish interest rates are lower than most and the banks are competing to offer mortgages that are competitive by any nation's standard. Furthermore, with the euro down against the pound, a Spanish mortgage in euros looks attractive.

Keep in mind also that foreign lenders are always reluctant to lend against property located in another country. European unity has not yet reached the stage where it is as easy for a bank in the UK to repossess a Spanish property as one in York.

Transfers of cash, gold and bearer cheques

Let's take a closer look at the regulations regarding transfers of funds in and out of Spain.

First we will take the rules regarding cash in any currency, gold bars, precious metals and bearer cheques, which you can carry in your attaché case across the border quite legally if you observe the regulations.

Any amount under the value of €6,000 is completely unregulated. You can carry this amount in or out of Spain without mentioning it, whether you are resident or non-resident.

Whether resident or non-resident, when bringing into Spain more than €6,000 in cash or bearer cheques, you are required to declare the sum to the customs authorities where you enter Spain, on form B-1. This form includes your personal details and a statement of what you intend to do with the funds.

If you are taking out of Spain more than €6,000 but less than €30,000, you must also fill in form B-1. You can do this at the bank where you obtain the cash or cheque, which will give you one copy for presentation to the customs agent at your point of departure, or you can make the declaration directly at the customs.

If you want to take out in cash more than €30,000, you must fill in form B-2 and request permission from the DGTE. This is routinely granted.

Both of these forms have a validity of 15 days only, so you will want to plan your trip accordingly.

If you are re-importing or re-exporting sums which you have previously imported or exported, you must also make the declarations, as long as they are more than €6,000.

Transactions through banks

The above refers only to cash, gold and bearer cheques. Transactions made through banks — the great majority of all money transfers in and out of Spain — are regulated more closely.

The top limit for absolutely free transfers is €600. That is, a resident or non-resident may obtain a bank cheque in foreign currency from his bank or effect a transfer in pounds sterling or US dollars up to this amount without any control at all, simply exchanging his euros for the foreign money.

In order to make a payment abroad of more than €600, the Spanish resident must declare to the bank the name and address of the recipient of the transfer or payment, and state the reason for the payment.

The resident must make this declaration to the bank before the payment is made, unless the payment is being made by a cheque in the name of the recipient, drawn on the resident's account, in which case the declaration may be made up to 15 days after the transfer.

So, even if you are just sending a cheque for €1,000 for an encyclopaedia you have ordered from London, you must fill in the form.

A resident who is receiving payments or transfers from abroad must also supply full information to the bank where the transfer arrives, including the name and address of the non-resident who sends the sum, and the reason for the operation.

This means that, if your pension cheque each month is more than €600, you must declare it each time. It takes only a moment to fill up the form at the bank.

The same declaration applies for transfers effected by debits and credits in your bank account to or from another bank account.

Residents who receive payments from non-residents, or make payments to them of more than €600 in cash or bearer cheques, must declare these payments on form B-3. This form includes the name, address and NIE of the resident and details of the non-resident and states the reason for the operation.

Note here that the resident who receives or makes the payment must make the declaration even when he is not the final recipient or the person responsible for the operation. This would include a fiscal representative who is receiving funds from abroad to pay his client's tax bill, for example, or a person who is acting as agent for another in making a payment abroad.

So, we see that transactions between residents and non-residents are documented for sums above €600 when they involve bank transfers, but cash and bearer cheques can be freely imported and exported up to €6,000.

We can begin to see why the banks have already complained about the paperwork involved. Even where it is not a question of permission being denied, the simple reporting takes a lot of time.

Operations between non-residents

Operations between non-residents transferring bearer cheques, euros or foreign currency must be authorised in advance. The original importation of the means of payment must be justified on form B-1, or declared on form B-3 if such means come from a resident, before the bank can carry out the operation.

This means that, when a non-resident buys a Spanish property from another non-resident, the purchaser must declare his importation of the foreign currency and its exchange into euros, or pay by a cheque on a non-Spanish bank in a foreign currency. This is perfectly legal, and many sellers prefer to be paid in their own currency.

For purposes of foreign exchange transfers, the resident may accredit his status by showing his residence card. If you have to prove that you are a non-resident, you must obtain a certificate from the Ministry of the Interior declaring that you are not listed as a resident, and this certificate must be dated at least two months before it is presented.

Bank accounts in Spain

Both residents and non-residents may freely open bank accounts in euros. The accounts of residents and non-residents are distinguished from each other, because different regulations apply to transfers for the resident and the non-resident. The non-resident account is called a *cuenta extranjera*, but for all internal purposes, is exactly the same as the resident's account.

In addition to your normal current account from which you write euro cheques to pay your normal bills in Spain, you may wish to take out a deposit certificate in euros or other currency. The interest rates will vary, because Spanish banks have cut back their interest on deposit certificates, in line with the general drop in Spanish interest rates. In fact, the banks cut back their own rates of interest before they cut back the interest rates they charge on mortgages.

Those residents who presently hold time deposit accounts in Spanish banks should check their interest payments now if they are on a variable-rate scheme. It might be time to discuss this with your investment advisers.

If you are a resident, 15 per cent of your interest earnings will be withheld and paid to the Spanish taxman in your name, just the same as for Spaniards. You may be eligible for a refund on this tax (see section on You and Your Taxes). If you are a non-resident, no tax will be withheld, but you will be liable for tax in your country of residence.

Any bank operation involving more than €3,000 requires that the payer and the receiver of the amount be identified.

Your normal current account may be paying as low as a miserable one-tenth of one per cent (0.1 per cent) on its average balance, and you will be paying some of the highest bank charges in Europe for routine services. You may be irritated when you discover that your bank has charged you €5 to make a draft for €60 worth of pounds in order to pay for a magazine subscription in your home country, so be sure to ask in advance what these charges will be.

And remember what we said in the first chapter about making sure of just how your pension cheque or funds from abroad will be transferred to you in Spain, and just how long it will take from the time of sending to the moment you can write a new cheque.

Many people have suffered greatly from delays in the transfer of funds, even when they have been sent from a British bank to its branch in Spain, so ask the bank manager how long it will take. You may wish to use one of the rapid bank transfer systems such as SWIFT, which assures you of quickly having the money sent. It costs a little more, but it is probably worth it.

There have been many complaints about high commissions charged on these transfers, as well.

Some people have been charged more than 4 per cent when sending money out of Spain. This would be €4,200 on a transfer of €120,000. Other banks charge fees of around €21 per €6,000 of transfer, a total of €420 on the same operation, or one-tenth of the charge.

No commission on pensions

Spanish banks have even charged exchange commission on direct transfer of British pensions. This is against European Union banking regulations, especially when the British send the pension cheques directly in euros to the Spanish bank.

If your bank is charging commission on your pension cheques, make sure that you are receiving them by direct transfer in euros. If not, arrange to do this — a simple letter is sufficient — and tell your Spanish bank that charging commission on pension transfers is against the EU regulations.

The British will send your pension cheque to you in euros through the Bank of Scotland, leaving the Spaniards no excuse whatsoever for charging commission. Make sure they don't.

Having said the above, many Spanish bank services function very well. Spain has one of the most complete and modern networks of electronic banking services, for example, where you can be sure of using your bank card to obtain cash from the electronic teller in all parts of the country, and in other countries as well.

If you have a complaint with your bank service and your local manager does not give you satisfaction, you will find that almost all banks have a *Defensor del Cliente*, who will hear your case and who must respond within two months.

More than half of all such complaints are resolved in favour of the client, reports the banking association. If you don't get any joy from your own bank, you can also complain to the Bank of Spain's *Servicio de Reclamaciones* in Madrid.

You will have to try your bank manager first, then the bank's own client department, and present your case in writing but the Bank of Spain helps hundreds of depositors every year. You can telephone them on 91-338 5068 for detailed information.

Writing cheques

Once you begin writing cheques on your normal Spanish account, you will find that many Spaniards prefer a cheque made out *al portador* ("to the bearer" or, as the Americans say, "cash"). The *portador* cheque is preferred by many because there is no record of who cashes it. You can either accept this practice or insist on making the cheque out in the name of the person for whom it is meant.

The post-dated cheque is no longer effective in Spain. That is, if you put a date one month or so in the future on your cheque, the receiver of it will be able to cash it at the bank immediately regardless of the future date you have written.

If you have a cheque written by a person with insufficient funds in the bank, you will be able to collect a partial amount up to the total of funds available. That is, if you have a cheque for €600 and the issuer has only €300 in his account, you can collect the €300 and the bank will note this on the cheque, which you can present again later in the hope that the rest of the money has arrived.

You will also find that personal cheques are not used quite as much as they are in most European countries for routine payments. Spaniards are still not quite used to the idea of personal cheques, though charge cards and credit cards are widely accepted. For many payments, especially instalment purchases of automobiles or major home appliances, the Spanish system prefers to use *letras,* or bills of exchange.

Take care with *letras*

For example, when you buy a car on instalments, you may sign 24 *letras* of €180 each, one to be paid each month. The auto dealer may send each *letra* to your bank, where it will be paid directly from your account, a system often used. Or you can go round and pay it yourself in person each month. The *letra* which you sign is a personal debt, so you want to be cautious.

And you want to make sure the *letra* is paying for what you think it is paying. There have been cases where someone selling property insisted that the buyer pay in *letras*, but had them made out to him personally and not to the company selling the property. So our buyer paid the *letras*, which the seller's agent was converting to his own use, and the poor buyer wound up having to pay for the property again, as the company had never received any money.

In another case, a man working for a company signed *letras* for a piece of machinery. The company went out of business but the man had to finish paying for the machinery, as he had signed the *letras*.

In yet another case, a man signed *letras* to pay for his new computer. He sent the computer back to the company because it was defective. The company made no problem, but the distributor who had sold him the computer went out of business, having already disposed of the *letras* to a bank.

The bank now held the bills of exchange and expected payment from the signer. Our buyer's only recourse was to bring a lawsuit against the bankrupt distributor, because the computer company had not received any money from him so could not return it to him, and the bank had made a deal in perfectly good faith to purchase the *letras* from the distribution company.

This practice of purchasing other people's *letras* is quite legal and normal. The bank or other institution buys them at a discount, because they will have to wait for payment, and the company accepts this in return for immediate cash. In the case above, however, it leaves our purchaser out in the cold.

Another useful service available from your bank will be the *domiciliación de pagos* or the "domiciling of payments".

The word "domicile" simply means home, and the domiciling of a payment is a standing order at your bank to pay your electricity bill, for example, or your IBI. This service is very useful for people who do not spend the whole year at their property in Spain, as it assures payment of necessary bills while they are away. You fill up a form at the bank. A copy goes to whoever is sending the bill and the bank keeps another copy as their authorisation to pay out directly from your account.

The disadvantage, of course, is that a bill may be paid which you do not want paid. The electric company or the tax authorities may make an error, which you would normally protest and refuse to pay. The bank will pay it unless they notice something terribly wrong.

The idea of *domiciliación* also applies when you are investing in Spain. This is a bit different, however. This official "home account" is one through which all your foreign transactions must pass. When you bring foreign exchange into Spain to make your investment, it comes into the officially domiciled account, and when you wish to repatriate your profits, you also do it through the same account. The *Dirección General de Transacciones Exteriores* can thus keep an eye on all cash movements related to your investment.

Investing in Spain

One of the simplest ways to invest in Spain, whether you are a resident or not, is with bank deposit certificates for varying periods of time. These pay different rates of interest depending on the amount invested, the time period fixed and the currency in which they are held. An official resident may now hold his deposit certificates in any currency he likes.

At today's interest rates, however, you will not achieve a very high rate of return on your investment.

An official resident will also find that the bank withholds 15 per cent of the interest to cover income tax. You get a receipt for this and when you go to pay your Spanish income tax, you deduct this prepaid tax from any income tax you may owe (see section on You and Your Taxes).

If you are not a resident, you may hold these deposit certificates in any currency and no tax will be withheld. The problem of withholding tax is one of the knottiest facing EU negotiators, who are trying to convince all member states to impose a 15 per cent withholding tax on bank interest.

You can also, resident or non-resident, purchase shares in Spanish companies on the *Bolsa*, or stock exchange, and you can purchase Spanish government bonds.

Spain does not tax stock-market profits

Spain does not tax profits made by an EU non-resident investor in the Spanish stock market. These profits from sale and income from interest on bonds are now considered as not arising in Spain. Dividends, however, remain taxable, when paid by Spanish companies.

But even dividends are free of Spanish tax when the EU investor puts his money into a foreign company which is quoted on the

Spanish stock-market, and there are many.

This freedom applies only to individuals who are resident in other EU countries, not to companies. It supposes that the non-resident investor is paying his taxes in the country where he resides.

You may also find new investment opportunities open up for you as a non-resident of your home country, such as certain British government stocks which are not taxed at source when the holder is a non-resident.

Expats find new hazards as well as new opportunities, however. If you are tempted to invest your pension capital in offshore funds that promise rapid growth, be warned that the independent financial advisers are completely unregulated in Spain.

Investments in the Spanish stock market are controlled by the *Comisión Nacional del Mercado de Valores,* a board which oversees the stock market. Insurance investment products are regulated by the national insurance board. The offshore funds, however, manage to fall outside the control of these bodies. Many of the funds provide good returns. But the investor should be warned that he has no comeback if things go wrong.

Invest in property

You can do what thousands of Europeans have done, and invest in real estate, especially on the Spanish coastline. This can take the form of buying large tracts of undeveloped land and waiting for the price to go up.

Or perhaps you want to develop it yourself and create your own urbanisation. You could chance across one of the last empty building lots in a town by the sea and put up your own apartment block. The Spanish real estate market has slowed down from its earlier boom but it is still a sound investment.

Perhaps you want to purchase a few apartments and make some income by letting them to holidaymakers. At the same time, your flats are increasing in value. This can be an attractive investment even though it involves much more administrative work.

You will be allowed, as a non-resident, to take out of Spain the rents you receive for your property.

Of course, you have to pay Spanish tax on this income arising in Spain. Legally, 25 per cent should be declared on form 210 and paid to *Hacienda* before you are allowed to take the rest out of Spain.

If you rent regularly to tourists on a short-term basis, providing linens and cleaning services to holiday-makers, you must also charge IVA, or value added tax, at 16 per cent, and register your business as tourist letting.

Your accountant or property consultant or management company can steer you right on these taxes. You also get to make a number of deductions for property maintenance on your income tax which are not available to home-owners who inhabit their property.

Now that you are a rather international sort of person, you may find that offshore banking and investment have advantages. There are perfectly legal ways to increase your income and avoid certain taxes by keeping your assets in investments located in tax havens such as the Channel Islands or Gibraltar.

There is a big push in Gibraltar to offer banking services and the formation of "offshore" companies which are non-resident in Spain. These companies are legally empowered to own property in Spain. They offer the advantages of secrecy and the legal avoidance of some Spanish transfer taxes, because when the time comes to sell, one does not sell the property, but only the company. Hence, no transfer has taken place in Spain, as the same company continues to own the property.

This system can also avoid Spanish — or any other — death duties and can be useful where property is bequeathed to a non-relative (see chapters on Making A Will and You and Your Taxes for more information on off-shore companies and their taxation).

Avoidance and evasion

"Avoiding" taxes, by the way, does not mean "evading" taxes. To evade a tax that you are legally liable to pay is a crime. But taking advantage of your change of residency in order to avoid taxes is only sensible.

In any case, you must look into the possibility of an offshore company before you purchase property. And remember, the formation of the company also incurs expenses. Such offshore ownership is not for everyone. You'll need expert advice to determine what's best for you.

For example, British emigrants should establish both residency and legal domicile (two different things) in Spain before they sell up their business in Great Britain. They can often, though not always, avoid British capital gains tax this way. There are similar advantages for those of other nationalities, but you need to take expert counsel.

This book cannot replace an individual investment adviser who studies your particular circumstances and plans the wisest course for you. Each person's situation and needs are different, requiring different strategies. The formation of a family trust or corporation based in Andorra or another tax haven, which would own all your property and pay you an income, might be best for some people. Such a family corporation has great advantages in tax reduction, with the useful provision that it attracts no death duties.

All of these schemes have disadvantages as well, remember, and some people have been tricked out of their savings by unscrupulous operators, so be alert.

GLOSSARY

Bolsa – Spanish stock market or stock exchange
Cheque – cheque (see talón)
Comisión Nacional del Mercado de Valores – national board regulating investments in companies registered with Spanish stock market.
Defensor del Cliente – Defender of the Client, bank ombudsman
Dinero – money
Domiciliación de Pago – standing order to pay a bill
Letra – bill of exchange
Cuenta Corriente – Current account
Dirección General de Transacciones Exteriores – General Directorate of Foreign Transactions
Divisas – foreign exchange
Efectivo – cash
Portador – bearer, cheque made out to "cash"
Talón – cheque
Talonario – chequebook
Transferencia – transfer

TAXES ON PROPERTY 9

SECTION 1 – CAPITAL GAINS

CAPITAL GAINS TAX	166
RESIDENT SELLERS WILL PAY MORE	166
BAD NEWS FOR LONG-TERM OWNERS	167
RESIDENTS OVER 65 EXEMPT	168
RESIDENT ROLLOVER CREDIT	168
HOLDERS OF USUFRUCT	168
LONG-TERM OWNERS	169
TRANSITIONAL SELLERS	169
RESIDENT PAYS AS INCOME TAX	170
NON-RESIDENT PAYS 35 PER CENT	171
INFLATION CORRECTION TABLE	172
TODAY'S SELLERS	172

SECTION 2 – TAXES YOU PAY EVERY YEAR

PROPERTY OWNER'S IMPUTED INCOME TAX	173
WEALTH TAX	173
PATRIMONIO TAX RATES 2006	174
NON-RESIDENT FORM 214	175
ANNUAL REAL ESTATE TAX	176
RENTAL OR BUSINESS INCOME (FORM 210)	177
COMMUNITY CHARGES	177
YOUR FISCAL REPRESENTATIVE	177
NON-RESIDENT FISCAL IDENTIFICATION Nº	177
SPECIAL TAX ON OFFSHORE COMPANIES	178
FORMS 211-212-213-214	182-189

Section One
CAPITAL GAINS TAX

For 2006 and 2007 there is bad news and good news and bad news for property owners. Spanish lawmakers have been busy.

The bad news for long-term property owners in Spain is that they are no longer free of capital gains tax when they sell their Spanish property. Those who bought before December 31, 1986 applied a reduction factor and had no capital gains tax at all.

This total exemption was annulled on January 20 of 2006. Now the long-term owners must pay. Their original reduction is still in force, so they will pay only for the percentage of profits gained after January 20, 2006, but they must pay something.

The government's proposed tax law for 2007 plans drastic changes in Spain's capital gains tax that will affect every property owner. These measures will almost certainly be passed into law and one of them is already in effect. Nevertheless, be alert for possible last-minute changes.

The good news for non-resident foreign property owners is that non-resident capital gains tax will be slashed in 2007 from its present 35 per cent to a less painful 18 per cent. This means that, as of January 1, 2007, non-resident sellers will face only half as much tax when they sell their property. Non-residents are the great majority of holiday homeowners on the Spanish costas.

The tax cut comes in response to a sharp reprimand from the European Union that the rate of 35 per cent discriminated against non-resident EU property owners in Spain, when residents were taxed only 15 per cent.

Resident Sellers Will Pay More
The bad news is that resident property owners will be subject to the same 18 per cent tax on capital gains instead of their former 15 per cent, also starting in 2007. Further, the 15 per cent presently in effect is the maximum rate. Resident sellers can pay even less if their incomes are modest because the capital gains tax is charged as part of a resident's income tax.

Under the 2007 plan, all residents will pay a flat rate of 18 per cent. The 18 per cent also affects all income from capital assets, such as the interest on bank accounts, dividends and profits from sale of stocks and shares. For residents this means that the bank will withhold 18 per cent from their miserable interest payments on their current accounts in Spanish banks.

These measures are contained in Spain's proposed budget for 2007. The budget has not yet been enacted but no one expects the Congress to vote any major changes in the government's plan.

Bad News for Long-Term Owners

The bad news for long-term property owners has already happened. As of January 20, 2006, a series of reductions and exemptions from capital gains tax have been cancelled.

Until January 20, 2006, a property seller who made his purchase before December 31, 1986, faced no capital gains tax at all. Those who bought after 1986, up until 1994 had a partial reduction of 11 per cent per year of ownership.

This meant that both residents and non-residents who owned their property before the end of 1986 owned it for 10 years before 1996 and had no capital gains tax. Buyers between 1986 and 1994 had partial reductions. This reduction was cancelled in 1996. However, the early buyers retained their right to the reduction.

They retain their reductions up to January 20, 2006. After that they face capital gains tax of 18 per cent on the portion of their profits generated after January 20.

The draft law for 2007 will not be final until December 31 of 2006, so change could still happen. It is unlikely, but be alert.

The draft law establishes a system of the number of days of ownership to calculated how much of your profit was gained after January 20, 2006. If you owned your property for 20 years or so, let's use nice round numbers. Say you owned it for 7,000 days before January 20. Two months later you sell it. Let's call that 70 days worth of tax.

We say 70 days is one per cent of 7,000 days. As a long-term owner, you are exempt from capital gains tax for 7,000 days, but you must pay tax on 70 days. If your profit is 100,000 euros, you will be taxed on 1,000 of those euros, or one per cent.

At 18 per cent, this means total tax of 180 euros.

The end of the total exemptions, which also affects other assets, like stocks, was put into effect quite stealthily and suddenly. The government did this in order to avoid a wave of quick sales.

Protests have already started against the retroactive nature of the new law.

All sellers, both resident and non-resident, still have the right to use the inflation correction factor which helps to reduce their taxable profit but never eliminates it.

Resident sellers 65 years of age who sell their principal home, where they have lived for a minimum of three years, continue to be exempt from capital gains.

There are three special situations in which a property seller is not liable for capital gains tax. Let's see if you are among the lucky ones.

Residents Over 65 Exempt

An official resident of Spain 65 years of age and over, who has lived in his principal residence for three years, is not subject to capital gains tax when he sells the residence.

If you are 65 or over and hold a Spanish residence permit, you can buy a principal residence this year and sell it in three years for a fat profit in today's brisk real estate market, and have no capital gains tax to pay.

Residents Get Rollover Credit For New Home

An official resident of Spain who reinvests all of the proceeds of his house sale to purchase another Spanish home as his principal residence will get complete relief from this tax. He must have lived in the home for three years to qualify. If he uses only a portion of the total amount of his house sale, he will get a percentage of relief up to the amount reinvested.

One typical situation is where an older couple sell their large villa, which they no longer need, and move into a smaller apartment, using the rest of their profits to improve their life style. If we suppose that the couple originally bought the villa for €120,000 and sell it today for €320,000, they have a profit of €200,000.

If they buy a new flat for the whole of the €320,000 selling price, they will have no Spanish capital gains tax to pay. But if they buy a small flat for €160,000, and keep the remaining €160,000 in cash, they will have used only one-half of their sale proceeds to purchase a new principal residence. Thus, they get to deduct only one-half of their profits. Half of €160,000 is €80,000 free of tax.

Holders of Usufruct

A recent change in capital gains regulations exempts elderly persons who use the "inherit from yourself" schemes in which you sell your house but retain the right to live in it until your death.

A person 65 or older who contracts with a company to sell his principal residence in exchange for the lifetime right to inhabit the dwelling, along with a monthly payment, will not be taxed on any capital gain involved. This makes such deals to turn your home ownership into lifetime income more attractive for older persons of modest means. The right to inhabit the property is called a *usufructo*.

If you do not fall into one of these groups, you will be liable for capital gains tax when you sell your property.

We can distinguish three possible situations for sellers of Spanish property today. These are:

1. Long-term Owners: The long-term owners who bought their homes before December 31, 1986, meaning they have owned them for 10 years before December 31, 1996. They now must pay Spanish capital gains tax, but only on the period starting January 20, 2006, as described above.

2. Transitional Sellers: Those who bought in the period from 1987 through 1994. They have the right to the 11.11 per cent per year reduction, starting after the first two years of ownership, but only up to 1996. Those who bought in 1995 have no reduction because their initial two-year period of no reduction runs up against the December 31, 1996, cut-off point. These sellers can also apply the inflation correction factor (see below).

3. Today's Buyers: Those who purchase today (and really, since 1995) have no 11.11 per cent reductions at all. Their only help is the application of a coefficient that corrects for inflation. Nevertheless, it is a help because it is applied to the entire amount of your original purchase price, rather than to the amount of your profit.

If you sell your Spanish property today, you will fall into one of these categories. Let's take them one by one.

Long-term owners

If you are a long-term owner who bought before December 31, 1986, your situation is described above.

Transitional sellers

If you are a "transitional seller", you have the most complicated calculation. Here is a step-by-step example.

1. Find the price you paid for your property originally. This will be the price entered on your *escritura*. If you did as many other Spanish buyers did a few years ago and entered a price lower than the price you actually paid, you will suffer for it now. Let's suppose you bought in 1990 and your registered price is 15 million pesetas.

2. Convert this price into euros. It comes to just over €90,000.

3. Now add onto your price all the official expenses you had in acquiring the property. After your purchase was complete, you should have attached the receipts for the taxes, fees and other expenses to your title deed for your files.

Add to your original purchase price the amount of property transfer tax you paid at the time, at 6 per cent, or at 7.5 per cent if you bought a new property from a developer, thus paying IVA instead of transfer tax. Enter expenses for notary, property registration, the plus valía tax if you as the buyer had to pay it, and lawyer. You need the official receipts for these payments in order to claim them.

4. Convert these peseta expenses into euros. Let's suppose that these expenses total just over 10 per cent of your price, or €10,000. You add them in, making a total acquisition cost of €100,000.

5. Apply inflation corrector. Your purchase was in 1990 and the money has become worth less today because of inflation. You can apply the inflation correction factor from the table below to bring that €100,000 to today's values. Looking at the table we see that any purchase before 1994 has a factor of 1.1924. Multiply this by €100,000 and you get €119.240. Those of you who are mathematically minded will notice that this does not really correct for all the inflation since 1990. However, the tax man knows that you transitional sellers will also have the reduction factor of 11.11 per cent per year to apply. I told you it was complicated.

6. In order to apply your reductions, you have to calculate your profit. You are selling today for €330,000, tripling your money in 15 years. Not too bad. And you are declaring the full amount on the contract. Subtract selling expenses from

your total. You can reduce your total selling price by any justified expenses. If you have a bill from your estate agent, with IVA, you can deduct this. If the commission is five per cent, that is €16,500 and you deduct it from your price. If your total acquisition cost, corrected for inflation, is a round €120,000 and your reduced selling price, as declared, is €315,000, this makes your profit on paper €195,000.

6. Now you get to apply the reduction percentage to this profit. If you bought in 1990, your factor starts in 1992, after your first two years of ownership. The factor ends in 1996, so you get four years worth. Four times 11.11 per cent is, rounding off, 44 per cent. Apply this to €195,000 and let's say you have €87,000 worth of reduction. Subtract this from €195,000 and you have a corrected and taxable profit of €108,000

So far, this operation applies to residents and non-residents alike, but now we see a difference in their taxation.

Resident pays as income tax

A resident pays his capital gains tax as part of his income tax. If you sell in 2006, you do noteclare this until May of 2007, when you file for Spanish income tax.

In Spanish, capital gain is called *incremento de patrimonio,* and there is a section of the tax form especially designed for it. The resident pays his capital gains tax at exactly the same rate as he pays his Spanish income tax. If you are of modest income, paying Spanish income tax somewhere around 12 per cent, you will also pay your capital gains tax at 12 per cent.

Even if your income is very high and your income tax rate is, say, 40 per cent, the absolute limit on capital gains tax for a resident is 15 per cent. This means that you could never pay more than €15,000 on a profit of €100,000.

However, as noted above, this applies only until the end of 2006. On January 1, 2007, the Tax Agency will apply the new rate of 18 per cent, so the resident seller will pay about €19,000 on his profit of €108,000.

Whoops, we forgot the extra tax due under the proposed 2007 tax law. The resident is taxed 15 per cent in 2006 and 18 per cent in 2007, on the part of the total profit generated after January 20, 2006. This will not be more than a few hundred euros so far, as we calculated in the opening paragraphs.

COEFICIENTE DE ACTUALIZACIÓN INFLATION CORRECTION TABLE	
PURCHASE DATE	**2006 SALE**
1994 and earlier	1.1924
1995	1.2597
1996	1.2167
1997	1.1924
1998	1.1692
1999	1.1482
2000	1.1261
2001	1.1040
2002	1.0824
2003	1.0612
2004	1.0404
2005	1.0200
2006	1.0000

Non-Resident pays 35 per cent

The non-resident, however, faces a tax of 35 per cent, at least until January 1, 2007. In our example, this gives him a tax of more than €37,000, almost double the resident's tax. To this must now be added the tax on the portion of his profit generated after January 20, 2006. This will be very small during 2006 but will start to add up during 2007.

If the non-resident is tempted to take the money and run, remember that the buyer does not pay him the full price. He must withhold five per cent of the total purchase price and pay it directly to the Spanish Tax Agency, filing form 211. The Notary demands to see the paid-up form 211 at the signing of the deeds, so there is no escape.

In our example, five per cent of €330,000 is €16,500. The seller still owes about €21,000 on top of this deposit. He is required to file Form 212 within 30 days and pay the rest of his tax. If he decides to become a tax dodger, he can leave Spain, owing the Tax Agency €21,000.

If the deposit of five per cent turns out to be greater than the amount of tax owed by the non-resident, you can also claim a refund on the same Form 212, which should be filed within 30 days of the transaction. The Tax Agency promises to return the over-payment within 90 days, but many report that they take as long as a year.

Today's sellers

Well, we told you it was complicated. If you fall into the third category of seller, those who bought after 1994, you have only the inflation correction factor to apply.

That is, if you bought in 1996 for €160,000, plus other taxes and costs of about €20,000, you have a cost of acquisition of €180,000. You look at the table of coefficients and you see that the inflation correction factor for 1996 is 1.2167. Apply this to €180,000 and you get a nice round €200,000 for a corrected cost of acquisition.

If you sell today for €300,000, you have a taxable profit of €100,000, taxed at 15 per cent for residents and 35 per cent for non-residents. As a non-resident, applying the correction factor took €20,000 off your profit, for a tax saving of €7,000.

Section Two
TAXES YOU PAY EVERY YEAR

All property owners in Spain are liable for three separate taxes every year. These taxes are:
1. **Property Owners' Imputed Income Tax**
2. **Wealth Tax (Non-Resident Tax Form 214)**
3. **Annual Real Estate Tax**

Property Owners' Imputed Income Tax:

Spain's property owners' imputed income tax is not charged on the owner's principal residence.

A non-resident must pay the yearly tax, however, because he is not resident in Spain, so his principal dwelling cannot be here. Residents who own more than one dwelling are subject to the tax on their second home or other property.

Persons subject to this tax have 2 per cent of the *valor catastral*, the official rated value, of their property attributed to them as a sort of imaginary income. This is 1.1 per cent if your rated value has been raised sharply since 1994 and many values have been raised. You must enquire locally to check your value.

Residents pay their tax on this notional income by having it added to their other income as if it were more earnings. This means that they pay tax at their normal income tax rate. If their incomes are modest they will pay 15 per cent and if their incomes are high they will pay 30 or even 40 per cent.

The non-resident is taxed always at the flat rate of 25 per cent on any income arising in Spain. Do not confuse this tax of 25 per cent on earnings with the capital gains tax of 35 per cent, which applies to profits from the sale of assets, such as a house or shares in a company.

If a non-resident husband and wife own a villa which has a *valor catastral* of €120,000 and a real value of €180,000, we find that the Spanish Tax Agency imputes to them separately an ownership of €60,000 each, half of the *valor catastral*.

We then calculate that 2 per cent of €60,000 is €1,200 of imaginary income. Taxed at 25 per cent, this gives a bill of €300.

Wealth tax

In addition to his income tax the Spanish resident - and non-resident property owner - is liable for Spain's tax on capital assets - the *Patrimonio* tax. The name "wealth tax" may not sound like proper legal terminology, but it is an adequate translation of the Spanish name, as it's exactly that: a tax on all your assets and property; your total wealth.

In Spanish, the name is *Impuesto Extraordinario sobre el Patrimonio,* the extraordinary tax on assets. This tax started in 1978 as a special measure to force many Spanish citizens who had been hiding their wealth, especially property, to bring these assets into the open.

Hacienda placed a very small tax on these assets, amounting to only .002, that is two-tenths of one per cent, or two-thousandths of the taxable base, up to assets of €108,182. After that, the rate goes up as assets go up.

Wealth tax is based on the real sale value declared in the contract, which is almost always higher than the *valor catastral*.

You declare for this tax when you declare for your income tax, on the simplified Form 214 if you are a non-resident with only one property or on the separate Form 714.

Wealth tax affects residents and non-residents differently. A resident is required to declare his world-wide assets while the non-resident declares only his property and assets in Spain.

These taxable assets can include bank deposits, stocks, shares, bonds, ownership of a business, gold bars under the mattress, automobiles, yachts, private airplanes, works of art unless they are owned by the maker, jewels, luxury fur coats or anything else that can be considered wealth. Your home furnishings are exempt unless they are valuable antiques. There are deductions available for debts against your business, mortgages on your property, and any tax of a similar nature paid in a foreign country.

PATRIMONIO TAX RATES 2006
(In euros, rounded to nearest euro)

TAXABLE BASE	TAX	RATE BAND	MARGINAL RATE %
0	0	167,129	0.20
167,129	334	167,123	0.30
334,253	836	334,247	0.50
716,581	2,507	668,500	0.90
1,337,000	8,523	1,337,000	1.30
2,673,999	25,904	2,673,999	1.70
5,347,998	71,362	5,347998	2.10
10,695,996	183,670	excess	2.50

The principal deduction for a resident of Spain is that he pays nothing on the first €108,182. A husband and wife each have an exemption of €108,182, and each must make an individual declaration. Further, if the asset in question is a principal residence, each person has an exemption of €150,253.

If a husband and wife own together a property valued at almost €300,000, they each declare half the value, take their exemption of more than €300,000, and have no *patrimonio* tax to pay.

As Spanish law views property as individually owned, for wealth tax purposes, this means that a husband and wife who own their home together, must each file a wealth tax declaration declaring 50 per cent of the value as their property.

Non-resident Form 214

None of the exemptions above apply to non-residents. They must pay from the first euro of valuation. The non-resident, however, is taxed only on his assets located in Spain.

Non-residents declare on their own special tax Form 214 every year (see forms at end of chapter).

In our example above for non-resident property tax, the sale value of the property is €180,000. Two-tenths of one per cent of this is €360, or €180 for each of the husband and wife half-owners.

Add to that €600 of Spanish non-resident property owner imputed income tax, divided into €300 each, and you get a total of €480 due to the Spanish tax man from each of the co-owning spouses, or €960 total from both spouses. This is in addition to your annual real estate tax (see below).

If we imagine that your annual real estate tax, IBI, on the villa is €240, this means that it will cost you €1,200 a year in Spanish taxes simply to own the place.

Non-residents using Form 214 can declare at any time during the year.

Keep in mind that, if you own two properties in Spain, you cannot use Form 214 and must declare on Form 714 for wealth tax and Form 210 for imputed income tax, and you must declare in the period between May 1 and June 20.

If you own two properties, you are still required to name an official *representante fiscal,* a tax representative in Spain. If you fail to name a representative, you can be fined up to €6,000.

One owner who applied for Form 214 was annoyed to discover that he was not eligible because he had purchased his garage separately from his house. Because he has two separate title deeds, he must fill out the standard forms, declare in the regular time period and name an official tax representative.

In addition to this, both residents and non-residents pay the annual real estate tax.

Annual real estate tax (IBI)

The annual real estate tax on your Spanish property must also be paid. This tax, based on your *valor catastral,* can vary widely from town to town for the same type of property because it is a municipal tax. You can expect to pay much more for a townhouse in Marbella than you would pay for the same accommodation in an inland provincial town. If you live in a typical village house set back from the coast, your annual real estate tax could be as little as €60. If you have a well-positioned villa on a large lot you could pay as much as €3,000.

This real estate tax is called the IBI, the *Impuesto sobre Bienes Inmuebles.* The tax is raised every year, in line with inflation.

If you are a non-resident, the best solution for you is to have the tax *domiciliado* in your bank. This is a standing order to the bank to pay the tax — and you can include any other municipal charges as well. You obtain a form at the bank which authorises them to pay the tax bill, and you deposit a copy of the form with your *ayuntamiento.* This tells them where to send the bill. You are thus assured that your taxes are paid when they are due, the same as the telephone, water and electric bills.

If you prefer to pay the bill in person, you will have to go to your town hall and pay it each year. Some towns offer a discount for early payment, so be sure to ask.

In addition to the *valor catastral,* the assessed value of your property for tax purposes, the IBI also lists your *referencia catas - tral* number, which will locate your property at the *Catastro* office, along with its officially measured dimensions. This can be important in buying and selling property because sometimes the physical description does not agree with the description given in the property title.

If you think that you can simply forget about these three taxes because you are not a Spanish resident and some day will sell your home in the sun anyway, think again.

The Spanish tax agency, *Hacienda,* will check the books at the time of the property sale. They will be holding that deposit of 5 per cent of your total sale price, remember. It is a guarantee against the owners' imputed income tax and wealth tax obligations for the last four years, as well as against the capital gains liability. You will also be required to present the current real estate tax receipt, the IBI, when you sign the sale contract.

Community charges

The fees charged annually by your community of property owners, to pay for your share of maintaining the community property, are not taxes of course, but they need to be factored into your totals when you are calculating the annual running costs of your Spanish property. These fees might be as little as €400 a year for a small flat or more like €4,000 a year for a luxury villa on an elegant estate in Marbella.

Rental or business income - Form 210

All non-residents who are making money by renting out their Spanish property are subject to tax on this income arising in Spain. They are required to declare their Spanish income on Form 210. They are supposed to declare within 30 days of receiving the income, but they can apply to make their declarations quarterly to save paperwork.

Such non-resident income is taxed at the flat rate of 25 per cent.

If you are a non-resident but you own and operate a business in Spain, such as a restaurant, or a bar, or a cement factory, you are also liable for Spanish tax on your profits.

Your fiscal representative

The non-resident property owner of only one property is no longer required by Spanish law to name a fiscal representative who is resident in Spain. Those who own two or more properties must do so, however, under penalty of fines that can go as high as €6,000 if he does not comply.

The fiscal representative assures the Spanish tax authorities that they can have a reliable contact inside Spain for the non-resident taxpayer.

Although most non-residents name their tax consultant or lawyer as their fiscal representative, it can be anyone, even a foreigner, as long as he is officially resident in Spain. Any *gestoría* or tax office has the simple forms necessary.

Non-resident's fiscal identification number

If you are a non-resident property owner, you will have the above-mentioned taxes to pay and perhaps a fiscal representative to name. In order to pay these taxes, you must apply for a *Número de Identificación de Extranjero* (NIE), which is your Spanish tax identification number. Residents of all nationalities also have a number.

In fact, you should apply for this number when you purchase your property. The number identifies you to the Spanish taxman and is required when you pay your taxes or have any dealings with *Hacienda*.

To obtain it, simply present yourself at the nearest police post, or *comisaría*, with a foreigners' department, along with a photocopy of the first pages of your passport. Fill in the form and wait a few weeks for your number to be assigned. You can also have your *gestoría* do this for you.

Then you will be registered with *Hacienda*'s central computers just like the rest of us in today's electronically observed society.

Special tax on offshore companies

During the property boom of the 1980s thousands of luxury homes on the Spanish coast were sold on the basis of ownership through a non-resident company. Many of these offshore companies are located in the so-called "tax havens" where little or no local tax is charged and the names of the owners are confidential.

On the Costa del Sol, entire urbanisations were marketed with Gibraltar companies already formed to own the property. The buyer purchased the Gibraltar company, in Gibraltar, and his real name never appeared on any Spanish documents, only the name of the Gibraltar company.

Estimates are that at least 12,000 companies exist, in Gibraltar alone, without mentioning other offshore tax havens, for the sole purpose of owning property in Spain. These companies were created, quite legally, as a means to slide around a number of Spanish taxes while concealing the identity of the true owners of the property.

Other non-resident companies are located in European countries where they are subject to tax like any other company, including tax on their assets in Spain.

There is nothing incorrect about this sort of operation, and it means that all Spanish transfer taxes — which can amount to 10 per cent of the price — are bypassed when property owned by such companies changes hands. This is because only the offshore company is bought and sold, a transaction which takes place outside Spain. As far as the Spanish government is concerned, the property is still owned by the same company, and no change has taken place, so no tax is due. This offshore company ownership also avoids Spanish inheritance tax. The company is not registered in Spain, even though it possesses an asset here, so no Spanish inheritance tax is charged when the company is bequeathed to its inheritor, who then continues to own the company through Gibraltar, the Channel Islands, or some other country.

This is all perfectly legal. Nevertheless, it is not quite cricket and the loss of tax revenue irritated the Spanish authorities so much that they finally enacted a special tax on offshore companies. They were not the first to do so. In fact they were just about the last country in Europe to permit these operations.

Special tax is 3 per cent

This special tax on offshore companies is 3 per cent of the *valor catastral*. This means that, if your property is valued at €100,000 (with a real market value of perhaps €150,000), your annual tax is €3,000.

For companies registered in Gibraltar or other tax havens around the world, there are absolutely no exemptions. Spain's tax ministry has a list of jurisdictions regarded as "tax havens".

When both the company and its real owners are fiscal residents of "normal" countries which have taxation treaties with Spain, the company can claim exemption from the tax of 3 per cent by revealing all details of the owners, and presenting certification that the company pays its taxes in its country of registration.

The law is designed to crack down on those persons taking advantage of secrecy provisions in tax havens while permitting normal EU companies to continue to own property in Spain as long as they pay their taxes at home.

This leaves perfectly legitimate owners of tax haven companies, however, in the position of either having to pay the stiff tax or divest themselves of their companies.

If they "sell" the property to themselves as the new individual owners, this operation attracts tax at about 10 per cent of the total operation, just like any normal property sale. Some lawyers have been able to wind up the Gibraltar company and distribute its assets to the owners, under a small business tax of one per cent, plus a few other charges that bring the total expense to about 3 per cent.

This leaves you as an individual owning your home in Spain,

just like almost everyone else, and subject to all the usual Spanish taxes we have discussed.

As the tax is based on the *valor catastral,* the assessed value, paying the tax might be a viable option in situations where this value is much lower than the real value. There are still cases where properties that are worth €200,000 on the market have an assessed value of €50,000.

In such cases and where the individual has special need for confidentiality in his ownership, it could be a possible course of action. Be warned, however, that Spain continues its process of raising the *valor catastral* towards normal market prices. Furthermore, European Union commissions are now studying the possibility of stricter controls over tax havens as part of the EU campaign to discover where black money obtained through various types of illegal operations is hidden.

Each case will need individual study and some careful planning.

GLOSSARY

Ayuntamiento – town hall, where you pay IBI
Coeficiente de Actualización – inflation correction factor
Contribuyente – taxpayer
Formulario – form, as in tax form
Impuesto – tax
IBI Impuesto sobre Bienes Inmuebles – annual real estate tax
Impuesto sobre el Patrimonio – wealth tax, capital assets tax
Incremento de patrimonio – capital gain
Modelo – type of form, as in *"Modelo* 211"
NIE (Numero de Identificación de Extranjero) – foreigner's tax identification number.
Paraíso fiscal – tax haven
Patrimonio – capital assets, wealth
Referencia catastral – reference number for property inscription in the *Catastro* Registry
Representante fiscal – official tax representative of foreigner
Valor catastral – rated value of property for tax purposes
Usufructo – usufruct, right to inhabit propert

FORM 211

This is the form used for declaring your deposit of five per cent paid to Spain's Tax Agency when you purchase property from a non-resident.

Datos del Adquirente: Here you enter name, address and details of the buyer, including his NIE, his tax identification number in Spain, even though Form says NIF. If you have Hacienda stickers, etiquetas, you can use these instead.

Devengo: Date of the sale.

Datos del Transmitente: Enter details of the non-resident seller. Where it says: "Clave País", a separate sheet gives you a three-digit number code for every country.

Representante: If you have a fiscal representative in Spain (not required if you own only one property) you enter his details here.

Descripción del Inmueble: Description of the property, including the address, whether or not it is being transmitted through a private document or a public document signed before a Notary, and, if so, the Notary and his registration number of the contract. Finally, enter the Catastral Reference number, found on the IBI receipt.

Liquidación: The liquidation is the calculation of the amount. Here you enter the declared price of the sale and calculate five per cent of it.

Adquirente: Buyer signs, with date.

Ingreso: Enter your form of payment, whether in cash or by certified cheque made out to "Tesoro Público".

Modelo **211**

Agencia Tributaria — Impuesto sobre la Renta de no Residentes — DECLARACIÓN/DOCUMENTO DE INGRESO

FORM 212

This is the form on which the non-resident declares his capital gain or loss when he sells his Spanish property. On this form the non-resident seller either applies for a refund, if the deposit of 5 per cent is greater than the tax, or makes an extra payment, if the deposit is less than the tax due.

Contribuyente: List your name and address and fiscal number, or, if you have them, affix one of your tax labels here. F/J is "F" for a person and "J" for a company. If spouses declare together, give percentage of ownership. "Código Extranjero" is for your tax number in your home country.

Cónyuge: Fiscal number and name and percentage of ownership of the spouse.

Representante: If you have a Fiscal Representative in Spain, enter his details here.

Adquirente: List details of the buyer.

Descripción: Description of the property. Give the name of the Notary before whom the contract was signed and list his Protocol Number for it.

Liquidación: Liquidation is the calculation of the tax on your capital gain. First, list the number of the Form 211 on which your buyer registered his five per cent deposit. Enter in Box 1 the net price you received after deducting all your expenses involved in the sale. In Box 2 enter your original cost of acquiring the property, adding in all your expenses at the time, such as taxes and legal fees. You apply the inflation correction factor at this point. See the text for examples of calculations. In Box 3 you enter the difference. If you bought your property before Dec. 31, 1994, you now apply the 11.11 per cent per year factor, as described in the text, in order to get your tax base, entered in Box 4. The second table is for any additions made to the property. Box 4 will then be your taxable base, entered again in Box 9. Your tax rate will be 35 per cent as a non-resident.

Enter total tax in Box 11. Subtract 5 per cent, shown in Box 13, and you have the "Cuota Diferencial", the amount you must either pay or claim back on the second sheet of Form 212 (Not shown).

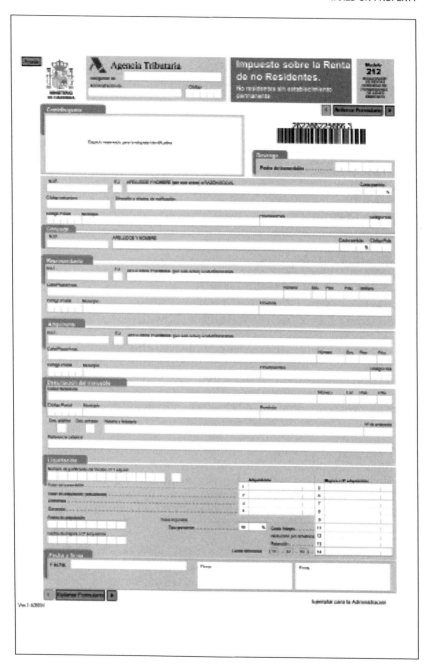

FORM 213

This is the form on which you either declare and pay your annual tax of 3 per cent on the valor catastral, or rated value, of your Spanish property owned by a non-resident company, or on which you cite your non-resident company's exemption from the tax.

Entidad Sujeta: Either paste in your Tax Agency label, or fill in the details of the non-resident company. "Código Extranjero" is the tax number, if it has one, in the country of registration.

Devengo: Enter year for which tax is being paid.

Representante: If the company has a fiscal representative in Spain, enter his details here.

Exenciones: Companies which are exempt from the tax check the appropriate box here. If your company is not located in a tax haven, and it pays its taxes in a "normal" country, check Box 1, and so on. Only those non-resident companies located in tax havens must pay.

Liquidación: Your "Base Imponible" is the valor catastral of the property. Tax rate is 3 per cent of that value. If you have owned the property less than a full year, you will have a proportional reduction. Otherwise you pay the full tax. When a company has several owners, some of whom are entitled to exemption and others not, there is a reduction as well.

NOTE: FORM 213 has two other sheets, one of them for listing all properties owned by the company, and another for entering the details of persons owning the company when exemption is requested because the company pays its taxes in a normal jurisdiction and discloses the names of its real owners.

Agencia Tributaria

MINISTERIO DE HACIENDA

Impuesto sobre la Renta de no Residentes

Modelo **213**

DOCUMENTO DE INGRESO

Entidad sujeto a gravamen

Exenciones

Liquidación

Base imponible

Cuota

Porcentaje de reducción
Reducción de la cuota

Cuota a ingresar

Negativas

CUOTA CERO

Declarante

Fecha:

Firma:

Ingreso

FORM 214

This form is used by non-resident property owners to declare their Spanish capital assets tax, the patrimonio, also called wealth tax, and their non-resident property owner's imputed income tax, on the same one-page form. Residents are not subject to this tax on their principal dwelling.

Contribuyente: Stick on your Tax Agency printed label, or fill in the form with your name and address. Put your NIE where it says NIF.

Devengo: Enter the year.

Liquidación Patrimonio: For patrimonio tax, you enter the real declared price of the property in Box 1. (See Tax chapter for values you may declare). Enter any debts against it, such as mortgages, in Box 2. The difference is your taxable base, Box 3. The percentages of the tax are given in a table on the back of the form and also in this book.

Liquidación Renta: To get Box 5, you apply to the *valor catastral* of the property either 2 per cent, or 1.1 per cent if your property has been sharply valued upward since 1994. Box 5 is your imaginary income. To this you apply 25 per cent, the non-resident income tax, to get Box 6, the amount of the tax.

Total: Add your two taxes together.

Vivienda: Enter details of the property, including the catastral reference number from your IBI receipt.

Representante: If you have a fiscal representative, list him here.

Declarante: Sign your name, with the date.

Ingreso: Enter your form of payment, cash or certified cheque.

SPANISH INCOME TAX

10

SIMPLIFIED SYSTEM FOR WAGE EARNERS 191
FOREIGN RESIDENTS MUST DECLARE 192
AVOIDING DOUBLE TAXATION 194
RETIRED CIVIL SERVANTS 195
HOW TO DECLARE YOUR INCOME TAX 197
NO IMPUTED INCOME TAX ON MAIN RESIDENCE 198
TAX RATES FOR 2006 199
DEDUCTIONS FROM INCOME 200
MORTGAGE DEDUCTION 202
WEALTH TAX FOR RESIDENTS 203
WEALTH TAX RATES 2006 203
RESIDENTS EXEMPT FOR €108,182 205

FOR the 2006 tax year, payable in May of 2007, the Spanish tax administration has corrected the income tax table for inflation. They have deflated the scale by 2 per cent. This does not quite make up for the real inflation but it certainly helps the taxpayer.

Simplified system for wage earners
Spain has also introduced a simplified system for wage earners, bringing their withholding tax more into line with the tax they actually owe, so that fewer workers have to make a tax declaration at all.

If you are a salaried worker earning less than €22,000, you probably don't need to make a tax declaration on your own. *Hacienda*, the

Tax Agency, will do it for you. As a result, almost 80 per cent of taxpayers do not need to file a return in the year 2007, nor in the immediate future. This does not mean they are not paying income tax. It means that their withholding tax, taken out of their wage during the year, has been carefully calculated to match their liability by taking into account the number of dependants in the family and other factors.

Workers earning up to €22,000 a year can escape making the tax declaration under this plan, as long as their incomes have already been subject to withholding tax.

The Spanish Tax Agency itself calculates their tax, sends them a special form to sign, and makes any refunds to them by the end of April, before the rest of us even get a chance to make our declaration. This system is called the *Devolución Rápida,* the Rapid Refund plan.

If you are in this situation, the Tax Agency should send you Form 105 to fill out in early 2006 for the 2005 tax year. If you agree with their calculations, you simply check the right box and return the form.

Foreign residents must declare

Foreigners with incomes from outside Spain, but under €22,000, should not get over-excited, however. Any foreign resident who has the right to apply a double taxation treaty cannot take advantage of the plan and this includes almost every foreigner in Spain.

Another of the conditions for the €22,000 limit is that all the income must proceed from one source only, and it must have been subject to prior Spanish withholding tax.

The Spanish tax ministry, which is now known as the *Agencia Estatal de Administración Tributaria — Agencia Tributaria* for short — has been making efforts to ease the taxpayer's burden when he goes to declare.

The agency, which we still call *Hacienda,* has inaugurated new telephone information services and has beefed up its own assistance to taxpayers who declare early and use *Hacienda's* own computer programme. This programme is ominously called PADRE, but the initials stand for *Programa de Ayuda a la Declaración de la Renta,* which sounds much more friendly.

You can take your pension receipts, your bank statement, the title deed and real estate tax receipt for your house directly to the tax office, where staffers will help you plug the data into the PADRE program, just as they did for millions of taxpayers last year.

You can rest assured that your declaration is in proper form and *Hacienda* also declares that users of the PADRE program will be first on the list to receive any refunds — *devolución* — coming to them.

In many areas, taxpayers can make a previous appointment by telephone to make their PADRE declaration. You will be assigned a time to meet with a staffer, who will help you to plug your declaration into the programme. You must take all necessary papers with you (see below). In tourist areas, there is usually someone who speaks English.

The general number to telephone in order to make this appointment is 901-223344.

Furthermore, you don't have to go in person to your tax office. The forms can be presented directly at your bank, whether they require payment or not.

Your own bank, in many cases, has the PADRE forms in its computer, and a bank staffer will help you to make your declaration, as part of the bank's service.

If your tax picture is complicated, however, do not hesitate to consult a Spanish tax consultant, the *asesor fiscal*, who will be able to advise you in detail on the circumstances of the foreign resident in Spain. Most of these tax consultants use the PADRE programme as well. You don't have to go the tax office to take advantage of it.

And, whether you are resident or non-resident, you can telephone *Hacienda*'s own consultation number — 900 333 555 — to have your doubts settled by the tax man's own consultants. This telephone call is completely free, but users report that the number is often engaged. In other cases of telephone consultations, callers are sometimes asked to leave a message describing their problem, and *Hacienda* will call back with the answer. Try also 901 200 345.

All these user-friendly innovations at the tax ministry sound just fine, but they don't mean that *Hacienda* is not serious about enforcing the law and collecting its money. Let's sound a word of warning.

As recently as 10 years ago, tax evasion was a way of life in Spain. People put ridiculously low values on their assets for property taxes, and anyone who talked about paying income tax on his real income was regarded as a kind of innocent fool.

Well, those good old days are gone forever. Spanish show business stars, football players and high-flying business tycoons find the taxman at their doors with a list of embarrassing questions.

Some Scandinavian governments have been known to inform the Spanish tax authorities that certain taxpayers have gone off their books and they have even included specific income information. Many new British residents of modest income have found they pay just as much tax in Spain as they paid in the UK.

The Spanish taxman: has slammed the door on single-premium insurance policies and secret bank accounts; has exposed a gigantic ring of IVA (VAT) fraud; will tax offshore companies owning property in Spain when the ownership is not revealed; and requires a 5 per cent deposit when non-residents sell property.

Tax consultants and accountants who used to advise their clients to bury income and not declare dividends are now warning people that Big Brother, aided by the most modern computers in Madrid, really is watching everyone. This means you, so let's take a look at your possible tax obligations in Spain.

Avoiding double taxation

When you stay in Spain for 183 days in one calendar year, you become legally liable for Spanish income tax, whether or not you take out a formal residence permit. On the morning of the 184th day, the Spanish treasury ministry, *Hacienda*, considers you a resident for tax purposes, and this means income tax on all your income, wherever in the world it may arise.

You also become liable for Spanish tax on your world-wide income when you take out a residence permit.

But what if you've just left the United Kingdom or Germany, where your pension has already been taxed? Do not worry too much. Spanish income tax regulations provide relief in cases where double taxation may arise. Spain has agreements with many countries to avoid double taxation and, where there is no specific agreement, relief is available through direct deduction of foreign tax paid or by a formula called *compensación extranjera,* or foreign compensation.

Even if you are not a resident of Spain and spend less than 183 days in the country, you are still liable for Spanish tax on any income arising in Spain, such as from the letting of your flat on the

Costa Blanca. In this case, you may be taxed in Spain and will have to apply for relief when you pay income tax in your home country.

Scandinavians, Dutch and Belgians find Spanish income tax a relief. Most other Europeans will pay about the same as they paid at home. United States citizens will find that they still have to file for their US taxes because it is one of the few countries in the world which bases tax liability on nationality rather than on place of residence. Americans will also find that they have some Spanish income tax to pay on top of their US tax because Spanish rates are a bit higher than the American rates. They can, however, turn around and deduct most of the Spanish tax from their US tax.

The Spanish authorities make adjustments to avoid double taxation in this way: if you have already paid abroad a tax much higher than the one you would pay in Spain, you will not have to pay more. But if your income tax in your home country is less than it would be on the same income in Spain, you will have to pay the Spanish government the difference.

So you are taxed in Spain at Spanish rates. But you are not doubly taxed. It seems fair enough. These are general principles, and you can read all about them in a Spanish Ministry of the Treasury booklet called Taxation Regulations for Foreigners.

If you are now liable to pay income tax in Spain, you will find that international agreements make all your income taxable, including your old-age pension, investments, interest, and any other source of income. The only exceptions to this are the pensions of civil servants. They are taxable in the home country which pays them.

Retired civil servants
However, the type of tax-free status varies from country to country because of the differences in Spain's treaties with each nation.

UK civil servant pensions are totally tax-free in Spain. A tax office information officer has declared that, as far as *Hacienda* is concerned, these UK civil service pensions "do not exist", and need not be declared. They include the pensions of municipal employees as well.

For the Dutch, however, a retired civil servant will find that the amount of his civil service pension must be declared to the Tax Agency, which will add the sum of the pension to the declarer's other income, in order to calculate his tax percentage bracket. Then the amount of the pension will be deducted, but the remaining income will be taxed at the new and higher tax percentage.

Retired United Nations civil servants do not receive the benefits of this exemption, but they have formed an association to protest this apparent discrimination.

And so it goes, with other variations for other countries. If you are a retired civil servant, obtain a copy of your double taxation agreement with Spain in order to find your particular situation.

How to avoid double taxation

For British citizens who have recently arrived to take up residence in Spain, a double taxation problem arises almost immediately.

The British tax inspector requires that a person be absent from the United Kingdom for a full tax year at least, before he is no longer liable for British income tax.

The UK tax year runs from April 6 to April 6. whereas the Spanish tax year is the natural year, from January 1 to January 1.

This overlapping of dates often means that a Briton is subject to tax both in the UK and in Spain during the first year of his Spanish residence.

If you have suffered income tax in both Spain and the UK, you can claim a return of your British tax from:

Inland Revenue, Inspector of Funds,
Lynwood Road, Thames Ditton,
Surrey KT7 0DP, England.

From this address you may also obtain forms on which to claim exemption from British income tax once you are an official resident of Spain. The form comes in both Spanish and English.

When you pay your Spanish tax, you present the two forms to *Hacienda* which stamps one for return to the British tax authorities as proof you have paid your Spanish tax.

You may also need to claim exemption for interest payments in the UK, where tax has been deducted at source, and on other investment income.

A number of shares and bonds are taxed differently when a Briton becomes non-resident in the UK. Great savings may be available if you get professional advice. Remember that you will not get any exemptions or reductions unless you apply for them.

How to declare your income tax

You do not have to file a declaration if your income for 2006 is less then €6,000 a year. This applies to married couples and retired people as well. If husband and wife each have income and declare separately, they each have a 6,000 limit.

The only condition on these limits is that no more than €1,500 of this income is from investments. If your income is less than €6,000 but it all comes from investments rather than work or pension, you will have to declare.

If you are running a business or working as a self-employed professional in Spain, you will have to declare no matter how low your income is.

Non-EU foreigners resident in Spain will need to present a Spanish tax declaration when they renew their residence card. Not to worry. You can present your declaration even if you do not owe any tax and this will meet the requirement.

The €6,000 limit includes total income of husband and wife and any children still living at home (as stated above, if husband and wife declare separately, they each have a €6,000 limit). Remember, this is world-wide income, not just Spanish income.

Let us suppose that you are retired and a resident for tax purposes in Spain, and you are legally bound to make a tax declaration. In many cases, it is best to consult a tax adviser. This may be a lawyer who specialises in tax matters; an *asesor fiscal*, who is an accountant and tax consultant, or a *gestor* who is experienced in tax matters.

These advisers will be up to date on new regulations and current practice. They will charge you a fee ranging upwards from €60 for this service, depending on how complex your return is, but their advice can save you many times that.

If your situation is simple and your income is from one basic source, such as a pension from your former employer, with perhaps a little income from stocks, you can do what millions of Spaniards do every spring, and walk into your local *Hacienda* office — which in major resort towns will be modern and well-equipped and staffed by young and helpful people — and ask for the *Información al contribuyente* section. Here you will probably find an English-speaking staffer who will advise on the preparation of your tax return and help you plug into the PADRE programme.

The usual dates for declaring Spanish income tax are from May 1 to June 30.

You need to present the following documents:
1. Your pension slips showing the amount of your income.
2. Your end-of-year bank statement, which will show any interest you have been paid and your *saldo medio*, your average balance.
3. The interest is part of your income and the average balance, or your balance on December 31, whichever is larger, is counted as part of your assets for Spanish wealth tax (see section on wealth tax). You probably will not be liable for wealth tax, as residents have an exemption on the first €108,18218 of assets.
4. Take any papers relating to deposit certificates, stocks or bonds or any other asset you own, wherever such assets may be located. Remember that you as a resident are subject to Spanish income tax on your world-wide income.
5. Of course you need your passport or your residence permit.
6. If you are claiming any deductions for invalid relatives living with you, for mortgage payments and interest on the purchase of your Spanish home, or for any other reason, take the appropriate documents.
7. If you have paid income tax in another country and are seeking relief from Spanish tax on that account, take the receipts or copies of your foreign declaration.

No imputed income tax on principal residence

Residents are no longer subject to the property owners' imputed income tax on their principal dwelling. For this tax, 2 per cent of the official rated value of your property, the *valor catastral,* is calculated as if it were income and added to your total. If your rated value has recently been raised sharply, the figure will be 1.1 per cent.

This tax on imaginary income for the taxpayer's principal residence ended in 1999. If, however, you own two homes in Spain, you will have to pay the tax on the second residence.

Non-residents remain subject to the tax as, by definition, Spain is not their principal residence. They file on Form 214 as described in the preceding chapter on Taxes on Property.

The 2 per cent or 1.1 per cent of value is not a tax. It is added to your other income just as if you had received the cash.

If your property is valued at €120,000, for example, 2 per cent will be €2,400. If your income is modest, €12,000 a year, you add this sum to it. Now your income is €14,400.

You are paying Spanish income tax at about 20 per cent, so the extra €2,400 of income produces an extra tax bill of €480.

If you are fortunate enough to own two properties in Spain, take along your receipt for this year's IBI, the *Impuesto sobre Bienes Inmuebles*, the annual real estate tax. This slip shows the official rated value of the property which is not your principal residence, so the tax officials can calculate your imputed income tax.

The *Hacienda* staff will counsel you on the proper way to fill in the forms, on your basic deductions, any credit for foreign tax paid, and so forth. But they cannot work miracles for you and, if your situation is complicated, you may need the services of a professional tax consultant.

SPANISH INCOME TAX RATES FOR 2006
(in euros, rounded to nearest euro)

Taxable Base	Tax	Rate Band	Marginal rate%
0	0	4,161	15
4,161	624	10,196	24
14,358	3,071	12,485	28
26,842	6,567	19,976	37
46,818	13,958	excess	45

The tax table refers to the year 2006, payable in May and June, 2007. Although it is divided into one share for the Spanish state and another for each autonomous region, we present the total scale. The same scale is used for individual or joint declaration. This is balanced by providing greater family deductions in the joint declaration.

How much it will cost you

As Spain continues its de-centralisation, it passes many areas of public administration to the individual regions. To pay for this, a part of the national income tax is also assigned directly to the autonomous regions. In order to simplify our calculations, however, we are not dividing the tax table into two sections.

In a complete revision of the tax system in 2000, an entire series of time-honoured tax deductions, for medical expenses and others, disappeared. They were replaced by a reduction directly from income on the philosophy that each human being needs about €3,400 a year simply to survive and that this survival minimum should not be subject to tax.

Thus, a single person of modest income can reduce his tax base by €3,400, while a married couple can combine their survival minimums and take €6,800 off, plus €1,400 or more for each child.

In this way, the system favours — just a little — married couples of modest incomes declaring jointly. The rates are about the same as most European rates, though the complex marginal system of taxing the difference between the successive rate bands is different.

To find your tax, consult the table. The first column lists your taxable income. The next column gives the amount of tax for that bracket. The third column refers to the amount of excess income until you reach the next step, and the last column tells what percentage is applied to that excess amount.

It works like this:

If you are a married couple of pensioners trying to live decently on one pension of €14,000, you first consult the list of deductions.

If both of you are over 65, your personal minimum is €4,200 each. Times two gives €8,400. If your pension is over €12,000, you are entitled to the wage earner's deduction of €2,400, which gives total deductions of €10,600.

Deducting the €10,600 from €14.000 gives €3,400 taxable income. You look at the table and see that no tax is due up to incomes of €4,080, so you have no Spanish income tax to pay.

Above that you will have to pay, at rates ranging from around 20 per cent for modest incomes up to 45 per cent over €45,900.

Deductions from income

From your total income you can deduct:

The total amount of your payments into the Spanish Social Security system during this year.

Seventy-five per cent of any *plus valía* tax you may have paid during the year on a property transfer.

Your personal or family minimum exempt from tax. This minimum varies according to the person and the family.

For example:

For the first child, €1,400.

For the second child, €1,500.

For the fourth child, €2,300.

For any child under three years of age, a further €1,200.

Further deductions for handicapped children range from €3,000 to €5,400 depending on the seriousness of the handicap. The children draw this deduction until they are 25 years old, as long as they are living at home and not earning themselves more than €1,200 in a year.

Any aged parents over 65 living in the family unit draw a deduction of €800 as long as they do not earn more than the minimum wage, no standing at €530 a month.

Any person over 65 has a reduction of €4,200 personal minimum instead of the normal €3,400.

A handicapped person may have a personal minimum exempt from tax up to €8,000.

One-parent families and the handicapped have a higher range of all these deductions.

Wage earner deductions

The wage earner can deduct €3,500 from income up to incomes of €8,000. This deduction goes down on a sliding scale as income rises to €12,000, when it is fixed at €2,400. It is also fixed at €2,400 when there is income of €6,000 from sources other than wages

Pension income counts as wage earnings, so nearly all pensioners would have the benefit of this deduction. If both husband and wife receive pensions, they each can deduct.

Better rate for annuities

There are tax reductions for those who receive regular payments from lifetime annuities, called in Spanish *renta vitalicia*. Reductions depend on the age at which you begin receiving payments.

The amount to be taxed goes by the following table:

45 per cent when the recipient began receiving payments at the age of 39 or less

40 per cent when he started between 40 and 49

35 per cent between 50 and 59

25 per cent between 60 and 69

20 per cent over the age of 69

So, if you began receiving your annuity payments at the age of

65, for example, you declare the entire amount but you are taxed on only 25 per cent of the income. This applies only to annuities constituted by purchase on your part. It does not apply to other pension plans.

A five-year annuity pays on only 15 per cent of the income, a five to 10-year annuity at 25 per cent, an annuity of 10 to 15 years will be taxed on 35 per cent of the income, and any annuity of a longer period will be charged on 42 per cent of the payments.

Mortgage deduction made from tax due

The only tax deduction remaining from the old system is that for purchase of your principal residence. This is basically 15 per cent of all expenses involved in buying your home, including mortgage repayments and the interest on the mortgage, up to a limit of 15 per cent of €9,000 per year.

If the mortgage loan exceeds half the value of the dwelling and no more than 40 per cent of it is to be paid back in the first three years, the deduction can be 25 per cent of the first €4,508 and 20 per cent of the rest,up to €9,000.

This means a maximum deduction of €2,028 per year. Remember, however, that this comes off your tax payable, not from your income, so it has a large effect.

Foreign tax deduction

If you have already paid income tax abroad, you can also deduct that from your Spanish tax bill. The procedure is to calculate the amount of Spanish tax you would pay on your income.

If you can show the amount of tax you have already paid abroad, this is entered as a possible deduction. But first, your tax consultant or adviser in *Hacienda* will make a little calculation, to find out what your *compensación extranjera* will be.

It involves some complicated arithmetic.

This calculation is made by dividing your *base imponible,* or tax base, into your *cuota líquida*, the amount of tax actually payable, times 100.

This gives a percentage called the *tipo medio,* or average rate, which is then, in turn, applied to the tax base, giving a new tax payable figure. You then deduct from your Spanish income tax either the full amount of the tax you have paid abroad, or the results of the *compensación extranjera* calculation, whichever is less.

The reason for this tricky arithmetic is to make certain that the Spanish tax authorities do not find themselves in the position of having to refund to you tax money which, for example, you have paid to the Swedish Treasury.

Taxes in Sweden are higher than those of this country and Spain simply cannot permit you to deduct that very high payment, which would result in Spain having to pay you back money it had never received.

The application of that calculated *tipo medio* means that your Spanish tax payable never falls below zero.

This does not mean that people never get money back from the Spanish Treasury. Millions of people do every year, foreigners among them.

This refund is called a *devolución*, and more than half of all Spanish taxpayers get money back at the end of the year.

PATRIMONIO TAX RATES 2006
(in euros, rounded to nearest euro)

Taxable Base	Tax	Rate Band	Marginal rate%
0	0	167,129	0.20
167,129	334	167,123	0.30
334,253	836	334,247	0.50
716,581	2,507	668,500	0.90
1,337,000	8,523	1,337,000	1.30
2,673,999	25,904	2,673,999	1.70
5,347,998	71,362	5,347,998	2.10
10,695,996	183,670	excess	2.50

"Wealth tax" for residents

In addition to his income tax the Spanish resident — and non-resident property owner — is liable for Spain's tax on capital assets: *Patrimonio* tax. The name "wealth tax" may not sound like proper legal terminology, but it is an adequate translation of the Spanish name, as it's exactly that, a tax on all your assets and property.

Do not be alarmed, however. A resident of Spain has an exemption of €108,182 of valuation, which rises to €150,253 when the asset is the principal residence. This means that a husband and wife whose principal asset in Spain is their home are exempt from the tax up to €300,506 if both their names are on the title deed.

In Spanish, the name is *Impuesto Extraordinario sobre el Patrimonio*, the extraordinary tax on assets. This tax started in 1978 as a special measure to force many Spanish citizens who had been hiding their wealth, especially property, to bring these assets into the open.

Hacienda placed a very small tax on these assets, amounting to only 0.2 per cent, that is two-tenths of one per cent, or two-thousandths of the taxable base, up to assets of €167,129. After that, the rate goes up as assets go up (see tax table).

The idea was that anyone who did not then declare his assets would be in violation and subject to fines. Further, any difference between assets declared at that time and such assets as later came to light would be treated as income for that year and taxed as such, at the much higher income tax rate, of course, going as high as 48 per cent.

The "extraordinary" tax worked more or less as projected, and many formerly hidden assets came to light. However, the state found it a good means of keeping track of people's wealth, so they have not discontinued it and it has become all-too ordinary and normal.

You declare for this tax when you declare for your income tax, on the separate Form 714.

Wealth tax affects residents and non-residents differently. A resident is required to declare his world-wide assets while the non-resident declares only his property and assets in Spain.

These taxable assets include anything he owns, not just real estate. They can include bank deposits, stocks, shares, bonds, ownership of a business, gold bars under the mattress, automobiles, yachts, private air-planes, works of art unless they are owned by the maker, jewels, luxury fur coats or anything else that can be considered wealth.

Your home furnishings are exempt unless they are valuable antiques. There are deductions available for debts against your business, mortgages on your property and any tax of a similar nature paid in a foreign country.

Real market value is used as the basis for Spanish capital assets tax. Unlike the property owners' imputed income tax, where the rated value is used, wealth tax is based on the current market value, or the declared price on property deeds.

Residents exempt for €108,102

A resident of Spain pays nothing on the first €108,102 of valuation of any assets he owns. In addition, a resident has a further exemption of €150,253 for the value of his principal residence. So he can own €100,000 of stocks and shares, plus a flat worth €150,000 and pay no *patrimonio* tax.

A husband and wife each have the exemption and each must make an individual declaration. If they own together a property valued at almost €300,000, they each declare half the value, take their exemption of €150,000, and have no *patrimonio* tax to pay.

For most of us, our principal wealth is our home, so most residents and Spaniards pay nothing in wealth tax.

But, as you see from the table, if you have world-wide assets of about a million pounds sterling, that is, over 1.6 million euros and you are a Spanish resident, you will have to pay wealth tax of almost €12,000 each year.

GLOSSARY

Agencia Estatal de Administración Tributaria – Spanish State Tax Agency
Base imponible – taxable base
Compensación extranjera – compensation for foreign tax paid
Contribuyente – tax payer
Cuota líquida – tax payable
Declaración de la Renta – income tax declaration
Devolución – refund
Devolución rápida – rapid refund plan
Hacienda – Ministry of the Economy
Impuesto sobre el Patrimonio – capital assets tax
IRPF (Impuesto sobre la Renta de las Personas Físicas) – income tax for individuals
PADRE – tax payers' help programme

Plus valía – municipal capital gains tax on property
Renta vitalicia – lifetime income, annuity
Saldo medio – average bank balance
Tipo medio – average tax rate
Valor catastral – rated value of property for tax purposes

WORKING AND STARTING A BUSINESS

11

EUROPEAN UNION REGULATIONS	207
CUENTA AJENA	209
CUENTA PROPIA, AUTÓNOMO	209
NON-EU WORK PERMITS	210
HOW TO APPLY FOR WORK PERMIT	210
AUTÓNOMO WORK PERMIT LIST	213
WHAT IT WILL COST	214
SPANISH SOCIAL SECURITY	215
INTERNATIONAL TREATIES	217
STARTING A BUSINESS	218
FORMING A SPANISH COMPANY	218

COUNCIL of Europe regulations provide that European Union citizens can work in Spain under exactly the same conditions as Spaniards.

The key words of the regulations are "equal treatment" and "non-discrimination". The *autorización de residencia y trabajo*, which is a work and residence document, is still required, but it is now much easier to obtain if you are an EU citizen.

In fact the residence card is no longer strictly required if you are working in Spain and paying into the Spanish Social Security system. It is still a good idea to obtain a card because it is useful in many other situations, such as obtaining a Spanish driving licence.

Spain cannot refuse a work or residence permit to any family members of the EU worker. Spouses and children under 21 years of age, or who are dependent on the worker, have full rights both to reside in the country and to obtain employment, either as hired persons or as self-employed.

This right applies even to family members who are not EU nationals. If a Briton working in Spain is married to a US national, for example, the non-EU spouse will have full rights to residence and employment in Spain.

All of these rights, and more, are set out in EU Regulation 1612/68,regarding the free circulation of workers within the European Union.

Among these rights are:

- The children of foreign workers will have the same rights to trade school education and apprenticeship programmes run by the state as nationals of that state.

- Any clause in the employment contract or in any trade union agreement which is discriminatory against EU citizens will be considered null and void. EU workers in other countries may vote and be elected to office in unions at a local level.

- Article 9 of Title II of the regulation notes that such EU workers will enjoy the same priority of access to public or sub-sidised housing as Spanish nationals. That is, where low-cost housing is available to workers, the EU member will be able to enter his name on the waiting list under the same conditions as a national.

- Title I of the regulation specifically prohibits any country from applying rules that limit or put unusual conditions on the employment of EU foreigners, or that set out any different or special rules for hiring foreigners, or that oblige employers to advertise jobs differently for foreigners and nationals, or that force foreigners to register with employment offices before they can obtain work, or that make any obstacles for the hiring of EU nationals who may not yet reside officially in that country.

- Article 5 of Title I requires that any EU foreigner looking for work in another EU country shall receive the same help from state employment offices as its own nationals seeking work.

All of these regulations add up to non-discrimination and equal treatment for all workers throughout the EU. They even mean that the foreign worker, should he lose his employment in Spain for reasons beyond his control, can have access to unemployment payments — the Spanish dole — just like a Spanish worker.

Once he has found employment, he will then need to register for his work and residence permit. Employees require a work permit called *cuenta ajena*, which means "on another person's account". Those seeking to work on a self-employed basis need another sort of permit, called *autónomo, or cuenta propia,* "on your own account".

Cuenta ajena

In practice this means that an EU citizen who is looking for a job may enter Spain without any more formalities than the presentation of his passport, and remain as a "tourist" for a time, until he finds work. The EU job-seeker should present himself at the nearest office of the INEM, the *Instituto Nacional de Empleo,* the National Employment Institute, where he registers as a *demandante de empleo*, a person looking for work. This is exactly the way Spaniards do it. The time limit for this is the normal tourist visit of six months.

When our job-seeker obtains employment, he must present his work contract and Social Security registration to the Spanish police and to the national government's sub-delegate office of the province, as well as to the *Delegado de Trabajo,* the provincial director of the Labour Ministry, who should routinely issue his *Tarjeta comunitaria,* his EU citizen's residence and work permit.

The first work permit will be for one year and renewals will be for five years. Your new employer will make the arrangements for your registration and payment into the Spanish *Seguridad Social* (Social Security) scheme. Remember that it is illegal to work in Spain without being registered for Social Security.

There are short-term permits as well, called *Permiso A,* running for three-month, six-month, or nine-month periods. The normal work permit is called *Permiso B.*

Those who have found jobs in Spain should also read the next chapter (Employing others) for a full discussion of their rights as workers.

Cuenta propia — autónomo

The other sort of work permit applies to persons like plumbers, carpenters or business operators, who wish to work as self-employed. This is called working "on your own account" the *cuenta propia.* It is often called *autónomo* as well, because the worker pays into the Spanish Social Security system under a different plan from the employee.

Unfortunately for these self-employed persons, their situation is a little more complicated, but it is no more complicated than it is for Spaniards themselves. Remember that "equal treatment" means that those persons applying for self-employed permits will have to go through a series of fiscal licences, opening permits and inspections just like Spaniards trying to start a business. The red tape has driven more than one Spaniard round the bend and foreigners will find the same frustrations (see the section of this chapter entitled How to Start a Business for more details).

European professionals who want to work in Spain now find it much easier to have their professional qualifications standardised to Spanish regulations and to set up their practice in Spain.

Doctors, dentists, nurses, veterinarians, architects, lawyers, insurance agents and hairdressers now experience fewer difficulties when they want to render their services in Spain. Other professions also will find restrictions relaxed.

The recognition of foreign qualifications has been greatly simplified and speeded up. Even the professional colleges can no longer act as either open or covert obstacles to the practice of professions by EU citizens who hold the proper titles in their home countries.

Non-EU work permits

Unfortunately for those citizens of non-EU nations, the situation has not changed. Such third-nation citizens as Americans and Canadians still need the *Visado de residencia,* the special visa which they must obtain from the Spanish consulate in their home country even before they come to Spain.

There are seven classifications of these visas, so be sure you get the right one when you apply. There are visas for people who only want to retire in Spain, visas for people who are going to start a business, visas for those who have found employment, visas for top-level executives, visas for students and visas for teachers.

Applicants who intend to take up employment will have to show a proper work contract, along with proof that the position has been advertised with the Spanish employment institute and that no adequate Spanish candidate can be found for the job.

In many areas this is a serious obstacle, but in specialised fields such as computers the Spanish authorities accept that the outside worker can make a positive contribution to Spain's development. Executives in sensitive positions and teachers usually have few problems in obtaining work permits.

Those non-EU applicants who wish to go into business will have to demonstrate that they have about US$18,000 to invest in their Spanish business and that they will provide work for Spanish nationals. Often enough, the Spanish consulate will insist that the investment be made, the employees hired and the business ready to operate before they will grant the visa. Remember that you need this visa even before you go to Spain to apply for the work permit itself, so things can get complicated.

These restrictions seem harsh, but try to understand the point of view of the Spanish labour authorities.

Unemployment has been high until very recently so the Ministry of Labour is very concerned with the creation of employment for Spanish nationals. If your business idea will bring employment to three or four Spaniards, your application will be looked upon most favourably.

Is there any way you can either earn a living or stretch your pension without having a work permit? Not really. The law says that anyone who carries out any activity with *fines lucrativos*, i.e. to gain money, is required to have a permit.

Painters may paint in Spain without a work permit. But, if they sell any of their paintings, they must have a permit. An established painter selling his work through a Madrid gallery will have no problem getting a permit. A young street artist who peddles his works to the tourists in the restaurants will probably never get a permit.

A musician contracted to give one concert does not need a work permit, though he is liable for Spanish income tax on any money he earns in Spain. A musician contracted to perform regularly in a night spot will require a work permit.

There are also temporary work permits, up to six months, for people such as tour guides and specialists who work in Spain for short periods without intending to take up residence. This is the sort of permit often arranged for those timeshare sales people, the OPC, or Off-Premises Contact. The company that hires you should provide you with this permit.

How to apply for a work permit

If you are an EU citizen, you can enter Spain as a tourist, go to the INEM (the National Institute of Employment). Then you look for work.

Once you have found your job, you go to the nearest police station which has a *departamento de extranjeros*, taking your job contract, your passport, and two photos. Fill in the application forms and wait for your permit to be granted. The requirements have been greatly simplified, but may vary somewhat from province to province.

Along with the *tarjeta comunitaria*, you will be issued a NIE, a *número de identificación de extranjeros,* your tax identification number. You must also be registered by your employer for Social Security.

In fact, your employer will steer you through the entire process. If you later change jobs, your new employer will handle the paperwork.

If you are opening your own business, things will be more complicated, so be prepared to face a jungle of permits if you want to open a bar on the Costa Blanca. However, once you have obtained your *Licencia de Apertura*, your opening licence, you will be issued a work permit. For more details on starting a business, see next section.

If you are seeking a self-employed work permit, you will have to register yourself with Social Security as an *autónomo*.

Non-EU citizens

If you are a non-EU citizen, first you obtain your visa from the Spanish consulate in your home country. Without it, you will never obtain the work permit.

You will need a police certificate from your home province or state stating that you have no prison record. This is called a *Certificado penal*. If it is not in Spanish, it must be translated and legalised by a Certificate of Apostille before the Spanish authorities will accept it. Ask the Spanish consulate in your country for the proper forms.

Once in Spain, you need to get your health certificate, the *Certificado médico*. It shows that you have no contagious diseases. Forms are available from the *gestorías* and government offices, as well as the authorised medical centres.

Then you need a certificate of registration with the consulate of your home country in Spain, showing that you are registered with their office.

Then you need photos, five of them if you are a non-EU citizen. One photo stays with the police, one with the *Sub-Delegado del*

Gobierno office of your province, one with the *Delegación de Trabajo* file, one goes on the document itself, and I forget what happens to the other one.

As one veteran resident of the Costa del Sol remarked: "They must have nearly a hundred photos of me by now. I wonder what they do with them?"

They keep them. They really do. I asked a labour official that same question and he led me to a room lined with shelves. On the shelves were the files. In every file were the photos.

This is a complicated, time-consuming and frustrating procedure. You will need some expert advice from the *gestoría* or a lawyer.

Autónomo permit list

Not all of the items on this list will be required in every case, thank goodness, but it gives you an idea.

1. Title or degree. If you wish to practise medicine or architecture, you must present your titles and certificates from EU institutions. If your titles are from outside the EU, they will have to undergo a lengthy process to be validated.

2. IAE or *Impuesto de Actividades Económicas.* This is your business licence, formerly called the *Licencia fiscal.* Now it is called the Tax on Economic Activities. This was formerly a municipal tax but is now administered by the central tax office. The IAE costs nothing if your turn-over is under €600,000, but you must register for it to obtain the correct code number *(epígrafe)* for your specific activity.

3. Your registration with Social Security as a *trabajador autónomo,* a self-employed worker. You register at your nearest *Seguridad Social* office, and in 2006 you will pay €241.20 every month minimum. It is illegal to work in Spain without paying into its Social Security system.

4. A *Licencia de Apertura,* an opening licence, will be necessary if you have business premises, such as a shop or a workshop installation. This municipal licence comes from your town hall and authorises you to operate your particular business in that particular location.

5. A written explanation of the activity you will carry out. This is called a *memoria de actividades*, and it describes just what work you will do as a self-employed person.

6. Passport and photocopy.
7. Four photos.
8. Title deed and lease contract for business premises and photocopy.
9. If a company has been formed, the incorporation charter.
10. Filled-in form *(solicitud)* requesting permit.
11. Any other permits relating to your special profession. If you are going to work as a cook in a restaurant, you will need a food handler's certificate, for example.

What it will cost

The cost of a work permit depends on a number of factors, principally on whether you use a *gestoría* or a lawyer or feel that you can handle the application on your own, and whether you have found a job or will work on your own account.

If you have a job, your employer will pay most of the expenses and will probably steer you through the entire process. If you are self-employed, you had better figure €500 to €700, including all the taxes and fees.

If your Spanish is reasonably good, you can handle the matter yourself. Obtain the forms from your local police station or from the *Delegación de Trabajo,* fill them out, and wait to see what happens. The first step is for the police to clear your residence permit application. This can take a month or more. Then the papers go to the Labour Ministry office in your province, where they rule on your work permit request. The Government Sub-Delegate (formerly Civil Governor) office also vets it. If granted, you then receive a combined work and residence permit.

The application forms themselves, the *solicitud,* are free, but they are the only item on your list that is. By the time you have added your first Social Security payment of €241.20, plus any possible costs for opening permits and other fees, you are looking at a real expense.

Few foreigners, however, will feel confident enough about their Spanish and their familiarity with bureaucratic ins and outs to handle their work permit application on their own..

Perhaps you will turn to a competent *gestoría*. The only way to find one is to make enquiries among people who have work permits and who recommend a particular *gestor.* Their advice can be invaluable.

As in any country, there are right ways and wrong ways to go about things, and a good *gestor* will know the right way. He will also be up to date on recent rulings of the Labour Ministry, and can advise you on whether or not you are likely to get a permit. He may suggest that you word the application in a certain way, for example.

For a work permit, one gestor recently charged the rock-bottom figure of €200, with the taxes and fees added to this.

Or you can use a lawyer. This, of course, can cost you €300 or more, in addition to the fees and taxes. Nevertheless, if you are starting a business, employing others, purchasing property for commercial use, or if you feel your particular case may need a little extra explaining, this fee can seem quite reasonable.

A lawyer will be able to advise you on many questions outside the competence of the *gestoría,* such as aspects of investment procedures. Again, make enquiries among people working already to find a lawyer who has given satisfaction.

Social Security — self-employed

All those European workers who are now free to seek employment in Spain on equal terms with Spaniards will want to know what the Spanish Social Security system will cost them and what it has to offer. It's never too soon to start thinking about your old age.

Many complications arise in the calculation of Social Security payments and benefits, depending on the age of the worker, time of payment, dependents and other factors, but the short version goes like this:

If you are a self-employed worker such as a plumber or a business operator, you are required by law to pay into the Social Security system in the *autónomo* scheme. In 2006, the minimum rate was €241.20 a month. You can choose to pay more each month in return for a higher pension later.

The minimum time to qualify for a minimum retirement pension is 15 years, but you need to pay for 35 years to get a full pension.

If you had paid into the Spanish system at this minimum rate for the last 35 years, reached the age of 65, had a wife — or husband — under your support who received no other State pension, then you would receive a pension of €565 a month during 2006.

But watch out. If you paid only 15 years, yes, you still qualify for a pension, but it is reduced by the number of years less than 35 that you have paid into the system. So, a person who paid 15 years will get half of €565 per month.

Remember that you will receive 14 of these payments, not 12. It's just like workers' pay. You get an extra month each at Christmas and in the summer.

Salaried worker

If you are a normal salaried worker, your Social Security payments and benefits can vary widely.

The minimum salary base for paying into the system is more than €600 and a basic percentage of about 30 per cent of this is calculated as the monthly payment for Social Security.

A very small part of this is deducted from the worker's salary. The employer pays the greater part directly to the Social Security system in the name of the worker. These payments, with their extra charges, come to an absolute minimum of more than €200 a month for a low-salaried worker.

The system is much more complicated than the outline above and amounts and percentages vary according to the type of employment.

Once the salaried worker has paid into the system at the minimum rate for the same period of 35 years, he also will receive the same minimum pension of €565 a month as the self-employed worker who retires at 65 with a spouse to feed.

So far we have discussed only the minimum payments and benefits of Spain's Social Security system, but workers may pay more into the system and qualify for higher pensions at 65.

A self-employed worker can choose to set his salary base as high as €2,987 a month, meaning he would pay more than €1,000 a month into the system, in order to qualify for the maximum permitted pension of more than €2,232 a month after 35 years. A salaried worker earning that sum can also pay the maximum in order to get the maximum.

Those fortunate enough to be earning higher incomes find that no more Social Security payments can be made on the additional income.

The employed worker's monthly contributions include the possibility of the dole, his unemployment payments if he should lose his job for reasons beyond his control. Self-employed workers only receive payments if they are medically incapacitated for work.

Recent cutbacks in benefits mean that many unemployed

workers receive only 75 per cent of the minimum wage as their unemployment benefit. The minimum wage in 2006 was set at €540.90, so that unemployed who had not paid into the system for a full year would receive only €405 a month. What is worse, they lose their credit towards a retirement pension as well.

Both *autónomo* and *cuenta ajena* workers are entitled to medical benefits through the Spanish National Health scheme, which is going through the same sort of financial and overburden crisis as national health plans in most European countries.

Nevertheless, Spanish Social Security hospitals are just as modern and well equipped as those in other countries and their medical staff are just as well trained. If the Social Security hospital on the Costa del Sol was good enough for Melanie Griffith to have her baby there, it should be good enough for you.

If a worker is ill, he will also continue to receive a portion of his salary, depending on various factors. The self-employed person can also receive sickness pay, at the same rate of 75 per cent of the minimum wage, as long as he can present a doctor's certificate testifying that he is incapacitated for carrying out his profession.

The Social Security system also sets out a schedule of payments for major disability, such as losing your legs in an industrial accident, for orphans and for other areas, and generally functions much like the system in other European nations. It has much the same worries about how the system will continue to work in the future, with more and more retired people having to be supported by a smaller percentage of active workers.

Domestic workers have a special scheme, in which they pay at a lower rate but receive the same minimum benefits as other workers after 15 years. That is if they are working on their own account, for two or three families. If they are employed full-time with one family, then they must be paid the minimum wage and have their Social Security under the normal scheme (see next chapter for details).

International treaties

For most foreign workers in Spain, not only EU citizens, there are treaty agreements with many nations to ensure that a worker who has laboured in several different countries does not wind up without enough years of paying Social Security to qualify for a pension in any country.

These agreements usually provide that the total number of years paid into social security systems in various countries be added together to enable the worker to qualify for a pension, which usually is paid proportionally by each country.

Starting a business

The first thing you should do if you are starting a business in Spain is to bring money — lots of it — and open a bank account.

Make contact with a good *gestoría* to advise you on all bureaucratic procedures. Find a good *asesor fiscal*, the tax consultant, to handle your bookkeeping. Consult a lawyer to make sure you understand your contracts. A good adviser in one of these categories will save you time, trouble and money. Many speak English.

Locate your premises and arrange to purchase, rent or lease. The Spanish lease was formerly called a *traspaso* and is now called a *cesión*. It can be bought and sold under certain conditions.

When you buy a going concern with a *traspaso* or *cesión* for the premises, be aware that the operator of the business who sells you the leasehold may not own the premises. The actual owner will have a right to re-negotiate the *traspaso* when the lease is up. If you lease directly from the owner, you have the right to renewal when the term is up.

Should you wish to sell a business you have started, along with the lease for the premises, you must offer it to the landlord first at the same price as your prospective purchaser has offered. The landlord always has first refusal. The whole business of *traspasos* and *cesiones* has many ins and outs and you will need expert legal advice to avoid pitfalls.

Begin to purchase your equipment and stock and decorate your premises. Also begin to keep careful records of your start-up expenses because the costs, and the IVA that you have paid, will become deductible from your taxes on your business earnings later.

Apply for your *Licencia de Apertura,* your opening licence for the business, which is granted by the town hall. This can cost you as little as €100 for a small shop, €200 for a bar or restaurant, and up to €5,000 if you are opening a bank branch. Be prepared for sanitary and technical inspections, and in some localities be ready for long waits as well.

In the city of Málaga, some establishments have waited as long as six months before receiving their licences. Many of them, of course, simply opened without the licence after a time. In fact, in Benalmádena, on the Costa del Sol, it was recently discovered that more than 1,000 of the 5,000 businesses operating there had no licence at all. That's all right for Spaniards, but you will need your licence to apply for your work and residence document.

In addition to the other papers, you may need a food handler's medical certificate or other document, depending on the business you choose. You will also be assigned your NIE, your foreigner's tax identification number, which identifies you to the Spanish taxman. Spaniards have a number, too. You can obtain this NIE without having a residence permit if you need it for your operations before your final permit is issued.

You need to acquire two more documents at this time. One is your Spanish Social Security card. As a self-employed businessman you will be called a *trabajador autónomo* (see above). You also need to register yourself as a businessman or professional for the IAE — the *Impuesto Sobre Actividades Económicas* — the tax on economic activities.

This IAE has replaced the former *Licencia fiscal,* the fiscal licence, though many people continue to call it *Licencia fiscal.* In a move to stimulate small business, the government has:

1. Reduced the tax to zero for professionals and businesses that turn over less than €600,000 a year.

2. Removed the administration of this tax from local municipalities and returned it to the central Tax Agency. Now you must apply to register at your *Hacienda* office, not your town hall.

You must still register for IAE because you must have a tax code assigned to you for your business or profession. A dentist has a different code number (*epígrafe)* to a plumber or travel agency.

If you employ others, you will find that a worker costs you at least €1,000 a month. This is based on the low salary of €600, plus Social Security payments of about 30 per cent of that, plus extra payments at Christmas and in the summer, and assorted other expenses. See next section on Employing Others for more details.

There are many complications with hiring workers and making contracts. Remember it is illegal to hire any worker without paying his Social Security. Perhaps you can take advantage of some of the tax breaks offered to those who create new jobs for younger or older workers or for workers who have been unemployed for long periods.

Be alert as to how much it will cost you to make the worker

redundant if your business fails to prosper.

Keep accurate books of expenses and income, noting all your payments of IVA, Spain's Value Added Tax, plus your expenses for *gestoría,* accounting and legal advice, and get ready to make your first quarterly tax payment, your *pago fraccionado.*

Most small businesses will find that there are two options for paying your business tax, one of which is called *módulos,* or modules, and the other *estimación directa,* or direct estimation.

A small business is obliged to start by using the modular system. In the case of bars and restaurants the Tax Agency itself decides what your income should be, based on a complex analysis of how many tables you have, how many waiters you employ, your location, the square metres of your premises, and other factors.

You will be charged business tax on this assigned amount each quarter. At the end of the year you file your complete return of actual income, making deductions for business expenses. If the Tax Agency owes you money in return, and they probably will, you claim the refund.

The only advantage of this system is that you do not have to maintain a detailed set of accounts in order to present your quarterly statements. This is helpful for small operations dealing in hundreds or thousands of little transactions every day. Of course, you must present your totals at the end of each year.

After the first year, you can decide if you wish to pass to the direct estimation system, which requires complete book-keeping, with every *factura* in its place. The advantage, of course, is that you are paying tax on your real business earnings each quarter. If you choose this system, you must continue to use it for three years.

Spain's company tax is charged at 35 per cent for large companies and 30 per cent for small companies. The budget planned for 2007 will lower these taxes to 30 per cent and 25 per cent respectively.

It begins to sound as if you definitely need the services of a tax consultant and business specialist here. Very few can handle this paperwork on their own.

Forming a Spanish company

If you intend to carry out any large-scale activity, you may wish to form a Spanish company, or a branch of a foreign company, in order to do business in Spain. You are permitted to do this as either a resident or a non-resident. If you have €60,000 in capital to invest, you can form a Spanish *Sociedad Anónima,* the equivalent of a British limited company (a plc), or an American corporation (an Inc.), where liability is limited to the amount of capital each investor has subscribed. These companies have "S.A." after their names.

S.A. companies must have their books audited yearly and register these audited accounts with the Mercantile Registry as public documents, available for inspection by any citizen. Thus you can consult the Mercantile Registry for information about any Spanish company with which you intend to do business. You can find out the names and addresses of the principal officers of the company and see its profits and losses for the previous year. Failure to file such an audited statement or to falsify any information it contains is an offence, punishable by fines.

Under the old system, which required very little capital for the formation of a company, hundreds of thousands of companies were constituted with no obligation to publish their accounts. It was easy for an unscrupulous businessman to form a company, conceal its profits, and later disappear, owing money to his creditors, which they had no way of recovering. The present system is designed to correct these abuses.

You can also form in Spain a *Sociedad Limitada,* a simpler form of incorporation with a reduced number of shareholders and capital, or you can undertake a legal partnership or make a Spanish branch company, a *sucursal,* of a parent company already existing in your home country.

If you form a company, its articles of association must be signed and registered with a Spanish Notary and of course the Mercantile Registry. Formerly, one needed three shareholders and three directors to form a company, but under the new legislation, a single person can incorporate himself.

If you form a company, you may be employed by it as a director, even if you own the company completely. The company will be liable for Spain's corporate tax of 35 per cent on its profits.

You will need the best legal advice you can get — in your home country before you start your Spanish company and in Spain before you form the company — to make sure you get the best tax and business breaks available when you transfer funds. There are many tax complications and opportunities when you set up a company, so study the requirements carefully before you begin.

Such questions as whether you set up your company while you are still a non-resident of Spain and whether you liquidate your foreign holdings before or after becoming a resident will become important considerations.

There is a maze of regulations and opportunities around foreign investment, and you will need a lawyer skilled in these matters. The foreign investment will be vetted by the *Dirección General de Transacciones Exteriores*, the general directorate of foreign transactions, better known as the DGTE, the authority which continues to keep a controlling eye on foreign exchange, even though it has fewer powers to deny money transfers..

You want to be sure that your Spanish company will be able to take its legal profits out of Spain, and also that it will have access to bank credit just like any Spanish company.

Spain's *Ministerio de Economía y Hacienda* publishes several booklets in English which are "must" reading for anyone thinking of starting a business here. The series is called "A Guide to Business in Spain". Among the titles are *Foreign Investments, Forms of Business Organisations,* and *Labour Legislation.* The Spanish consulate in your home country may be able to supply you with copies, or you can write directly to the *Dirección General de Transacciones Exteriores,* Calle Almagro 34, 28010 Madrid.

GLOSSARY

Autónomo – self-employed
Certificado de Antecedentes Penales – certificate of criminal record
Certificado médico – medical certificate, for work permit application
Cesión – leasing of any sort
Cuenta ajena – "on another's account", an employed worker
Cuenta propia – "on your own account", a self-employed worker.
Delegación de Trabajo – provincial office of Ministry of Labour
Demandante de trabajo – jobseeker
Dirección General de Transacciones Exteriores – General Directorate of Foreign Transactions, regulates foreign investment

Estimación directa – direct calculation of income for tax purposes.

Impuesto sobre Actividades Económicas – tax on business activities

Instituto Nacional de Empleo – National Employment Institute

Licencia de Apertura – opening licence

Memoria de actividades – description of activities, when applying for business licence or permit.

Ministerio de Economía y Hacienda – Ministry of Economy and Finance

Módulos – modules, a form of estimating business income for tax purposes.

NIE (Número de Identificación de Extranjero) – foreigner's tax identification number.

Pago fraccionado – quarterly tax payment for businesses

Registro Mercantil – Mercantile Registry, where companies are inscribed.

Sociedad Anónima – limited liability public company, plc, or corporation.

Sociedad Limitada – limited liability company, simpler form of incorporation than an S.A.

Solicitud – application

Sub-Delegado del Gobierno – provincial representative of national government.

Sucursal – branch office

WHAT TO DO

IF YOU ARE INVOLVED IN AN ACCIDENT

The first warning is: do not sign the responsibility agreement form that both parties to an accident fill out together.
Second, do not admit to any fault. Such admission can give your insurance company reason not to pay out.

This accident report form is actually a European Union form, which comes in all EU languages. If you are carrying a form in Spanish, issued to you by your insurance company, you can obtain the same form in English or another EU language.

In Spanish it is called a *Declaración Amistosa,* a friendly declaration. The parties must agree on how the accident occurred and mark the diagram accordingly. If they cannot agree, then the insurance companies or the courts must decide who is at fault.

There is no legal obligation to sign the form. You should not sign it because the form signed by both parties is valid for presentation in court. If you admit any fault, the decision is likely to go against you. Unless you speak perfect Spanish, even an honest misunderstanding can work against you.

It is likely that the other party, especially if they are at fault and this is not crystal clear from your description, will insist that you sign the form. Even the traffic police will urge you to sign it because it clears their agenda.

We repeat. Do not sign it. Fill it in but do not sign it. Remember to obtain the licence number and all personal details of the driver of the other vehicle.

Keep in mind that it is not necessary to call the police if there is no personal injury. It may be a good idea but it is not a legal requirement.

After the accident, inform your insurance company immediately and give them a copy of the accident report. A good local agent will help to steer you through the process.

You have two months to bring a formal charge against the other driver if you wish to do so.

IF YOU GET A TRAFFIC FINE

If you are a law-abiding citizen and you feel that you have been caught fair and square, you just pay the fine. In fact, normally if you pay up within 10 days, you get a discount of 30 per cent. (Note: the time allowed for payment and the amount of discount can vary, depending on the municipality.)

If, however, you feel that the fine is unjust, or if you are one of those people who makes the administration work to get anything out of you, you can just wait.

In purely legal terms, the police do not fine you. They report the violation and issue a ticket. You must receive written confirmation from the court that you have been fined. If you do not receive a written fine from the court, you cannot be held liable.

The traffic department is required to notify you by certified post at your residence. If your parking ticket is 91 euros or less, this qualifies as a minor violation and it lapses after three months. If the fine is between 92 and 300 euros, this counts as a "serious" infraction and it lapses after six months. Thus, if you have not received notification by post of your infraction, it lapses after three or six months.

In more than a few cases, this written fine never arrives. This is one of the few instances when the slow pace of Spanish courts can work in your favour.

When you do receive a *Boletín de Denuncia* (a ticket for speeding ticket or other infraction), you have 30 days to pay. You can do so by money order at the post office. If you are convinced that your fine is not fair, you can present an appeal (*recurso*). You will need professional help to prepare your appeal in the correct form directed to the traffic department.

When your case is called, you go to court. If you convince the traffic judge, your fine will be dropped. Sometimes there are errors of form in the original documentation, or the police officer may not appear.

Between 20 and 30 per cent of those who appeal win their case or have it dropped. Another 20 per cent or so lapse because of faulty notification, meaning that about half of all traffic fines issued in Spain are never collected.

There are also professional firms which undertake to appeal fines.

IF YOU BUY A LEMON

Mrs. García bought a shiny new washing machine, but only five weeks later it stopped working. The machine was covered by guarantee so a repairman came and re-did the programme. But a few weeks later the motor stopped and had to be replaced. Then it de-programmed itself again.

These breakdowns continued, and Mrs. García knew she had bought a "lemon", a unit or an automobile that comes with factory defects. It would never be right.

Her initial attempts to have the machine replaced with a

new one instead of endlessly repairing it failed. The shop simply refused. Mrs. García obtained the *hoja de reclamación,* the complaints sheet, and filed a complaint with her local OMIC, or consumer office (see chapter on How to Complain for full details).

Her complaint was being processed but it got no immediate result. She still had no washing machine. Then she contacted the consumer organisation she had joined the previous year. They contacted the manufacturer directly and within two weeks Mrs. García had a new washing machine.

The shop itself was required by law to replace the defective machine, but they refused to do this. The manufacturer would have eventually replaced her machine in any case, but it seems clear that the call from the consumer organisation had some effect.

Mrs. García feels that her annual dues of 40 euros to the consumer group is money well spent.

WHEN IT IS TIME TO MAKE A WILL

If you own property in Spain, you should make a Spanish will. The Spanish will must say that it refers only to your property in Spain.

Take these steps:

1. Go to see a Spanish lawyer.

2. Establish the tax value of your property today. It will be real market value or something near it. See Section on Inheritance Tax. Your lawyer can calculate this.

3. Decide on the terms of your will, taking your

lawyer's advice.

4. Calculate the inheritance tax your heirs will face. Your lawyer can do this. Your heirs will know they must pay the tax.

5. Go the Notary, make the will, and register it. The Notary will always have a copy available for you or your heirs. It can be changed.

6. Inform everyone involved.

WHEN A CLIENT OWES YOU MONEY

Clients and customers who do not pay what they owe you are infuriating. Often, the professional or small business will simply abandon the debt rather than go to the trouble and expense of bringing a lawsuit.

The Spanish legal system has developed a plan for lawsuits without lawyers at minimum expense, similar to the Small Claims Court in the UK.

If the debt is less than €9,000, you go to your nearest First Instance Court, the *Juzgado de Primera Instancia,* and apply for the forms to initiate a *proceso monitorio,* a civil action claiming money from a debtor.

You must present evidence of the debt, such as invoices, work orders, or written agreements, preferably with the signature or the stamp of the debtor, though this is not strictly necessary. You need the address of the debtor for official notification and you must bring your case in the district where the debtor resides.

The two keys to the system are rapid verbal hearings and immediate action.

Once you have presented your claim, the judge should call your case within a short time, citing both parties to appear. At the hearing, the two parties present their arguments to the judge. This may be recorded on video.

If the debtor fails to appear or if the judge decides he has no valid reason for not paying, he will order the debtor to pay up within 20 days. If the debtor does not pay, the judge will order his assets, such as a bank account, seized to cover the debt.

IF YOU ARE ABUSED

The Spanish legal system has finally begun to take spouse abuse seriously. Until just a few years ago, most spouse abuse was classified as a simple infraction and any action to protect a battered wife was extremely difficult.

This has changed, both in public opinion and in the legal system. If you are in immediate physical danger, call the police. You should get a rapid and sympathetic response. If you have been beaten, go to the hospital for treatment. Have photographs taken.

You can then go yourself to the duty court, the *Juzgado de guardia,* and present charges against your attacker. If you have a lawyer, talk with him first.

There are centres of attention for battered women in all major cities, with telephone help lines listed in the newspapers. If you are of low income, you have the right to free legal assistance.

In most cases, a court will rapidly issue a restraining order against the offending spouse. If the spouse violates the order and approaches his victim, he can face prison.

IF YOU ARE ACCUSED OF ABUSE

The other side of the issue of spouse abuse is that wives sometimes use the new laws as a weapon against a husband who may have angered them but has not really abused them.

A husband will then find himself in a difficult position. Basically, in today's new climate, no one will believe him. The police will haul him into court even if the wife retracts her earlier charge.

The principal danger for the falsely accused spouse comes if he accepts a *juicio rápido,* the quick hearing. This type of hearing, without full legal preparation or the presentation of much evidence, is useful in many cases, such as drunken driving or petty theft.

However, it can lead to a hasty judgement where the court simply accepts the wife's declaration and rules the husband guilty. He is issued with a restraining order that forbids him to enter his own home, a fine, and a gaol term of 90 days.

The fine and gaol term are suspended but the husband is now on record and will be a second-time offender if he comes again before a court. The husband's only defence is to insist on a full hearing at a later date.

The court will seek more severe penalties against him at this full hearing, but the husband will have his own lawyer and the full protection of the law if he is truly innocent of the charges.

IF THE CONTRACTOR'S WORK IS DEFECTIVE

So you hire a kitchen installer to re-do your ancient kitchen. However, even before you have made the final payment, cupboard doors start to warp and hinges pull off. The whole job is a botch.

So, you hold back the final payment, right? Wrong. If the contractor refuses to make the job right, you must make the final payment. Then you have completed your part of the bargain and you can go to court against him.

If you do not make the final payment, then you also are technically at fault and the contractor will go to court against you, thus complicating the issue.

You will probably want a *perito judicial,* a court-certified expert witness, to testify that your kitchen installation is truly defective and to put a value on it.

TO FIGHT THE ELECTRIC COMPANY

A recent study showed that something like 20 per cent of all electric metres in Spain do not function correctly. Nevertheless, this could actually work in favour of the consumer.

One problem area can arise when you buy a re-sale property from a private owner, who still owes an electric bill. Sometimes the company does not even read the metre for months and months, charging only the base fee. Then they read the metre and charge for four months or even six.

If you are a new owner, you are not responsible for the

bills of the preceding owner. The company will try to charge you for it, however, saying they will cut off the electricity.

Let them cut it off. Then make a new contract with the company in your own name. This new contract starts from zero. The company cannot deny you a new contract, no matter what they say.

Another problem is damage arising from power cuts. This could be food in the freezer or damage to your electrical appliances. You go first to the company itself with some proof of the damage. If they do not pay, you go to the consumer office, the OMIC, and file a claim there.

Spanish electric companies pay out millions in damages every year. Recent consumer legislation requires them to give you five hours of free consumption for every hour you have been without power.

IF YOUR TENANT REFUSES TO VACATE

Suppose you usually rent out your property to tenants on short-term contracts. One tenant stays for six months, then stays another six, making a total of 12 months. As you now need to use your property, you tell him that you will not renew the contract and he must vacate the flat.

But the tenant finds out about Spanish law and declares to you that he is now entitled to rent the place for five years because it has become his home.

You must go to court to seek an eviction order, *una Orden de Desahucio*. Your lawyer will present your six-month contracts, which ought to say *"Por temporada"* on them, meaning a short period of time. Or perhaps they are only agreements in English which must be translated.

The tenant will say that he really lives in Spain and the property has become his real home and that you, the greedy landlord, forced these short-term contracts on him. If he can make a case, it is just possible that he will be awarded the right to stay. This is unlikely. It is far more probable that the court will rule in the landlord's favour.

There is no quicker way to do this.

IF YOU CANNOT RE-SELL YOUR TIMESHARE

There is nothing wrong with the idea of timeshare. A purchaser gets his holidays at a reasonable price, with the chance of going somewhere different every year on the exchange plans offered.

In practice, however, many problems can arise. Aggressive sales methods, refusal to return deposits and management difficulties at the resort are among these problems.

Or perhaps a person simply has to sell his timeshare for personal reasons. The company has promised to help you with the re-sale but somehow it does not work out.

Beware of the following scenario: you locate on the Internet a company which offers to sell your timeshare weeks or points at a good price. They require a few hundred pounds in advance, however, for their expenses. Months pass and you hear nothing but excuses from them. Finally they disappear entirely. Yes, it was a scam.

Then someone contacts you to say that he represents an association of victims of the first company, and they promise to get your money back, but they need a few hundred pounds for their expenses. You're right. It's the same people, with a scam on top of their scam.

The only way to re-sell your timeshare is to do it yourself, or through people you know and trust. Expect to get less than you paid for it.

IN ANY EMERGENCY CALL 112

The telephone number 112 is gradually coming into effect as the standard European Union all-purpose emergency number.

Your call goes to a regional centre where they should speak English and other languages, too. They are equipped to trace your call and find your position.

If you can describe the nature of your emergency they will immediately contact the appropriate emergency service, whether it is medical, fire or police.

EMPLOYING OTHERS

12

MAIDS AND GARDENERS 225

MINIMUM WAGE 226

WARNING TO EMPLOYERS8 227

DOMESTIC WORKERS SOCIAL SECURITY 227

HANDYMAN NEEDS INSURANCE 228

BUSINESS EMPLOYEES 229

BEWARE "INDEFINITE" CONTRACTS 230

FINES FOR UNREGISTERED WORKERS 231

RIGHTS OF EMPLOYEES 232

EMPLOYER PAYS SOCIAL SECURITY 232

Employing others

Most foreigners will at some point employ Spanish or other foreign workers. Property owners need odd jobs done and the growing number of foreign residents starting their own businesses need employees. Here are a few things you should know about labour relations in Spain.

Maids and gardeners

Though Spain is no longer the low-priced paradise it once was for northern Europeans, many new residents find they are still able to afford at least a part-time maid and gardener.

As in many countries, most part-time maids, cleaning women and garden workers in Spain are working illegally, whether they are employed by foreigners or by other Spaniards. By "illegally", we mean they are not covered by Social Security, and are not making payments into the system. These workers do not make a lot of money anywhere, and their work is easy to hide.

In Spain the law says that all workers — absolutely all — must be covered by Social Security.

A full-time employee has most of his Social Security paid by his employer under the terms of his employment contract.

A worker such as a handyman, maid or gardener, who provides services to several employers, must be covered by Social Security as a *trabajador autónomo*, a self-employed worker, or under a special scheme for domestic workers.

Minimum wage

The law stipulates that all such domestic workers shall be paid at least the *salario mínimo interprofesional* (€540.90 a month in 2006). You may, of course, pay more if you wish. The law also stipulates a 40-hour work week.

This minimum wage, less than €4 an hour, will seem low to most foreign residents who cannot find a part-time cleaning woman for less than €8 an hour, but remember it is a minimum for full-time workers.

When employment is less than 40 hours a week, payment should be proportional. That is, if the maid works 30 hours a week, she should get three-quarters of the wage, and if she works 20 hours a week, she gets half of it.

A domestic employee receives 30 days of paid vacation each year. This means a month's holiday, in addition to weekends. Full-time maids receive two extra payments each year, of 15 days' salary each.

An employer and a domestic employee may make a written contract. If the employer chooses not to renew the contract at its expiry, he must pay the employee seven days of salary for each year worked.

If there is no written contract, the law assumes that the verbal agreement is for one year. At the end of this year, or at any other time, the employer can dismiss the worker, giving at least seven days' notice and paying the seven days' salary for each year or part of a year worked.

The law provides a 15-day trial period for new employees. It sets a 3 per cent increase in salary for every three years worked, or one per cent per year, which seems very little. The minimum wage itself rises more than that to keep up with inflation.

An employer who provides a live-in maid or other domestic employee with housing and food may deduct as much as 45 per cent from the cash payment to cover this food and lodging.

Labour legislation requires that all workers have Spanish Social Security. Some foreigners have been slapped with stiff fines and been forced to pay Social Security payments for years back when reported by the maid or gardener who seemed so nice at first, so be wary.

In one case, a home-owner who employed a gardener in his village for many years without any papers at all, decided to sell his property and dismiss the gardener.

The gardener, who had always seemed so pleasant, and so ignorant, went to the Labour Court on the basis of the implicit verbal contract and obtained a settlement of almost €18,000. The owner could not sell his property until this was paid.

Warning to employers

One veteran labour expert at a *gestoría* in Marbella warned employers of maids and gardeners in the following way:

"Let's imagine that a villa owner decides to sell up and leave Spain. He has a maid and gardener who have never had a contract or in fact anything at all written down. He simply paid them in cash each month or each week.

"Now the maid and gardener come to see me. To be blunt, I just might suggest to them that not only do they put in their case for Social Security payments, they sue the owner for a year's wages.

"In reality, they have been paid these wages, but there are no receipts to indicate this. For my nasty cleverness, I just might take a commission of 20 per cent of whatever they are able to get. Unscrupulous agents do this every day.

"And that is why I urge all employers of Spanish domestic help to require that at least the employee sign a receipt for his pay each time, even if he doesn't have a contract."

Domestic workers' Social Security

For their Social Security, domestic employees have special regulations.

A maid, for example, need pay only €138 per month for complete Social Security health coverage and a minimum pension after 15 years. For a full pension, 35 years is required. The law says that the employer should pay 83 per cent of this and the employee 17 per cent. In practice, the employer usually pays it all.

If two or three families share a maid, she can enter herself on the Social Security books under the *Régimen Especial de Empleados de Hogar*, the special scheme for domestic employees.

She herself is responsible for her Social Security payments, but they are also €138 a month under this scheme, against more than €200 for a normal industrial worker making a low salary.

Her Social Security card will state that her work is to supply *servicios domésticos de carácter parcial o discontinuo,* domestic services of a partial or discontinuous nature. In this way, she is protected in case of accident or illness.

One great risk in employing an uninsured maid is that she may have an accident while working on your property. You can be held responsible if she sues you for damages. Your homeowners' insurance policy will not cover any claims from a person working on your property. It covers visitors and passers-by, but not workers.

The gardener or chauffeur is in a similar situation. If he works for several employers, he must be a *trabajador autónomo* also, but he comes under the general regulations and his payments each month will be €235.

Handyman needs insurance

You may also become an employer of Spanish nationals when you have some work done around your property, such as building a wall in a corner of your garden. If you hire a man on an hourly basis to carry out this work, as is often done, you will probably have no problem.

But take care. Such hiring in theory makes you an employer and the worker an employee, and can make you liable if there is an accident on the job.

Your best protection is to ask any such worker for a *presupuesto,* a bid, for the job you want done. This bid should include the worker's NIF, which is his tax identification number, and it should specify the price, along with the amount of IVA, or value added tax.

That, technically at least, makes him an independent contractor, responsible for his own insurance and Social Security. This written *presupuesto* is a good idea in any case to make sure that both parties understand the terms of your agreement.

As with the maid or gardener, the hitch here is accident insurance. As the property owner, you could find yourself sued if the worker suffers an accident.

Your home-owners' insurance policy will not cover a worker injured on your property. Your protection against this is to ask to see the worker's Social Security card when you contract him for the job. Even better, deal with a registered building contractor. This will surely cost you more, but it is the only way to be completely safe.

Remember also that you must have a proper bill — a *factura* — including the fiscal identification number of the contractor, the price and the IVA, if you wish to deduct the cost of home improvements from your profits when you sell your Spanish property.

Sometimes the friendly offer of "no bill, no IVA" represents a false saving in the end.

Business employees

Spain's membership of the European Union means that an EU citizen starting a business in Spain no longer must provide employment for Spanish nationals in order to obtain a work permit and business licence. He can hire any workers he chooses.

Even so, a foreigner new to doing business in Spain may very well decide he needs at least one Spanish employee to assist in serving his Spanish clients.

Keep in mind that just as many Spaniards spend their holidays on the Spanish Costas as do foreigners.

Whether your employees are Spanish or foreign, they will be entitled to all the benefits of Spanish labour legislation. This means that you will pay Social Security payments for your employee, and redundancy pay if you let him go. It confronts you with all the changing complexity of Spanish labour law.

One surprise for employers from other countries is that Spaniards are often paid 14 months' salary for 11 months' work. This is because the custom of an extra month's pay at Christmas and again in July persists in many cases, with the employee also entitled to a month's vacation. This is in addition to his 14 paid holidays.

Another of the principal problems of employing workers in Spain is the difficulty of firing a worker. Spain is only beginning to relax its strong protection of the worker's right to job security. Many workers are protected and cannot be fired for any reason other than gross incompetence, without being paid a large redundancy sum.

Many Spanish businessmen have pointed out that the rigidity of this system actually works against full employment because it makes bosses reluctant to take on extra employees when things are going well for fear of being stuck with them later.

It also makes life difficult in seasonal businesses like hotels, and generally cramps enterprise, especially in small concerns where the wages of one or two employees make the difference between profit and loss.

The government has passed a series of measures to make the labour market "more flexible". They include provisions for hiring workers on short-term contracts. The employer must pay the usual Social Security contributions, but he is liable only for a very small redundancy payment should he choose to let the worker go.

So many Spanish employers have taken advantage of these plans that 75 per cent of all labour contracts at one point were such "provisional" hirings. The trades unions call these *basura* contracts, "garbage" contracts, because the worker can be thrown out like rubbish.

Further measures were then enacted to discourage the short-term contracts and encourage long-term hirings. They added an indemnity of eight days' pay for each year worked on such temporary contracts, and relaxed the indemnity for workers let go from long-term contracts from 45 days' pay per year worked to 33 days' pay per year.

Another plan provides tax breaks for employers taking on workers over 45 years of age who have been out of a job for more than one year.

There are many plans designed to help small businesses, and the foreigner starting an enterprise in Spain could find them quite useful. Unless you get competent legal advice, however, you could miss out on the benefits. In many cases, Spanish labour law continues to regard the relation between employer and employee as legally binding, even if there is no written contract, and the worker becomes protected from dismissal, no matter how poorly your business goes.

Beware of "indefinite" contracts

Be wary, in particular, of "temporary" contracts which do not give a definite time period or state a date on which the contract lapses unless renewed. In some cases Spanish employees have taken advantage of this type of contract in the following way:

The employee works for a time at his new job. One day he simply fails to show up for work and the employer is unable to contact him. Months later the employer receives a notice from the Spanish labour court that he is being charged with unfair dismissal by the missing employee.

The former employee wants his Social Security paid for six months or a year and he wants an indemnity of €10,000 or so to make up for his suffering.

All this is an invention of course, but the Labour Court (see below) has a long history of favouring the employee against the employer, so some unscrupulous workers have learned to take advantage of this, and the employer faces a long and expensive process to prove he is right.

Very often the employer will simply give up, even though he is being taken for a ride, and will make an out-of-court settlement to the "worker".

The employer's only protection here is to formally dismiss the worker when he fails to appear. He must be informed at his home address — a telegram constitutes legally acceptable notice — that he has been fired for failing to appear at his job.

Whether he responds or not, a copy of this telegram will help the employer in his court case later. Some employers have failed to make this official dismissal for cause, to their later sorrow.

Make sure your contract is clearly understood when you take on any new employees.

Fines start at €3,000 for unregistered workers

You will be right if you think that situations like the above have produced a sort of paranoia in small business owners, who in turn are tempted to hire workers without any contracts or Social Security or any papers whatsoever.

This is illegal, however, even though thousands of Spanish as well as foreign employers are doing it right at this moment.

Labour inspectors do check on establishments and fines start at €3,000 for such unregistered employees, whether they are Spaniards or foreigners. Especially in coastal bars and restaurants, inspectors discover hundreds of cases every year, and fine the owners.

Rights of employees

Among the rights of employees is included the payment of the official minimum wage, which is different for different sorts of work. The absolute minimum is €540.90 per month in 2006. It is quite low, however, and most employees are paid more.

The standard work week is 40 hours, though this varies from one occupation to another. There is an official 40 per cent increase for overtime, with double time for Sundays and national holidays.

In a changing Spain, one is never quite certain what the national holidays will be next year. They even differ from Catalonia to Andalusia.

Workers are entitled to 14 paid holidays a year, 12 of them national and two of them local, such as the town's fiesta. The annual vacation is a minimum 23 days. In many cases, "fixed" workers are entitled to a leave of absence with pay of 15 days should they get married, and two days when a relative dies or is seriously ill. A woman may be entitled to 16 weeks' leave for child-bearing, but the Spanish Social Security system will pay a large portion of her salary during this time. A new father gets two days off and the mother can choose to pass up to two weeks of her maternity leave to the father.

These are guidelines which do not apply to all workers and you should consult a competent *gestoría* or lawyer who is expert in labour law to find out just what applies in your individual field.

The Spanish custom of special payments in July and at Christmas, or even more often in some cases, continues to apply. These are called *pagas extraordinarias* and their original purpose was to make sure that workers had some funds in hand for Christmas and summer holidays. These payments are often stated as one month's pay each time, but the actual amount depends on a number of factors, such as seniority, the type of work, and individual contract.

Employer pays Social Security

The principal expense you will have with any worker you employ in your business, whether on one-year contracts or "fixed", will be the payment of his Social Security contributions. As an employer, you will have to pay this for yourself, as well.

The payments are split between the employer and the worker,

but the employer pays by far the greater share. Your payment is based on the *nómina*, the official salary for your type of work. If you employ a waiter or a shop girl on the absolute minimum wage of €540.90, you will find that your payments are based on the lowest official *nómina*. This is almost €600 and you will pay about 35 per cent of this, i.e. more than €200 each and every month in addition to your worker's salary. This is a rock-bottom figure. Most employers pay higher wages and higher Social Security payments.

Remember that this includes complete health care, accident and disability insurance, unemployment payments, and the worker's state retirement pension.

Spain, like most other modern industrial nations, is concerned about its Social Security system and where the money will come from as the number of pensioners in the population steadily increases.

An employer can fire a worker without compensation if the worker is repeatedly absent or late, if he does not obey reasonable orders, or if he is drunk or otherwise in a condition which affects his work.

A worker can quit and seek compensation if he feels that the employer has not held to the contract, has substantially altered working conditions for the worse, or has not paid the agreed wages.

Disputes about these matters are taken to the *Magistratura de Trabajo*, the Labour Court, which will decide who it thinks has the right and make judgement accordingly. Compensation payable to a worker varies, but he might get 33 days' pay for each year he has worked if the court rules he has been unfairly dismissed.

If a company goes out of business, one guideline holds that its employees are entitled to 20 days' pay for each year they have worked.

The labour laws are complex and vary widely according to the field of work. You will do well to consult a specialist to find out what rules apply to your specific situation.

GLOSSARY

Factura – bill, invoice
Fijo – "fixed", a worker on an indefinite contract
IVA – VAT, Value Added Tax
Jardinero – gardener
Magistratura de Trabajo – labour tribunal
Mujer de limpieza – cleaning woman
Obrero – worker, labourer
Paga extraordinaria – special payment
Presupuesto –estimate for a job of work
Régimen Especial de Empleados de Hogar –
  Social Security Special Scheme for Domestic Employees
Salario Mínimo Interprofesional – minimum wage
Seguridad Social – Social Security
Trabajador autónomo – self-employed worker

BIRTH, DEATH, MARRIAGE AND NATIONALITY

13

BIRTH IN SPAIN	*236*
NATIONALITY OF CHILD BORN IN SPAIN	*236*
CHILD BORN IN SPAIN HAS TWO NAMES	*237*
DEATH IN SPAIN	*237*
FUNERAL DIRECTOR	*238*
CREMATION AVAILABLE	*239*
FUNERAL COSTS	*240*
MARRIAGE IN SPAIN	*241*
MARRYING IN GIBRALTAR	*242*
GAY MARRIAGE LEGALISED	*242*
COMMON LAW COUPLES	*243*
DIVORCE IN SPAIN	*243*
NATIONALITY	*244*

AS all nations do, Spain requires that births, marriages, divorces and deaths be officially registered.

A baby born in Spain needs a Spanish birth certificate, regardless of the nationality of its parents. If the parents are not Spanish, they should also register the birth at their own country's consulate.

A death must also be registered, both in Spain and with the consulate of the country of the deceased.

A civil marriage between foreigners can be celebrated in Spain and will be recognised in other countries as valid. One of the partners must be an official resident of Spain.

Married foreigners can be divorced in Spain, regardless of where they were married, as long as one of the parties is resident, and the divorce will be recognised in other countries.

Let's take a look at each of these events and the necessary formalities in Spain.

Birth in Spain

By law, all births in Spain must be reported and registered. Even if you unexpectedly have your baby while you are on holiday in Spain, the birth must be reported here.

This is done at the *Registro Civil*, the civil registry, of the town where the birth takes place. The attending physician or other official of the hospital certifies the birth, though a registered midwife may also do this if the birth takes place at home with only the midwife in attendance.

The report must be made within eight days and include the hour, date and place of birth, the child's first and last names, the full names of both parents, and the doctor's certificate. This information will go on file at the civil registry.

The parents can then request for their own records one of two forms of the birth certificate. One is called the *Extracto de Inscripción de Nacimiento,* which gives the birth date and inscription number and the names of child and parents. This abbreviated "extract" form is sufficient for most legal purposes.

You can also get a *Certificación Literal*, which is more complete and contains all of the items in the declaration, such as the exact place and hour, the attending physician, and so on. This one will cost you a little more, but neither of the forms is expensive.

Armed with this certificate of birth in Spain, you can then go to the consulate of your home country in Spain and report the birth. Some countries, such as Great Britain, require the literal certificate before they will issue a birth certificate of their own country. You may also need your passport, your own parents' birth certificates and your marriage certificate. Procedure and necessary documents vary somewhat depending on your country of origin. Your consulate will then issue a certificate of the birth of a citizen abroad.

Nationality of child born in Spain

A child born to foreign parents in Spain does not automatically acquire Spanish nationality.

If both parents are foreigners, the child will be a foreigner even if the parents are residents.

However, if the child should, between its 18th and 19th birthdays, choose to apply for Spanish nationality, it will certainly be granted, particularly if the child has been living in Spain during most of that time.

If either of the child's parents is Spanish, a child born in Spain is automatically entitled to Spanish nationality.

A child born in Spain out of wedlock, where the paternity is not disclosed, is also entitled to Spanish nationality, regardless of the nationality of the mother.

The laws about nationality vary from country to country and can be quite complicated in their attempts to cover the various possible combinations, such as a citizen-and-foreign wife or citizen-and-foreign husband, or a father born in that country who has since taken another nationality.

Make enquiries at your own consulate. Sometimes a country requires that a child of its own nationals who is born abroad must return to his parents' country for a certain time period in order to justify his nationality, for example.

CHILD BORN IN SPAIN HAS TWO LAST NAMES

When you register the birth of your child, you will come in contact with the peculiarly Spanish practice of using two last names. If you are John Smith and your wife's maiden name was Betty Jones, your son will be registered in Spain as James Smith Jones. The Spanish rule is that the last name of the father comes first, followed by the last name of the mother. A child may choose to use his mother's last name first when he comes of legal age.

Death in Spain

If you are resident in Spain and have no plans to return to your home country near the end of your life, you should take these steps:

2. Make your Spanish will with your lawyer.

3. Select a cemetery where you wish to be buried.

4. Make contact with a Spanish funeral director.

5. Share your arrangements with your partner and family members.

6. Perhaps take out Spanish burial insurance if you are not already covered.

Procedures in Spain are just about the same as in your home country, but it helps to be familiar with them.

If the death occurs in a hospital, a doctor on the staff will prepare and sign the death certificate, which must be officially issued by a Spanish judge. If death occurs at home, the attending physician can prepare the certificate.

The funeral director

The funeral director is probably the first person you'll want to contact if you are in charge of arrangements for a death.

Funeral directors in Spain, just as in other countries, are aware that family members are distraught when a loved one has died. So they aim to provide full service, including all the necessary paperwork, and you may need to make only one telephone call to set the process in motion.

Funeral directors in areas with many foreign residents usually have at least one English-speaking staff member. When they receive a call, they respond quickly.

If no doctor has officially pronounced the person dead, they will locate a doctor to do so and they will inform both the Spanish judge who officially issues the death certificate and the consulate of the person's nationality, as the consulate must issue a death certificate for that country.

You need both these death certificates for any insurance forms and for executing the will of the deceased. The funeral director takes the passport data of the deceased and of the person who is responsible for the body in order to prepare his own reports. He sees that the necessary official certificates are delivered to the family.

If necessary, the funeral director can then take the body to the nearest cold-storage vault. Such vaults exist in most larger towns in Spain.

Cemeteries are usually owned by the towns where they are located and a foreigner can be buried in most of them, whether or not he is Catholic.

Perhaps we shouldn't say "buried" as most cemeteries in Spain are, in fact, above ground, and the bodies are placed in niches. At a burial, the casket is eased into the niche and a pair of masons brick it in.

You will probably find that you need to be registered as an inhabitant of your municipality in order to be buried in the local cemetery. This is another reason to obtain that *Certificado de Empadronamiento,* or municipal registration, which we have mentioned before.

This does not represent any discrimination against foreigners. A Spaniard may not usually be buried in the municipal cemetery if he is not registered, either.

If your new home-town cemetery doesn't suit you, there are others available. In Málaga, for example, there is an English Cemetery and in Benalmádena there is an International Cemetery. These have the sort of burial plots to which northern Europeans are more accustomed. Funeral directors can make arrangements for the cemetery plot or niche. They can also contact a British, Danish, Swedish or German pastor, as appropriate, to perform the burial service.

If the body is to be returned to the deceased's home country, funeral directors can make the arrangements for the air transport as well as the embalming. Embalming is not a standard practice in Spain, but it can be done. The Spanish funeral director will see to the body's transport to the airport in the home country, after which you will have to make other arrangements to have the body picked up. A few funeral directors have corresponding agents in other countries who will see to it that the body is delivered to any town in that country.

Cremation is available

If your preference is cremation, you will find crematoriums available in many areas of Spain. Cremation – *incineración* – was almost unknown a few years ago but is now quite common. One peculiarity of the cremation procedure is that family members are not allowed to attend the cremation itself. They may hold a religious service before the cremation, with the body present, or after it, with the urn.

Cremation costs around 300 euros as a minimum.

For those who choose to donate their bodies to medical science, any medical school in Spain will be very pleased to make the arrangements in advance. Simply telephone the medical school and declare your intentions. You can either visit them to fill out the forms or they will send a representative to you. They will arrange with your funeral director for collection of the body. Their only conditions are that the body be available within 24 hours of death and that the death was not caused by an infectious disease or an accident which requires autopsy.

FACT: *In the province of Málaga more than half of all bodies, Spanish and foreigners, are cremated.*

The usual custom in Spain, where it's hot and bodies are seldom embalmed, is to bury the day after death. This is custom, not law. The law says only that a body may not be interred sooner than 24 hours after the death has occurred.

Where there is no cold storage, it must be buried within 72 hours. Where there is cold storage available, this limit does not apply.

Funeral costs

What will all this funeral service cost you? A basic rate would be around 2,500 euros, but this can rise quickly when transport costs, embalming fees, cold storage and cemetery fees are added in.

You should know that most Spanish cemeteries usually let their niches for varying time periods. The municipal cemetery rates are quite inexpensive, but it isn't the same as purchasing the plot forever. One Málaga cemetery quoted rates of 300 euros for the first five years, dropping to about half that rate thereafter, around 30 euros per year, or 1,500 euros for 50 years. If the rent is not paid, after a time the body is removed to a common grave-site within the consecrated cemetery grounds.

If you wish to purchase a plot, it can cost more than 3,000 euros for a double plot at the Benalmádena International Cemetery on the Costa del Sol, for example. You can ask at your own town hall for prices *en perpetuidad.*

If you wish to repatriate a body to the deceased's home country, you will find that prices for air transport of bodies are high. They go as freight and are charged by the kilo. Air transport costs within Europe can range from 1,000 to 2,500 euros. Prolonged storage will also add to your costs. Embalming costs around 1,500 euros.

It pays to plan ahead. Check now with a Spanish funeral director for his rates and services. If the first price quoted you seems high, don't hesitate to visit another funeral director and compare rates.

Burial insurance is also available in Spain.

Marriage in Spain

It is perfectly possible to be married in Spain — people do it every day. But remember that one of the parties must be a resident.

There is quite a lot of paperwork, however. Some evidence must be provided that the two parties are single, such as a certificate from the civil registry of your home country. Birth certificates are required. A widow or widower will have to present both the original marriage certificate and a death certificate for the deceased spouse. A divorced person will need to present evidence of a valid divorce.

All of these documents must be officially translated into Spanish and accompanied by the Certificate of Apostille (an "apostille" is an annotation), which verifies them. This internationally recognised certificate is issued by different authorities in different countries, so you will have to ask.

The marriage is held at the Spanish Civil Registry office, with the local judge presiding, although town mayors and deputised municipal councillors are also authorised to perform civil wedding ceremonies. It has become rather trendy, in fact, for couples to be married in places like Marbella, where the town hall has arranged a special and attractive wedding site in a municipal park.

If you are interested in being married in Spain and are not resident, be warned that you will have to come in person to present and sign all the forms and it will take about 30 days before these are processed and you can be married.

Roman Catholics, even though not Spanish, may also be married in church, following the practice outlined above for civil marriage along with the usual practice of the Roman Catholic church. Each partner will present a baptismal certificate and a declaration from their former parish priest that they adhere to the Roman Catholic faith and they are free to marry. After the ceremony, the priest gives the couple a certificate of marriage, which makes them man and wife, but they must still present this certificate at the Civil Registry to get an official marriage certificate.

If you marry a Spaniard, you receive a *Libro de Familia*, the "Family Book", which is a very important document in Spanish life. It is the official registration of husband and wife and their children. Spaniards present it: when they come of age and get their own identity cards; for identification to the Social Security officials; when they marry; and when they die.

If you marry a Spanish subject, you do not automatically become Spanish. A husband or wife will have to apply for Spanish nationality, which should be routinely granted, but does not come automatically.

Marrying In Gibraltar

Gibraltar is a less complicated alternative for wedding-bound couples of most nationalities.

Forms are available at consulates in Spain, or in your home country on which the parties to the marriage enter their personal details and apply for a special marriage licence from the Governor of Gibraltar. Again, the divorced or widowed will need to produce the appropriate certificates.

When the licence is granted, the couple may go to Gibraltar and be married in the registry office there. They will need two witnesses.

Gay marriage legalised in 2005

In 2005 Spain joined the few countries in the world to legalise same-sex marriages under the same terms as marriage between a man and a woman. Hundreds of couples have already been wed.

Thousands of other couples, gay and straight, have chosen to register their union in special registries created in various municipalities and autonomous regions. These registries record a *pareja de hecho,* partners, of the same sex or opposite sex, living together as families.

Registration in this list confers no legal rights, however. Same sex pairs have the same inheritance problem as unmarried parents (see below). They can leave their property to their partners but the inheriting partner will be subject to Spanish inheritance tax at double the percentage that an immediate family member pays.

In some autonomous regions, such as Andalusia, an exception is made.

Common law couples

There is no "common law" marriage in Spain. That is, a couple may live together for many years as man and wife and have children together, but this establishes no legal rights for either the man or the woman.

If the man dies, the woman has no claim to inherit any share of his property or to collect his pension. In the eyes of the law, there is no legal relationship.

Unless the man has formally recognised the children as his own, he is not required to bequeath his property to them.

The law regards these children as offspring of a single mother. Their births must be registered as such and they take their mother's two last names because she is their only legal parent.

If the unmarried father of the children chooses to leave parts of his estate to his unrecognised children, they will not have the right to apply the lower inheritance tax rate enjoyed by children of married parents, except in some autonomous regions, such as Andalusia.

Divorce in Spain

Through the Franco years there was no divorce in Spain. This was out of deference to the regime's special relationship with the Roman Catholic Church.

In 1981, however, the first divorce law went into effect and it is now possible to obtain a divorce in Spain on various grounds. The law has since been amended and modernised several times. The latest version, enacted in 2005, has made divorce by mutual consent speedier and easier.

Even foreigners who have been married in other countries can, if they are now residents in Spain, obtain a divorce here which will be recognised in their home country. In fact, only one of the parties need be resident in Spain.

If a man's wife leaves him and returns to her home in Belgium, say, he can, after a time, petition in Spain for a divorce. The couple must have been married for one full year before a petition for divorce will be heard, which seems reasonable enough.

The simplest sort of procedure is for the couple to request by mutual consent — or for one of the pair to request with the formal consent of the other — a legal separation. The separation document must be formalised before a Spanish *Notario*. The couple will need a lawyer.

Under the previous law they then had to wait one year in the state of legal separation. Under the 2005 revised law, procedures can be completed within three months.

At the time of requesting this legal separation, the couple will be required to settle their financial arrangements about who gets what share of their property, any child support or maintenance payments, visiting rights of children, and so on. At the end of the separation, there is a brief hearing, and if nothing has changed, the final divorce will be processed.

The 2005 revised law also offers the easiest and quickest divorce of all. The couple, by mutual consent, can settle their arrangements and proceed immediately to a full divorce with no period of legal separation required. This is popularly called *divorcio exprés*.

In addition to this "no-fault" sort of procedure, the standard grounds for divorce familiar to most Europeans also apply. They include adultery, desertion, cruelty, alcohol or drug addiction and mental problems.

You will want to consult a Spanish lawyer when seeking divorce on these grounds. If your income is modest, you may be entitled to free legal assistance, which you can find out by inquiring at your area's *Colegio de Abogados*, the law society (see chapter on Your Legal Advisers for more details).

Nationality

If you move to Spain, install yourself here, take out a Spanish residence permit, pay taxes in Spain, raise your children here and do business here, that does not make you or your children Spanish. You remain a Norwegian, American or Briton, unless you choose to formally renounce your nationality in order to take another.

At this point complications arise. Some countries permit dual nationality, and do not mind if one of their citizens takes on another nationality in addition to the one he was born with.

A British citizen, for example, can take another nationality without renouncing his British citizenship. The United States of America formerly did not permit dual nationality but has now changed. If one of its citizens takes Spanish nationality, this is no longer grounds for loss of his United States citizenship.

An American woman who marries a Spaniard does not lose her American citizenship, nor does she automatically become Spanish. It is also possible for a child born in Spain of a Spanish father and

American mother to have Spanish nationality through his father and place of birth and American nationality through his mother.

Until he reaches the age of 18, that is. Then he must make a choice. Spanish law does not recognise dual nationality for adults, so the child must then either renounce his American nationality, making a declaration to the authorities, or he will lose his Spanish nationality.

But if Spain does not recognise dual nationality, what about the British citizens who take Spanish nationality, but still are regarded as British in the UK? Well, Spain does not regard them as even the slightest bit British. They are now Spanish, all Spanish and only Spanish. If the UK chooses to regard them as British, that is no business of Spain's.

Marriage is another tricky area. In general, marriage to a foreigner does not automatically change the nationality of the partner. So a British woman who marries a Spaniard remains British unless she applies for Spanish nationality, which she can do immediately after the marriage and which will routinely be granted. A British man who marries a Spanish woman, however, will have to wait out a two-year residence requirement before he can apply.

Each nation has somewhat different rules regarding the retention and loss of nationality. Where marriage partners of two different nationalities are involved, perhaps living for long periods in yet a third country, it is best to make careful enquiries at your own consulate. When there are children, it can be even more complex, so it is best to get good advice.

The basic requirement for applying for Spanish nationality is a residence period in Spain of 10 years, even if you are a European Union citizen. This varies for South Americans, for example, who need not wait so long, and in the case of marriage. A number of Europeans who have settled here have taken out Spanish nationality, although members of fellow European Union nations have practically the same rights as Spaniards, and can now even vote in municipal elections.

If you decide to apply for Spanish citizenship, you will need your own birth certificate, your parents' birth certificates and marriage certificate, all translated into Spanish by official translators and authenticated by your own consulate.

You will need to show, by means of previous residence permits, that you have held a *residencia* for 10 years. The process will take up to a year before everything is cleared, and you will do well to have a skilled *gestor* or *abogado* handle your application, as they know the ins and outs of the paperwork.

Finally, you will be required to renounce your former nationality and you will swear an oath of allegiance to the Spanish Crown.

Then you will be Spanish, a citizen of a proud nation which once ruled vast portions of the globe and is today the world's ninth largest industrial power.

Your last will and testament must provide for your family according to Spanish law.

GLOSSARY

Apellido – last name
Certificate of Apostille - internationally recognised form by which the authorities of one country validate a document to another country.
Divorcio - divorce
Incineración – cremation
Inscripción de Nacimiento – birth certificate, comes in two versions, a short form called an **extracto** and a complete form called **literal.**
Libro de Familia – "Family Book" in which husband and wife and children are inscribed.
Nombre – first name
Matrimonio - marriage
Pareja de hecho – unmarried partners living together as family.
Registro Civil – Spanish Civil Registry, where births, deaths and marriages are officially recorded.

SPANISH WILLS AND INHERITANCE TAX

SPANISH WILLS	248
CHILDREN ARE COMPULSORY HEIRS	249
ANDALUSIAN RESIDENTS PAY LESS	250
DYING WITHOUT A WILL	250
ARE YOU BOUND BY SPANISH LAW?	251
MOST FOREIGNERS HAVE FREE DISPOSITION	252
LEGITIMATE INHERITORS CAN CONTEST WILL	253
FOREIGN WILL IS VALID	254
MAKING A SPANISH WILL	255
SECRET WILLS	256
INHERITANCE TAX	257
RESIDENTS GET 95 PER CENT REDUCTION	257
SETTING TAX VALUES	259
REAL ESTATE	259
PERSONAL EFFECTS	259
AUTOMOBILES	260
STOCKS AND SHARES	260
LIFE ASSURANCE	260
BANK ACCOUNTS	260
REGIONS CAN VARY	260
INHERITANCE TAX RATES 2006	261
CALCULATE YOUR TAX	261
WEALTHY PEOPLE PAY MORE	262

POWER OF ATTORNEY	*263*
FAMILY TRUST	*263*
OFFSHORE COMPANY	*264*
FOUR-YEAR LIMIT	*264*
USUFRUCT	*264*
GIFT	*264*

Spanish wills

There are four points to bear in mind in connection with Spanish wills:

1. You should make a Spanish will disposing of your Spanish property in order to avoid time-consuming and expensive legal problems for your heirs. Make a separate will disposing of assets located outside Spain.

2. As a foreigner, you will probably find that Spanish authorities do not oblige you to follow the Spanish law of compulsory heirs, in which you must leave two-thirds of your estate to your children. You can leave your estate to whomever you choose, as long as your own national law permits this. Your estate, however, will be subject to Spanish inheritance tax, which can be high when property is left to non-relatives.

3. There are very few ways around Spanish inheritance taxes and these legal ways require careful advance planning. Spanish law provides no large exemption from inheritance tax, such as most countries have when the family home is transferred. The tax is due after the first €16,000.

4. However, if you are an official resident of Spain leaving your property to a spouse or child who is also a resident, you may be eligible for a 95-per-cent reduction in the value of the property for inheritance tax calculation. This is not available to non-residents. The reduction applies only to the first €120,000 of value.

Let's look at these points in more detail.

Spanish inheritance laws

In order to protect the family and provide for the children, Spanish inheritance laws restrict the testator's freedom to leave his property to anyone he pleases.

It is almost impossible for a Spanish parent to make the classic threat that he will cut the no-good son out of his will. This is because Spanish law requires a parent to leave two-thirds of his estate to his children, even bypassing the surviving spouse.

In general, most people wish to provide for their children, so they have no problem in making a Spanish will in accordance with those provisions.

But let us first establish just what the estate consists of when a person dies.

In Spanish law, a surviving spouse keeps all assets acquired before the marriage, half of the goods acquired during marriage, and all personal gifts or inheritances which have come directly to this spouse.

Assuming that most of the couple's assets were acquired during their marriage, this means that about half of their assets do not really form part of the deceased person's estate. Half of the property continues to belong to the surviving spouse.

This is particularly true of real estate. If the names of husband and wife both figure on the title deed of the property, each has one half of the ownership. Thus, when one dies, only half of the Spanish property is transmitted. The living spouse continues to own his or her half, with his or her name on the title deed.

Children are compulsory heirs

Of the rest of the assets, only one-third can be freely disposed of, under the Spanish law of *herederos forzosos,* or obligatory heirs. When a person dies leaving children, the estate is divided into three equal parts.

One of these thirds must be left to the children in equal parts. Another third must also be left to the children, but the testator may decide how to divide it. That is, he can choose to leave all of this third to only one of his children or grandchildren. A surviving spouse has a life interest in this third. If the estate is a house or a piece of property, the child who inherits it cannot dispose of it freely until his surviving parent dies, because the surviving parent holds a usufruct over the property.

The final third of the estate can be freely willed to anyone the testator chooses.

Dying without a will

If a foreign resident dies in Spain without a will, his estate in Spain will be distributed according to the Spanish laws of succession.

As an example, let us suppose that a husband and father dies, leaving a widow and three children. The only property is the house. The widow continues to own half the house, because her name is on the title deed as half-owner. The other half of the house constitutes the estate.

This is divided equally among the three children. When the estate is settled, each child will have one-third title to half of the house, meaning that each one now owns one-sixth of the house, and the title deed has four names on it, the widow and each of the three children. The widow also holds a usufruct (*usufructo*) on the children's share. This means she can use their half of the property until she dies, as well as her own half. They must all agree and sign the deed if the house is to be sold.

It is this provision of the inheritance law that causes the situation frequently seen in the Spanish countryside and villages, where six brothers are part-owners of a *finca* or a *pueblo* house.

Dying without a will can cause time-consuming and expensive legal procedures for your survivors, so if you really want to care for them and if you have any definite ideas about how you want your estate distributed, you must make a Spanish will. It's easy and you will feel more secure.

NOTE: All our tax rates and exemptions here refer to the national inheritance law, which applies in most areas, but you may find some regional differences. The administration of inheritance law has passed from the central government in Madrid to the various autonomous regions. Some of these regions have different provisions in their laws.

If you live in Aragon, for example, it is half of the estate which must go to children, not two-thirds. If you live in the Basque country, you probably will pay no inheritance tax at all. Check locally for details.

Andalusians get tax break

Andalusian tax authorities have eliminated inheritance tax for family inheritors who are official residents of Andalusia and who receive less than €125,000. There are five conditions:

1. The testator must have been an official resident of Andalusia.

2. The inheritor, also a resident, must be a direct family member.

3. The total amount of the estate may not exceed €500,000.

4. The already-existing registered assets of each inheritor may not exceed €402,678.

5. Each individual inheritor may not inherit more than €125,000.

The bad news is that, once the total amount of the estate exceeds €500,000, or each inheritor's share exceeds €125,000, the entire exemption disappears, and normal inheritance tax must be paid on the full amount.

Andalusia already applies the hefty reduction of 95 per cent set out in national law on the testator's habitual residence when left to family members who are also residents. This reduction rises to 99.99 per cent when the home is also the main residence of the inheritor. This reduction applies only to the first €120,000 of value.

Unmarried couples and same-sex couples who are registered with the Andalusian registry of *de facto* couples, or *parejas de hecho,* can also take advantage of this reduction.

Are you bound by Spanish law?

The Spanish law of obligatory heirs in theory applies to foreigners with property in Spain, restricting the disposal of this property just as it restricts such disposal for Spaniards. This is because most nations apply the law of the place where the property is located.

However, Article 9 of the Spanish Civil Code provides that, when a foreign property owner dies, even if he holds an official residence permit, the disposal of any assets he has in Spain will be governed by his own national law, not Spanish law.

If his own country's law permits free disposal of the estate, this frees him from the Spanish law of "compulsory heirs" explained above. English law and United States law provide free disposition of assets. German law and Scottish law require that some portion of the estate go to surviving children. You must check your own national law here.

This article does not free the foreigner from Spanish inheritance taxes, however (see next section).

This freedom applies only when such foreigner has an existing foreign will or Spanish will. If he dies intestate, without having made a will, Spanish law will be applied to his assets in Spain and they will be divided equally among his children.

This is a powerful argument for making a Spanish will disposing of your assets in Spain according to your wishes.

For citizens of the United Kingdom, the first complication arises here. A number of countries, including Great Britain, have laws stating that the disposition of real property such as land, houses and apartments will be governed by the law of the country where such property is located. English law — which applies to Wales and Northern Ireland in this case, but not to Scotland — also states that other assets, such as investments, will be governed by the law of the country where the deceased is legally domiciled at the time of his death.

So Spanish law says that English law will apply, and English law sends the ball right back, saying that *Spanish* law will apply, because that is where the property is located. An Englishman in theory is subject to the Spanish law, which may mean he can freely dispose of only one-third of his assets in Spain.

A number of other countries have laws similar to the English law. Investigate in your home country to find out what law applies to the disposition of real estate, the law of your home country or the law of the country where the immovable asset is located.

All this is the theory but what happens in real life?

Most foreigners have free disposition

In practice, any foreigner can make a Spanish will bequeathing his Spanish property to any person of his choice as long as his own national law is ruled by the principle of free disposition of property by testament. The Spanish registrar of wills accepts this. When the time comes, the will is executed and the inheritor takes possession of his new property. Spanish lawyers routinely make such wills.

This means that, even if you are British, you can make a Spanish will leaving your Spanish property to whomever you choose.

The law also says that any foreigner officially resident in Spain is subject to Spanish inheritance law on his world-wide estate.

In practice the authorities simply do not ask whether the testator is an official resident or not. They accept as valid the Spanish will disposing of only the Spanish property. The only requirement enforced by Spain is the payment of Spanish inheritance tax on property or assets located in Spain.

So most foreigners will find no problem in making a separate Spanish will to dispose of their immovable property in Spain, even though the law seems to say otherwise, whether they are residents or non-residents.

Legitimate inheritors can contest Spanish will

One note of warning: All of the above relating to the foreigner's making a will that permits him to leave his Spanish property to anyone he chooses, thus avoiding Spanish inheritance law which requires him to leave at least two-thirds of his estate to his children, works perfectly well in most cases.

But, as we have said, it is not exactly in agreement with the law as written. It is more a matter of the Spanish authorities choosing not to enforce their own laws too strictly.

This means that, if you write your Spanish will leaving your lovely villa to your favourite daughter and cutting out your no-good son entirely, that son could get expert Spanish legal advice, contest the will on the grounds that the law stipulates that half of the inheritance is his, and win his case, thus getting title to half the villa.

So, if you foresee any possible challenge from one of Spain's legitimate inheritors, such as a child or a spouse, you should make other arrangements, such as transferring the title of the property to your chosen heir while you are still alive. You can always maintain the usufruct over the property, which gives you the right to use it as long as you are still living, although the title has formally passed to another person.

If you are quite certain that no possibility exists of successfully contesting it, then go ahead and make your Spanish will as you choose in the confidence that it will be executed as you have written it.

You also need to make a foreign will disposing of any assets you have in other countries. Be sure that any foreign will states clearly that it disposes only of your assets in that country and make sure to say in your Spanish will that it disposes only of your assets in Spain.

There have been unfortunate cases where a person has made one will in Spain stating that all assets are left to one inheritor and another will later made in Germany or Australia, saying the same thing, but leaving "everything" to a different person.

In one particular case, the testator intended to leave all her German assets to family members and her Spanish villa to the friend who had looked after her for years. She made a Spanish will leaving everything to her friend in Spain and then made a German will, dated after the Spanish will, also leaving "everything" to her German family members. These inheritors later had the German will translated and legalised in Spain, and took possession of the Spanish property as well.

They were able to do this because the German will made no distinction of country and it was dated after the Spanish will, so it took precedence. So, the testator's wishes were not carried out and the faithful friend who had looked after the ill and dying person in Spain did not inherit the villa as she was supposed to.

This story is a good argument for taking legal advice when you make your Spanish will.

Foreign will Is valid in Spain

Legally, it is not absolutely necessary for you to make a Spanish will to dispose of your assets in Spain. A Briton who owns property in Spain can bequeath his Spanish apartment in the same British will he uses to dispose of his property in England, and his will can be probated in Spain. However, there are a number of steps which must take place in order to do this.

If you have lived in Spain for a long time, it may be necessary for you to re-create a legal domicile in your home country for purposes of making a will. You may be able to do this by filing an official "letter of intent" with your lawyers. This letter states that, even though you hold a Spanish residence permit now, you really intend to return to your home country in the end. This should be sufficient for establishing a legal domicile in your home country and will allow its laws to apply.

Let us suppose that you do this. Your foreign will (which can be made at your consulate in Spain as long as the proper formalities are observed) must go through the following process before it can dispose of your Spanish assets:

1. A certified copy of the grant of probate must be legalised by the Spanish consul in the testator's home country, and a Spanish translation of this certified copy prepared. A Spanish lawyer must then be empowered to prepare a list of the assets in

Spain, see that the Spanish inheritance taxes are paid, and handle the rest of the paperwork involved in distributing the assets.

2. Two lawyers registered in your home country, or a Notary, or a Spanish consul-general in your home country, must prepare a certificate of law, a *Certificado de Ley,* which affirms that the testator had the legal capacity to make a will; that the will is valid; that the Spanish law of obligatory heirs and the dispositions relating to property of spouses do not exist in the law of your country; that the will has been duly proved, and that the trustees named have the correct legal powers to administer the estate.

3. Finally, your will is declared effective to dispose of your assets in Spain, and your Spanish lawyer can carry this out.

It's a complicated, time-consuming and expensive process, and it is clearly better to make a Spanish will disposing of your assets in Spain.

Making a Spanish will

You go to see a Spanish lawyer and explain your wishes to him. In the case of the death of one spouse, for example, you may wish to leave all possible assets directly to the other spouse, without any inheritance to the children. As a foreigner, you should be able to do this.

Even if surviving children inherit their legal portion, it is not usually necessary for the house to be sold and the proceeds divided, for example. The surviving spouse continues to live in the house and administer it for the good of the children still at home. If the house is later sold, the children can then get their legal share of the price.

The lawyer will advise you as to how the will should read in order to carry out your intentions. People sometimes say that they want their Spanish flat sold and the proceeds divided among the children, for example. Your lawyer will tell you that you cannot do this. You must leave the flat to the children in equal parts. They can then sell it and divide the proceeds, but you cannot order its sale in your will. There may be other provisions on which your lawyer can advise.

The will is made out in two columns, one in Spanish and one in English, or in whatever language the testator prefers. The will is then checked by the *Notario* and signed in his presence. Witnesses are not necessary. This is called a *testamento abierto,* an open will, which is the usual form. The Notary keeps the original in his files, gives you an authorised copy and sends a notification to the central registry in Madrid, called the *Registro Central de Ultima Voluntad.*

The certification numbers of all Spanish wills are kept on file here to ensure that a legal copy can always be found. If the will is lost or if you do not know whether the deceased person has made a Spanish will or not, you can apply to the central registry to find out if a Spanish will exists under that name. If it does exist, the registry will give you the number and the name of the Notary who made it in the first place. You can get a copy of the will from the Notary. Having a Spanish will certainly speeds up the legal processes of inheritance.

The Notary will charge around €60 for the will and the lawyer's fee could be about the same, a total of €120, although this could go much higher if the will is complicated or involves large sums of money.

Remember that husband and wife must each make separate wills, as they each own property separately.

You can also find out almost exactly how much inheritance tax your Spanish estate will attract. Your lawyer will consult the table of rates and then you will know what to expect.

All too often, the existence of Spanish inheritance tax seems to come as a complete surprise to foreign property owners. This tax is charged even when the inheritance is between spouses, with only a minimum exemption, as explained in the next section.

Secret wills

Should you wish to keep secret the provisions of your will, you can also execute a *testamento cerrado,* a closed will. It is, of course, important to have a Spanish lawyer advise you to make sure your wishes square with Spanish law. Otherwise, you might find your desires cannot lawfully be carried out. You take this closed will, in an envelope, to the *Notario,* who seals the envelope and signs it. He then files it, just as with the open will.

Other types of wills are also valid. You can make a holographic will, in your own handwriting, but this later has to be authenticated as genuine before a judge, which means more time, trouble and expense. You can even make a verbal will, in the presence of five witnesses. Each of the five witnesses then has to testify to the

Notario that these are truly the wishes of the deceased. The *Notario* then prepares a written will and certifies it.

Inheritance tax in Spain

Spain's *Ley de Sucesiones* provides no large exemption from inheritance tax when property is passed to a spouse or to family members, so many foreign property owners are dismayed to discover that some tax will be due. The present law provides a total exemption from taxes only for legacies under €16,000. To be exact, the exemption is €15,956.87. This long number results from the addition of yearly inflation to an original round number, plus the conversion from pesetas into euros. We shall call it simply €16,000.

The €16,000 exemption seems rather small, but it applies to each inheritor, not to the total estate. So, if you have a property worth €120,000, your half equals an estate valued at €60,000, and you leave it equally divided among your spouse and three children, each will receive an inheritance worth €15,000, and the bequest will attract no tax at all.

In addition, an inheritor under the age of 21 can have an exemption of up to €48,000. For each year younger than 21, he deducts €4,000 more, until he arrives at the maximum exemption at the age of 13.

This exemption applies to bequests between parents, children, spouses and brothers and sisters. For uncles, cousins and nephews, the exemption is cut by half to €8,000. For more distant relatives, or those not related at all, there is no exemption.

95 per cent reduction

Official residents of Spain leaving their principal residence to wife or children, who are also official residents, may be eligible for a 95 per cent reduction in their tax base. This is 99.9 per cent in Andalusia.

There are three conditions to be eligible for this reduction:
7. You must have held an official residence permit for at least three years.
8. The home you transmit must be your principal residence and you must have lived in it for at least three years.
9. The inheritors must undertake not to sell the property for 10 years. If they do, they are subject to tax.
This reduction applies only up to a maximum of €120,000. If

your inheritance is a property worth €120,000, you can reduce this total by 95 per cent, taking off €114,000. So you pay tax on only €6,000, meaning no tax at all.

But if your family home in Spain has a market value of €360,000, then half of that is €180,000. Your reduction stops at the maximum of €120,000, meaning you must pay Spanish inheritance tax on €60,000, which comes to just over €6,000 in tax.

This reduction is also available for a principal dwelling left to a brother or sister over 65 years of age who has been living with the testator for the previous two years.

The reduction does not apply to any other property, such as a car or a yacht or shares in companies, only to the home itself.

The inheritor, in turn, must keep the property for at least 10 years. If he/she attempts to sell it, he/she will have to pay any tax due on the original inheritance.

This measure forms part of a package of laws designed to help small family businesses rather than retired foreigners. Many small businesses in Spain have failed on the death of the founder because his inheritors were unable to deal with the inheritance tax on the property, such as a shop or a small factory. Now the children can freely inherit, as long as they continue to operate the business for 10 years.

That is the reason behind the 10-year requirement, which then causes problems for the foreign children who want to sell the property rather than keep it.

Retired foreign couples can also benefit, as described above, because the family home is included in the law. When one half of the couple dies, his or her share of the house or flat will be just about tax-free to the surviving partner.

Non-residents cannot take advantage of this reduction.

SETTING TAX VALUES

Spain has a set system for evaluating assets for purposes of inheritance tax. These are:

Real estate
Property is valued either at market price, or at the *valor catastral*, the rated value, or at the value set by *Hacienda* for purposes of

wealth tax, whichever is greater. So, in almost all cases, you will find that the declared sales price on your title deed, or today's market value, will be the value used. That is, if you bought your flat 20 years ago for €60,000, and it is worth €150,000 on the market today, Spain's Tax Agency will value it at €150,000 for purposes of calculating inheritance tax.

When you make your inheritance tax declaration, if you declare the flat as worth only €120,000, you might get away with it, or you might get a notice from *Hacienda* that they have valued it at €150,000 and you must pay tax on €30,000 more.

Remember that *Hacienda* has its own office of valuation and is perfectly aware of the market price of real estate. They will not fine you, but they will charge you the extra tax. They do this frequently.

If you disagree with their valuation, you can request an independent survey, a *tasación*.

Here is a useful tip for deciding what value to use when you wish to make your own inheritance tax calculation. Most autonomous regions maintain a valuation department. If you consult their web site, it will give you an acceptable value for your location.

The Andalusian regional government, for example, sets values at the following web site.

http://www.juntadeandalucia.es/economiayhacienda/ov/tributos/valoracion/val_urbana.htm

You might get a pleasant surprise to find that their acceptable value is actually lower than today's real market price.

Personal effects

The furniture, clothing, personal possessions and so on of the deceased are called the *ajuar*. For inheritance tax purposes they are routinely valued at 3 per cent of the price of the property. If valuable works of art or antique furniture pieces are included, they may be valued separately. In general, add 3 per cent of the property value to your estate.

Automobiles

Most property owners have automobiles, and these are included separately in the estate. Spain's Tax Agency publishes tables each year for the value of used cars. Other items, such as yachts or airplanes, will be valued separately.

Stocks and shares

Stocks and shares in companies or mutual funds or other investments are valued at their price on the day of the person's death.

Life insurance

If received by children, the total amount is added to the estate, after a reduction of €9,000. If received by surviving spouse, half of the amount is added to the estate, and the other half is taxed as a capital gain in the spouse's yearly income tax. Spouse also has reduction of €9,000.

SOME REGIONS CHANGE RULES

NOTE that some of Spain's autonomous regions have somewhat different tax scales for inheritance. Madrid, Catalonia and the Valencia Community, using their independence from the central government, have prepared their own inheritance tax scales. Madrid and its province, like Andalusia, allow unmarried couples listed in the registry of common-law couples to take advantage of the lower tax rates applied to married couples. This is not true in other regions.

Bank accounts

The balance on the day of death is added to the estate.

Calculate your own tax

You can calculate your own inheritance tax by using the tables shown here.

1. **Figure total value:** Figure your total value by referring to the section above on valuations.

2. **Reductions:** You can then subtract from this amount any debts owed by the deceased. This would include a mortgage still unpaid on the property, for example. You can also deduct the expenses of the last illness and the funeral and burial.

3. **Refusal of inheritance:** In cases where the debts of an

SPANISH INHERITANCE TAX RATES YEAR 2006
(euros — rounding céntimos)

Tax Base	Tax	Marginal Percentage
0.00	0.00	7.65
7,993	611	8.50
15,980	1,290	9.35
23,968	2,037	10.20
31,955	2,852	11.05
39,943	3,735	11.90
47,930	4,685	12.75
55,918	5,703	13.60
63,905	6,790	14.45
71,893	7,944	15.30
79,880	9,166	16.15
119,757	15,606	18.70
159,634	23,063	21.25
239,389	40,011	25.50
398,777	80,655	29.75
797,555	199,291	34.00

estate are greater than the assets, which could happen when a small business constitutes the estate, for example, the inheritors can refuse to accept the inheritance, thus being free of their parents´ debts.

4. **Calculation:** After you have made any deductions allowed you for the inheritance tax, such as your basic exemption of €15,956.87, if the estate is passing to close family, let's suppose that your final taxable inheritance is about €42,000.

Look at the table to find the nearest figure below that amount. In this case it is €39,943. The tax due on that amount is €3,735.

Now you need to consult the marginal percentage list, for the rate charged on the difference between the steps. In your case you find that you must pay 11.90 per cent of the difference between €39,943 and your inheritance of €42,000.

The difference is €2,057. Multiply this by 11.90 percent and this gives you another €244.78. Add the two together and you have a total tax of €3,980, a little less than 10 per cent of your base.

These numbers were originally nice round numbers like five million in pesetas, but they have been increased according to inflation since the law was originally passed, and even more decimals arose when they were converted directly and exactly into euros.

Rich pay more

From this table, it looks as if 34 per cent is the absolute top rate of Spanish inheritance tax. This is true when the estate is passed in direct line of descent or between spouses. But it can be much higher when bequests are made to more distant relatives or to non-relatives. And it can be even higher when the inheritor is already wealthy. Remember that the sliding scale of Spanish inheritance tax is designed to favour the poor and soak the rich.

This scale provides multiplying coefficients for the degree of relationship and also for the amount of existing wealth of the inheritor. To get the amount of tax due from those who are more distant relatives or non-related and those who already have sizeable fortunes, you must multiply the basic tax rates above by the coefficients given in the table below.

So, if you are fortunate enough to possess assets worth more than four million euros, and you inherit more than €797,555 from someone who is not related to you, the Spanish tax ministry will multiply the 34 per cent by the 2.4 coefficient and will demand a tax from you of 81.6 per cent.

This system penalises inheritance to non-relations because it is designed to protect the family structure as well as the poor. It has caused problems for same-sex couples and for couples who may have lived together for many years in a stable relationship but are not married.

Can you avoid Spanish tax?

The high rate of inheritance tax and low exemptions in Spain cause many to seek ways round paying it, some of which are legal, some not.

Power of attorney: A note of warning: Many foreigners have been misled by the reference in English to an "Enduring Power of Attorney".

Such a power of attorney does not mean that the power endures beyond the death of the person who grants it. A power of attorney dies with its maker, in Spain and in the UK. The "enduring" simply means that it has no other fixed date of expiry.

IN EUROS — ROUNDING CÉNTIMOS			
Existing Assets	**Spouses Children**	**Cousins Uncles**	**Non-Relatives**
0 to €402,678	1.0000	1.5882	2.0000
€402,678 to €2,007,380	1.0500	1.6676	2.1000
€2,007,388 to €4,020,770	1.1000	1.7471	2.2000
More than €4,020,770	1.2000	1.9059	2.4000

People sometimes think that such a power of attorney will allow them to dispose of property, such as a villa in Spain, after the death of the owner, thus avoiding the formalities of a will and inheritance tax.

This is not so. The power of attorney legally expires when the maker of it dies. Some people have used the trick of failing to inform the authorities of the death and then using the power of attorney to sell a property.

If swiftly done, the authorities are not likely to catch you, but it is against the law. Further, if someone had reason to protest such a sale, they could have it annulled as a fraudulent act.

Family trust: Among the perfectly legal possibilities is the formation of a family corporation or trust, in which the family's wealth passes into the hands of the company, with each family member becoming a director of the company. So when one member of the family dies, it involves only a reorganisation of the board of directors and a transfer of some of the company shares, attracting very little tax.

Off-shore company: For non-Spaniards, the constitution of a Gibraltar-based company or other offshore operation in order to own real property in Spain has been another way to avoid Spanish inheritance taxes. In this case, when the founder of the company dies he leaves his shares in the company to whomever he chooses, in a will made outside Spain. But as far as Spain is concerned, the same company continues to own the property and no transfer has taken place, hence there is no tax. See chapter on taxes for more information, but be warned that Spain has placed a special tax on properties owned by companies registered in off-shore tax havens. You will need expert legal advice on your individual circumstances and the possible disadvantages of this offshore ownership before you decide.

Four-year limit: Another trick takes advantage of the fact that the statute of limitations on inheritance tax, and all other taxes, runs out after four years. That is, the state cannot collect the tax once four years have elapsed. So the scheme is to "lose" the deceased's will for four years, not declaring the property for inheritance. At the end of four years, the inheritor "discovers" the will and takes possession of the property, free of any inheritance tax. Where the estate is large and the tax is high, this plan can be worth it.

Be warned, however, that Spanish law requires that an inheritance be declared within six months of the death. And, if you are found out, you can be subject to a surcharge of 25 per cent on the tax due, or even higher penalties if the Spanish authorities rule that deliberate fraud is involved.

Also be warned that the six-month period is included in the statute of limitations, so you really have to wait four years and six months for *prescripción*, the Spanish term for statute of limitations.

Gift: You can also make a gift of the property to your inheritors while you are still living, perhaps reserving the right to inhabit the flat as long as you live, but remember that the Spanish gift tax is exactly the same as the inheritance tax. The law in fact is called the Law on Inheritance and Gifts.

"Sell" property now: Or you might "sell" your property to your heir, again reserving the *usufructo* or lifetime right to inhabit it yourself. At property transfer costs of around 10 per cent, this could save your inheritor a sizeable sum when the valuation is more than €50,000 and the inheritor is a non-relative.

You have to go on living for at least five years after you carry out this operation, however, or the state will assume that you did it only to avoid tax and will charge you the full amount.

This particular method has many attractions for same-sex couples where one party owns the property and wishes to leave it to the other, without suffering the very high rate of taxation applied to non-relatives.

Each case needs individual study so it makes sense to consult a Spanish lawyer when making your will.

GLOSSARY

Ajuar – the contents of a home, furnishings and equipment
Certificado de Ley – Certificate of Law, usually certifying that the law of another country is applicable
Exención – exemption
Herederos forzosos – compulsory heirs
Pareja de hecho – unmarried couple living together as man and wife
Poder – power of attorney
Prescripción – time limit on legal action, statute of limitations
Registro Central de Ultima Voluntad – Central Registry of Wills
Tasación – valuation, of property or other asset
Testamento – will, testament
Testamento cerrado – secret, closed will
Ultima voluntad – last will and testament
Usufructo – usufruct, right to enjoy
Valor catastral – officially rated value of property

YOU AND YOUR LEGAL ADVISERS

15

YOUR *ABOGADO* — 267

LAWYER'S FEES — 268

CLIENT'S BILL OF RIGHTS — 269

HOW TO COMPLAIN — 269

FREE LEGAL ASSISTANCE — 270

YOUR *GESTORÍA* — 272

YOUR *ASESOR FISCAL* — 274

THE *NOTARIO* — 274

ADMINISTRADOR DE FINCAS — 275

HOW TO CHOOSE A LEGAL ADVISER — 276

WHO are these legal advisers we keep telling you to consult? What can the Spanish *abogado*, the *gestor*, the *asesor fiscal*, the *Notario* and the *administrador de fincas* do for you?

They can do a lot to steer you right and save you money while protecting you from a load of problems and headaches. Let's examine each of them.

Your *abogado*

Abogado means lawyer, solicitor or attorney. Do not be afraid to consult a Spanish lawyer. They are trained professionals whose job is to serve their clients within the law.

Many of them who practise in areas with many foreigners speak excellent English or German and are accustomed to dealing with foreign residents in Spain and their special problems.

Foreigners make up more than half the clients of many lawyers in Marbella and the surrounding area, for example. In Fuengirola, more than 40 per cent of all court cases involve foreigners. These Spanish lawyers make their living by serving their foreign clients, and they are prepared to serve you as well.

If you are purchasing property in Spain, starting a business, attempting to get a work permit, investing in a Spanish business, or making a Spanish will, you need a Spanish lawyer to advise you.

A lawyer will check the title of property you wish to buy in order to discover if the seller really holds clear title or if there are unpaid taxes on the property. He will vet your contract to make sure the provisions are the normal ones and do not contain any tricky clauses working to your disadvantage.

In a country where you do not speak the language, do not have any local knowledge and are not familiar with the law, it seems basic common sense to get expert help, for your own protection.

Doing it yourself is often penny-wise and pound-foolish. Yes, you can get a standard form to make a Spanish will and have the *Notario* register it for a small fee. But only the *abogado* will explain to you whether you can legally make such a will or not. Your terms may not be valid in Spanish law.

In any case, when it is time to probate the will and distribute the estate, a lawyer's services will be necessary, and the lawyer who prepared the will in the first place will be familiar with its terms and prepared to see they are carried out.

Spanish lawyers work with another professional, called a *Procurador*, who handles much of the complicated routine of preparation and presentation of documents to the court. The *Procurador* charges his fees separately. If a lot of paperwork is involved, they can be substantial.

If you instruct a lawyer to act for you in your absence, you can be sure that your taxes, fees and other matters will be correctly handled while you are away. If you employ a lawyer for one transaction, you will later find it easy to ring him up for five minutes of consultation. There are dozens of ways a lawyer can help you.

Lawyers' fees

Lawyers' fees vary widely because they depend on the amount of work involved. A half-hour consultation with a lawyer may cost you 60 euros and save you hundreds of thousands. Or it may cost you nothing, depending on the situation.

Handling a property purchase may cost you as little as 500 euros or it could run into the thousands if the lawyer discovers complications that need sorting out.

One rough estimate for property transactions is one per cent of the amount involved, although many lawyers will try to charge more.

Ask in advance, and try to establish an agreed fee or percentage before you assign your case to a lawyer. Many of them will agree to this and you can avoid unpleasant surprises later.

The *Colegio de Abogados* publishes a list of guidelines, setting minimum recommended fees.

Property purchase: One per cent of the total price is standard.

Residence and work permit: €150 for a married couple.

Disputes over money: There is a sliding scale. To claim €600,000, a lawyer will charge 10 per cent. For €300,000, the base fee is 5 per cent.

Divorce: Where there are no children and no property at stake, and the divorce is by mutual agreement, a minimum of €1,000.

Will preparation: Minimum €100, plus about €60 to Notary.

These are rock-bottom fees, remember, but they give you an idea.

A "Bill of Rights for Citizens before the Administration of Justice" (*Carta de Derechos de los Ciudadanos ante la Justicia*) provides for the *hoja de encargo*, a work order, which lists the services that the lawyer will provide and the fees he will charge.

The work order provision is part of a 41-point programme to make the citizen's contact with the legal system more user-friendly (see section on Courts for more details).

As lawyers are notoriously reluctant to tell clients what their fees will be, we can only hope that this laudable initiative works out in practice. On the lawyer's side of the case, it is difficult for them to know in advance just how complicated a case may turn out to be.

Nevertheless, it is certainly worth mentioning this Bill of Rights when you try to find out how much your lawyer will charge you.

How to complain

If you find that your lawyer is not giving you proper service, is there anything you can do? Suppose you have waited two years for your title deed and you hear nothing from the lawyer, and you wish to make a formal complaint.

The professional organisation which watches standards and defends the interests of its members is called the *Ilustre Colegio de Abogados* (the Illustrious College of Lawyers). You can complain directly to this body, which has branches in each province, about the activities of one of its members.

As in any country, one finds that the lawyers' watchdog committee is reluctant to condemn a fellow attorney, but they will hear your complaint and look into it. The *Colegio* publishes a booklet each year, listing approximate fees for various legal services, as mentioned above. Although these fees are not binding, they are supposed to represent a minimum charge, in order to prevent a lawyer from under-cutting his colleagues.

If the fee charged to you for a particular action is very much higher than the fees in the booklet, however, you may have a good case for claiming that you have been overcharged.

You will probably want to consult another lawyer, who will help you prepare a letter of complaint to the College. The College will question your original lawyer about the problem. Your original lawyer will then have to explain the basis for his fees.

If the explanation does not satisfy the College, you will get a reduction.

In serious cases, the College takes stronger action. A number of Spanish lawyers have been charged with failure to perform the services for which they were instructed, or for using their clients' money for their own purposes, or for participating in schemes to cheat their clients.

These lawyers will be fined, disbarred and even imprisoned. It does happen, so do not hesitate to make your complaint if you feel that you have been wronged.

Remember that it also helps to have your agreement with your lawyer written and signed. This will help both in negotiating fees and in establishing the facts if you have a complaint.

Free legal assistance

If you are a resident of modest means, you may even find that you are entitled to free legal aid in Spain.

The poor have been guaranteed free access to legal defence since the granting of the Spanish Constitution in 1978. Nevertheless, the system has been sharply criticised for the limited service provided, for abuse by persons falsely claiming to be poor, and for the fact that the state paid the public defenders too little and too late, which did not encourage them to work hard for their clients.

A new Free Legal Assistance law has been enacted to remedy these defects.

The law of *Asistencia Jurídica Gratuita* provides easier access to legal help, greatly widens the scope of the help available, and attempts to check the abuse of the system by persons who in fact have sufficient means to pay their own private lawyer.

For the foreigner, the good news is that even a non-resident of Spain may qualify for free legal aid. Resident foreigners of course are entitled.

Persons of incomes below 2.5 times the official minimum wage are entitled to free legal aid. As the Spanish minimum wage is a little more than 6,000 euros a year, this means families with incomes under 15,000 euros a year.

Furthermore, the *Colegio de Abogados* has installed its own offices in each judicial district in Spain. Those who are seeking free legal aid can present themselves at their local office and request the forms to apply for aid.

You will find the legal aid offices in your local court building, usually called the *Palacio de Justicia*. We say it's easy, but filling in the forms can be complicated.

In an attempt to identify false applicants, the forms require copies of your Spanish income tax declaration, or a certificate from *Hacienda* that you do not pay income tax. The form also requires a certification from your town hall listing any properties you own, and even a note from the Traffic Department giving details of any automobiles you own in Spain.

Workers and beneficiaries of the Spanish Social Security system also have the right to free representation before the labour court, so anyone who feels he has been mistreated by his Spanish employer can be sure of professional assistance to plead his case.

For the first time, the legal aid includes advice and planning before any court action takes place. This means that a poor person who feels that he must bring a lawsuit against a neighbour who has built a road across part of his garden can get legal advice and help before he takes any action.

Perhaps a pointed letter from the lawyer will settle the matter out of court, thus saving time and money for the taxpayers as well as the persons involved.

The law also provides free access to the services of court-appointed experts, those professionals who evaluate the costs of a botched plumbing or carpentry job, for example, so the judge can assign a value.

In Spanish such an expert is called a *perito judicial*. Even the threat of calling one can often make the offending supplier back off on his attempts to collect a bill for substandard work.

Even more important, the free legal aid law provides an exemption from the deposits necessary in many legal actions.

Often, you must make a deposit of a certain percentage of the amount you are seeking in order for the court to accept your suit. Although this aims to discourage people from making idle lawsuits simply for the nuisance value, it also has the effect of preventing persons of modest means from bringing some justified legal actions.

So, the exemption from deposit empowers them to sue when otherwise they would not be able to do so.

A false declaration of poverty or the concealment of financial resources can bring an order to repay to the State any expenses incurred on behalf of the person who has requested free legal aid. This is to prevent abuses of the system, which occurred all too frequently under the former law.

Your *gestoría*

All countries have bureaucracies and red tape, forms to fill in, certificates to be obtained, licences and permits but some people say that Spanish red tape is in a class all its own. Not only foreigners in Spain have to deal with this *papeleo*, or paperchase. Spaniards themselves have the same forms to deal with and are driven just as mad by their own bureaucracy. This situation has given rise to the *gestoría,* a peculiarly Spanish institution licensed by the government.

The *gestor* is the middleman between you and the bureaucracy. When you are standing in line waiting to present the papers for your residence renewal and you see a man with a folder of papers pass directly behind the counter and engage the attention of one of the clerks while you and the rest of the people wait, that is the man from the *gestoría*.

He is doing exactly what you are doing, but he is doing it for half a dozen or so people who have paid him to handle the matter. He receives prompt attention from the clerks not because he pays them bribes, but because he saves them work. They know that his forms will be properly filled in and all necessary documents present.

The *gestoría* can save you a lot of time and trouble, usually for a rather small fee. The *gestor* has no official powers, but he must pass an exam and is licensed by the authorities as a professional. He can be held to account if he mishandles your applications or charges for services he does not perform.

The *gestor*, if he is experienced, can do a great deal more than save you time in the queue. There are *gestorías* in large cities with 30 or 40 employees, where you find experts on one floor arranging the Social Security payments for a restaurant's waiters, while on the next floor someone is processing the papers to renew the tourist licence plates for a foreigner's car, and on the ground floor a messenger is picking up clients' property purchase contracts to take along to the registry office.

They carry out all the operations described in this book, and many more besides. They can advise you on all sorts of transactions.

If you are starting a business, you will definitely need a good *gestoría* to steer you through the complexities of licensing, administration, bookkeeping and taxation. There are also small *gestorías* which simply do not have the expertise to handle a lot of the often complex problems involving foreigners, so it is necessary to ask among old hands for a *gestoría* which has given them satisfactory service.

The *gestor*, as a licensed professional, also has a *colegio*, and if you feel that you have not received satisfactory service, you may lodge a complaint. Ask in advance what the fees are for the service you require. If they seem high to you, try another *gestoría*. The *colegio* sets fees, but these are minimums, not maximums, unfortunately, as their primary aim is to prevent a price war.

One note of warning: Although a good *gestor* can provide many services, including the arranging of rental contracts and the hiring and paying of employees, we advise you to use the services of a lawyer and a tax consultant as well, to make sure that you are fully protected.

Sometimes a busy *gestor* will apply a standard contract in a situation where legal or tax complications can later arise, so do not be lulled into a false sense of security when he says that your contract is the one everyone uses. He is probably right, but check with the lawyer and tax consultant just to be sure.

Your *asesor fiscal*
Literally translated, this is a "fiscal adviser", basically an accountant and tax consultant.

In the first stages of your residence in Spain, you may not need an accountant. But when it is time for you to declare for Spanish income tax, you should certainly consult an *asesor fiscal*. If you have any investments in Spain or are starting a business, you will also need an accountant or financial consultant.

He can save you money and see that you keep on the right side of the ever-changing tax laws as well. Again, you should ask among veteran residents to find a satisfactory *asesor fiscal*.

Otherwise, you may have the frustrating experience of one resident who, out of curiosity, consulted three accountants, two *gestorías*, and the information office of *Hacienda* about his income tax, and received six different answers.

As discussed in the section on You and Your Taxes, the income tax situation in Spain is gradually becoming stricter, and foreigners have the additional complications of taxes paid outside Spain or income arising outside Spain, which require expert advice.

In business, you will need to know things like just how much holiday pay your workers should get, what expenses you can deduct, how to reclaim Value Added Tax you have paid.

Most of these accountants are also familiar with labour legislation and can advise you on whether or not you may dismiss a worker, and how much compensation you will have to pay him.

Unlike the *gestor* or the *abogado*, anyone may set himself up as a tax consultant as there are no legal requirements. This means that, if you suffer loss through bad advice or service from your adviser, you have no easy recourse to a professional oversight body. Your only remedy will be to bring a civil lawsuit against him in the normal courts for the loss.

The *Notario*
The *Notario*, public Notary, is a public official, like a judge, and you cannot employ him as your agent or instruct him to act for you in the same way you engage a lawyer or accountant, although he can

give you useful advice.

His principal mission is to make sure that certain matters are officially noted and registered. These include wills, as discussed in the section on Making A Will, and various sorts of contracts, such as your purchase contract when you buy property. He will register your foreign money contribution when you buy your property. He also registers the charters of companies, and the official book of minutes of a community of property owners is presented for his stamp, which makes the book an official matter of public record.

You might also need a notarised letter when you notify the tenant of your property that you wish to end the rental when the contract term ends, or to make some other official notification.

The Notary receives fees from you for these services, but you cannot instruct him to act for you in the same way as a lawyer or an accountant. These fees are fixed by law.

They currently run about €75 for a will and about €300 for a property sales contract under €60,000.

For most foreign property purchasers, their big moment comes when they sign their contract at the Notary's office. The Notary or your lawyer then passes the contract to the Property Registry for inscription.

The original of your property contract, the *escritura,* stays in the Notary's office, where you can always request an authorised copy. He also keeps the original copies of Spanish wills made before him.

In the past, Spanish notaries did not hesitate to register sales contracts which obviously under-declared the real amount of the purchase price, nor did they involve themselves with payment of taxes.

Now, however, they are required to warn the parties to contracts that if they undervalue the purchase by more than €12,000 or 20 per cent, they will be subject to fines if *Hacienda* discovers this.

They must also verify that 5 per cent of the purchase price is withheld and paid to *Hacienda* when property is sold by a non-resident, as a guarantee against the capital gains tax.

The *administrador de fincas*

This licensed professional is a property administrator. He can handle all of the matters that come up with your property, such as seeing that taxes are paid, managing rentals and making sure that books are properly kept. He is licensed to serve as a paid administrator for property owners' communities.

Although there is no legal requirement that a community administrator be a licensed professional, it is often a good idea to employ an *administrador de fincas* because he will see that the community's affairs are handled professionally.

"*Finca*" in this case does not mean a little house in the countryside. It refers to all property in general. He can advise you about any aspect of owning and purchasing property.

Like the other professional groups, there is a *colegio* which oversees standards for these property consultants, and you can formally complain to this college if you feel your administrator has not given you reasonable service.

How to choose a legal adviser

Walk into the nearest bar or hairdresser and ask them to recommend a lawyer or a tax consultant. Anybody in business will have an opinion, whether they are foreign or Spanish.

Visit three establishments and you will have a list of professionals whom people love — and another list of advisers to stay away from. You will also have a fund of useful practical information about how things really work in Spain, because every new settler has a story and loves to tell it.

The consulates of all nations maintain lists of lawyers, tax consultants, doctors and other professionals who speak the language of their nation. These lists are not necessarily professionals whom the consulate is recommending. They are simply noted as speaking your language.

GLOSSARY

Abogado – lawyer, attorney, solicitor
Administrador de fincas – licensed property administrator and manager
Asesor fiscal – tax consultant and accountant
Asistencia Jurídica Gratuita – free legal aid
Colegio – official college of professionals
Gestoría – licensed administrative office
Hoja de encargo – work order, either for a plumber or a lawyer

Notario – public Notary
Perito judicial – court-appointed technical expert
Procurador – legal expert who works with lawyer

YOU AND THE SPANISH AUTHORITIES

16

YOUR TOWN HALL	280
REGISTER TO VOTE	281
EMPADRONAMIENTO	281
PROVINCIAL, REGIONAL AND NATIONAL AUTHORITIES	282
THREE KINDS OF POLICE	283
REPORTING A THEFT	285
IF YOU ARE ARRESTED	286
WHAT IS A *DENUNCIA*?	286
COURTS AND JUDGES	287
LAWSUIT WITHOUT LAWYER	289
JUICIO RÁPIDO	290
CITIZEN'S BILL OF LEGAL RIGHTS	290
YOUR CONSULATE	291
SPANISH CONSTITUTION	291
FOREIGNERS' LAW	291

IN your home country you are probably familiar with the various official authorities you come in contact with. These include the town hall, the state or provincial or county government, the police, the courts and judges, the Social Security system, the national government. Spain is organised in very much the same way as most European countries.

Your town hall

Your town hall, or *ayuntamiento,* will be important to you in many ways.

You pay your annual motor vehicle circulation tax here. If you build a house, it is here that you apply for a building permit. It is here — in the *urbanismo* department — that you discover how much your *Plus valía* tax will be before you buy or sell property. It is here that you register as an inhabitant of the town in order to exercise your right to vote in municipal elections.

All you have to do is find the right window or *ventanilla.* If your town is located in an area with a large foreign population, you will probably find someone in your town hall who speaks English.

Towns with many foreign residents, like Mijas and Fuengirola on the Costa del Sol maintain special departments to assist the foreigners. If you are fortunate enough to live in a town with a foreign residents' department, this will be your starting place for most queries.

The mayor is called the *alcalde* and the members of the town council are called *concejales.* You may make any complaints you have to these officials.

Individual *concejales* are responsible for each area of municipal services, rubbish collection, building permits and so on. Ask for the appropriate one, and he or she will give you a hearing.

As foreign residents make up a large part of both the population and the income of many towns, officials generally try to keep them happy.

They are now aware that European Union citizens resident in Spain have the right to vote in local elections, and even to be elected to the municipal government, which ought to establish your credentials. (See next page).

If your town hall does not have a foreigners' department or anyone who speaks your language, you should get some Spanish assistance and present your complaint or request in writing. This will be stamped as *recibido,* "received", when you present it.

Spanish regulations on local administration declare that all cases presented in this way must be acted upon, either positively or negatively, in a reasonable period of time. This "reasonable period" of time can seem quite long, but complaints about things like burning rubbish or noisy bars are read and registered. And, when enough of them pile up, something eventually gets done, just as it does in your home country.

Register to vote

If you are a European Union citizen, you are entitled not only to vote in the municipal elections in the town where you are registered but to be elected to office as well. This right applies even if you do not hold a Spanish residence permit.

Can you see yourself at the meeting of the town council as you propose the death penalty for riders of noisy motorbikes? At last you will be in a position to do something about it. Don't laugh too hard. Local Spanish politicians have started to recruit foreign candidates in towns along the Costa Blanca and the Costa del Sol where there are large foreign populations. A few have even been elected in recent municipal elections.

First, however, you must be registered as residing in your town and then you must make sure your name is on the list of voters. Go into your town hall with your passport, your residence permit or some evidence that you live in the municipality, such as a rental contract or a property deed.

WARNING: COSTA CRIME IS RISING

Although Spain is still a much safer place to live than the UK, for example, crime is on the rise, especially in coastal areas frequented by tourists. Be alert for persons who try to distract your attention in supermarket parking lots and at cash machines. Often, one of the gang will pretend to be a Spanish police officer in plain clothes. Another ploy is to puncture one of your tyres. The thieves offer to help, then snatch a handbag. Statistics show that the crime rate in Mediterranean tourist towns like Torremolinos is more than seven times higher than the national average. Police claim they are more than 25 per cent under-strength for the job.

Empadronamiento

You wish to inscribe yourself in the *padrón*, the list of local residents. You want to be *empadronado,* or inscribed, and receive a *Certificado de Empadronamiento*, a registry certificate for this municipality.

Town halls are generally happy to inscribe anyone residing within their limits because their slices of the national or regional tax pie are bigger when they can demonstrate a larger population. However, they will not register just anyone who walks in.

The principal requirement is that you spend more than six months residing in the municipality. This rule applies to both Spaniards and foreigners. Persons are prohibited from being *empadronado* in two municipalities at the same time. This requirement applies to Spaniards and to foreigners. If you are from the UK, for example, but you register as an inhabitant of a town in Spain, you will be required to vote for your European Union representative in Spain, not in the UK.

Once you are *empadronado* you can then request that your name appear on the *censo electoral,* the voter registration list, and you will be ready to vote for your local European parliamentary representative and for candidates standing in the next municipal elections, whether for mayor or councillors. Or you may even stand for office yourself. A number of non-Spanish EU citizens now sit on municipal councils.

In modern Spain where regional autonomy has become the order of the day, you may find, as Spaniards also do, some confusion above the town hall level. Many responsibilities formerly handled by the central government in Madrid have been passed down to the regional governments such as the *Junta de Andalucía* or the *Generalitat Valenciana.*

Provincial authorities

Each of Spain's 50 provincial authorities has its own legislature, called the *Diputación Provincial,* which is responsible for various areas, such as consumer complaints and some secondary roads. Through their tourism departments they promote the local attractions and they organise cultural events. They oversee projects which affect various municipalities, such as a province-wide sewage system, for example, or an urban development plan cutting across town boundaries.

Regional authorities

These regional governments set standards for property development and building. They usually operate the health care system and have the power to make changes in a number of national taxes. This means that a resident in Marbella gets health care from the Andalusian health service, not the national health service, and that inheritance taxes in the Valencia region may differ from those in Madrid. Both the Basques and the Catalans have their own special statutes granting them various degrees of autononmy, including the teaching of their own languages in the public schools and their own regional police forces. The governments of the autonomous regions also fight with the central government in Madrid over things like their share of the national taxes and whether they will get a high-speed train next year.

National authorities

The central government in Madrid has gradually been devolving powers to the autonomous regions. This includes the assignment of a share of the national taxes to each region to meet their expenses.

The Madrid government's chief representative in each province is called the *Sub-Delegado del Gobierno*. He is in charge of residence permits, among other matters, because immigration is a national policy.

Sometimes there are areas where municipal, provincial and regional authorities conflict and overlap. You may find that you are dealing with the national government when you could easily think it's the provincial one.

When you apply for a work permit, for example, you deal with the *Delegación Provincial* of the *Ministerio de Trabajo*. This is the office of the Labour Ministry located in your province, but it is not a provincial organ. And so it goes, with various state organisms in charge of different areas. Some will be important to you and others will not.

POLICE FORCES

Three different kinds of police, and sometimes four, may operate in the same areas, which can be confusing.

There are municipal police, national police and the Civil Guard. Some autonomous regions, such as the Basque Country and Catalonia, have their own regional police as well.

You most likely will come into contact with the local police when a young municipal policewoman puts a 30-euro parking ticket on your illegally parked car. The *Policía Nacional* (National Police) are in charge of applications for a residence card at your local police station, or *Comisaría*. If you drive too fast, you may be pulled over by a motor-cycle officer of the *tráfico* division of the *Guardia Civil*.

Municipal police

First, there are the municipal police of your town, called *Policía Local*. They are in charge of matters such as directing traffic and making sure bars close on time. As a general rule, you will find them polite and helpful.

In a situation where another citizen's activities disturb you or damage your property, you may make an official complaint or *denuncia* to the police. This could be neighbours fighting at the top of their lungs or when a bar plays loud music late at night.

If your polite protests to the offending parties are disregarded, call a cop. One visit from a policeman will show your neighbour that you are seriously annoyed, and this ought to take care of the problem.

The police have a device which measures the decibel level of the noise coming from a bar, and they can fine the proprietor if this noise is above permitted levels. They have even been seen in the streets applying this meter to the motors of those small 50-cc motorbikes that infuriate Spaniards and foreigners alike.

People often say that police do nothing about the noisy bikes, but in fact they confiscate hundreds of them every year and do not return them until they are fitted with proper silencers.

National police

The *Policía Nacional* are more thoroughly trained and are in charge of dealing with most crime. There are National Police posts in towns of any size. Here you find the *extranjeros* or foreigners' department where you apply for a residence card. The National Police are charged with the documentation and control of foreigners in Spain, including the wave of illegal immigrants pouring in from Africa. The National Police have specialised units dealing with matters such as organised crime rings, drug smuggling and money laundering. Organised gangs from Eastern Europe are the most recent threat.

FACT: **Almost one-third of all prisoners in Spanish gaols are foreigners.**

Civil Guard

Finally, there is the *Guardia Civil*. This body was originally organised to provide police protection in country areas, and they have little to do with large cities or even big towns. If you live in a village, though, there will be a *Guardia Civil* post instead of a National Police unit, and you report crimes to them.

Your principal contact with them will most likely be through their mission of patrolling the highways. They assist motorists in difficulty. On the other hand, they might be around a curve with modern radar equipment that times your speed, and identifies your licence number. You won't even know you have been clocked until you get the *multa*, or fine, in the mail.

You can choose to protest it or pay it, at the *Jefatura de Tráfico,* the provincial highway department You can usually pay a speeding fine by *giro postal,* a post office money order, which will save you a trip.

You may also have contact with the *Guardia Civil* when they mount a checkpoint along the highway, picking drivers at random to apply a breath test for alcohol.

The *Guardia Civil* have specialised units at borders, at sea where they pursue drug-smugglers and boatloads of illegal immigrants. They have bomb disposal experts and anti-terrorist specialists, and they also have teams of high-tech computer experts who try to keep tabs on sophisticated computer crimes.

Reporting a theft

You need to contact the police in case of a burglary in your home, a stolen car or a stolen purse on the street.

In large towns, you report thefts to the *Policía Nacional* rather than to the municipal police. In small villages or in the country, you will report to the *Guardia Civil* post. Procedures for reporting theft are much the same in Spain as in any country.

You may have to wait with others for the chance to make your report. A police clerk records the details. The sad reality in all countries is that most stolen items are never seen again. Nevertheless, every year the Spanish police recover thousands of stolen cars, and other items which can be viewed at the police station.

REPORT BY PHONE: Call police on 902-102112 and report a theft or loss. This report will be sent to your local police station where you must later sign it to obtain a copy.

Remember that you must make this report and obtain an official copy of it if you are going to make an insurance claim. In tourist-area towns, you may find the report forms available in four or five languages. In some cities, like Málaga or Fuengirola, there will be interpreters on the spot.

If you are arrested

If you are arrested by the Spanish police, you have the same basic rights you have in any modern democracy: the right to remain silent; the right to hear the charges against you; the right to legal counsel; the right to contact a lawyer.

You can be held for three days before being taken before a judge, but the judge must be informed of your arrest within 24 hours. That three-day provision may seem overlong but keep in mind that the judge must be informed within 24 hours, so at least one other official besides the police knows that the temporary, uncharged, prisoner is in gaol.

In practice, the police hold very few suspects for 72 hours without bringing them before the judge to be formally charged or set free. The police use this power normally to harass small-time crooks or offenders whom they are morally certain have violated the law but who will probably be freed by the judge either on technical grounds or for lack of solid evidence.

What Is a *denuncia?*

Sooner or later, you will hear the Spanish word, *denuncia.* Because it sounds so much like the English verb "to denounce" it is often thought by foreigners to have some special Spanish legal significance. It sounds threatening to them.

In Spanish legal terms, the word *denunciar* means only "to report, to declare". When your wallet is stolen, you go to the police post and make a *denuncia,* a report. So, when someone threatens to have you denounced, it only means he's going to have you reported, as one might report a neighbour's noisy television set or a wall being built which will cut off your protected view.

You should be aware that reporting an infraction to the police is not the same as bringing charges in court. If your neighbour's barking dog is disturbing you throughout the night, you can call the police and they may or may not pay him a visit. In most cases, the matter ends here.

But, if you go in person to the *juzgado de guardia* (the duty court) to present a formal charge of disturbing the peace, this is more serious. You must sign the charges and be prepared to back up your case. The judge will order the offending dog-owner to appear, along with yourself, to hear both sides of the story.

Courts and judges

With a little luck, you won't have anything to do with courts and judges in Spain.

Taking a case through a court can be frustrating and time-consuming. The mills of justice grind exceedingly slowly. Spanish courts have been reprimanded and fined by the European Union for the slowness of their proceedings.

The Spanish courts do function, however, and lawsuits are settled and judgements awarded.

If you intend to sue someone in Spain, you consult a lawyer, who explains either that you have no case in law for this or that reason, or who says that, yes, you have an excellent chance of getting the damages you seek. Your lawyer then prepares the papers and the process is set in motion.

Justice of the Peace

Maybe a neighbour in your village has begun to build a wall on your property or your landlord has denied you access to the roof terrace when your contract clearly states that you are entitled to it. The *Juez de Paz,* the Justice of the Peace, is often the first-level court in small disputes of this type.

At this level, neither party need be represented by counsel. Often enough, just the fact that you have gone to the Justice of the Peace and cited your neighbour to a hearing will be sufficient to solve the problem peaceably.

These Justice of the Peace courts exist only in small towns where there is no higher court locally available. They are empowered to settle only very minor matters.

Court of First Instance

The next step up in the court scheme is the *Juzgado de Primera Instancia,* the Court of First Instance. Here you can bring suit to recover unpaid debts and deal with more serious matters, such as breach of contract or divorce. A lawsuit is called a *demanda* and to sue is *demandar.* Now you need a lawyer.

In the First Instance Court you might sue a business client who has not paid his debts to you for goods and services. If your case is sound and the amount of the debts not too great, you may get a ruling in your favour within six months or you might wait three years — depending on the caseload.

Here also you can sue the contractor whose work has not met the standards specified in the contract or a repairman whose bill seems too high.

Perito Judicial: In many cases of this type, your lawyer may ask for the appointment of a *perito judicial,* a court-appointed expert on plumbing, electrical installations, or whatever the subject of thedispute. This expert will evaluate the quality of the work and the price paid. Again, in situations of overcharging a client, very often the mere threat of this *perito judicial* will be enough to cause settlement of the case.

Provincial Assizes & Supreme Court

Legal action usually begins in the Court of First Instance. Any case, however, can lead to a series of appeals and counter appeals to higher courts, such as the *Audiencia Provincial* (Provincial Assizes) with its four separate branches or *salas* for civil, criminal, administrative or labour cases and right on up to the *Tribunal Supremo,* the highest court of all.

If questions about basic constitutional rights are involved, the case will go to the *Tribunal Constitucional,* the Constitutional Court.

A case might even begin in one of these higher courts when serious criminal activity is involved or where large sums of money are disputed in civil matters.

So, there is a functioning legal system in Spain, which you can make work for you by obtaining skilled legal counsel. Just as in most countries, some Spanish courts function quickly and effectively, but most are slow and overloaded. Do not give up on the system. Even when you are told that the courts are so terrible that you may as well forget about your loss, do not believe this.

Plenty of horror stories exist about taking nine years to settle an accident claim against an insurance company, for example, but there is legal recourse for you, and the Spanish state is spending millions of euros to expand and modernise the court system.

Lawsuit without lawyer

Spain's revised Law of Civil Judgement, has made it much easier for businesses and services to pursue their cases against debtors who just won't pay up.

The law allows you to make your claim without a lawyer or procurator, filling in a simple form at your nearest court, for debts up to €30,000. The words to remember are *"proceso monitorio"*. This is the equivalent of a small claims court in the UK.

The creditor presents himself at the court with some evidence of the debt, such as an unpaid bill or a work order, preferably with the signature or stamp of the debtor, though this is not strictly necessary. The creditor must have the address of the debtor for official notification, and he must bring his case in the court district where the debtor resides.

The two principles of the new system are immediate action and rapid verbal hearings. Once you have presented your case, the judge should order a hearing within a short time, citing both parties to appear. At the hearing the two sides give their arguments in the presence of the judge and the process is recorded on video-tape. Yes, you will be filmed.

If the debtor does not appear, or if the judge decides he has not presented a valid reason for not paying the debt, he will order the debtor to pay within 20 days. If the debtor does not pay, the judge will order his assets seized by the court in an amount sufficient to cover the debt.

These assets will be seized even if the debtor appeals to a higher court. It is now easier for courts to act against assets such as bank accounts, which can speed up the seizure process.

Yes, all this sounds very well for creditors, but will it work in practice?

Most Spanish courts are simply unprepared to put the new law into effect. Not enough courtrooms have the required videotape and recording equipment, and there are not enough judges to handle all of the verbal hearings.

Furthermore, although the process can be started very simply for debts up to €9,000, if the debtor chooses to contest the case and the amount is more than €9,000, lawyers and procurators will then be required, meaning extra expense for the creditor.

Nevertheless, the new *"proceso monitorio"* should be a useful tool for small businesses and self-employed persons with outstanding debts.

It also enables communities of property owners to proceed immediately and effectively against owners who do not pay their community fees.

Juicio rápido

The *juicio rápido,* or "quick judgement" procedure, is another recent attempt to speed up Spanish court operations.

It can be applied to a number of situations, including hearings for traffic violators who face suspension of their driving licences, for those accused of spouse abuse and for most petty crimes.

One positive effect has been the rapid resolution of hundreds of serious traffic violations which formerly had to go through long court procedures, as well as the disposal of many petty crime cases. In spouse abuse cases the law has aided in speeding up injunctions against husbands who have committed physical abuse against their spouses.

An accused offender can choose to insist on a full hearing if he feels the abbreviated procedure will not bring him justice.

Citizens' Bill of Legal Rights

Whenever a poll is taken, Spaniards rate their justice system at the bottom of the list. In response, all political parties together have backed a "Bill of Rights for Citizens before the Administration of Justice", or *Carta de los Derechos de los Ciudadanos ante la Justicia.*

This 41-point list is designed to make the administration of justice seem more user-friendly and we can only hope that it is put effectively into practice. Any attempt to improve the present poor relations between citizens and their justice system can only be praised.

Some of the major points are:

Information: Citizens have the right to be informed by the court of any proceedings involving them and be advised of the probable length of time they will take.

Direct contact: Citizens have the right to direct contact with the judges and court secretaries involved in their case.

Compensation: Citizens' claims for compensation from the state for judicial errors shall have preferential treatment.

Lawyer's Estimate: Citizens may require a cost estimate from their lawyers in order to know approximately how much a legal proceeding will cost them.

Your consulate

Consulates generally carry out routine paperwork with your home country's government, such as the renewal of your passport. They usually have lists of English-speaking doctors, lawyers and so on. They help persons in distress, who have lost their passports and money, for example.

What your consulate *cannot* do is solve your personal problems in your new country. If you are accused of a crime and put into gaol, your consular representative may visit you, but he is not in charge of handling your defence.

If you have a dispute with your Spanish neighbour, this is not the consulate's line of work. They do, however, try to be helpful and often go far beyond the call of duty in emergencies.

You and the Spanish Constitution

Since King Juan Carlos I signed it into law in December, 1978, Spain has had a constitution similar to that of other European countries, enshrining all the normal rights and obligations of a modern, democratic state.

It guarantees the basic liberties of free speech and belief, equality before the law, freedom of religion, the right to due process of law for anyone accused of crimes, and abolishes the death penalty. It states that human freedoms will be protected by the law as set out in the Universal Declaration of Human Rights.

It declares that a person has a right to privacy and that his home may not be entered or searched without a warrant unless a serious crime is suspected. It establishes the right to a proper legal defence by a lawyer, and so on.

In Article 13, it declares that foreigners in Spain shall also enjoy all the rights established in the constitution. Article 13 first opened the door for the possibility of foreigners to vote in municipal elections where they reside in Spain.

Spain's law for foreigners

Foreigners in Spain can be forgiven if sometimes they are not quite sure where they stand under the law. Or even what law they stand under.

In January of 2000 the Spanish Congress passed a sweeping law called the *Ley de Derechos y Libertades de los Extranjeros en España*, the "Law for the Rights and Freedoms of Foreigners in Spain".

The law replaced the Foreigners' Law passed in 1985 and greatly liberalised the requirements for obtaining work and residence permits for non-European Union citizens. EU citizens already enjoy almost all of the rights of Spaniards themselves.

Together with the new Foreigners' Law came a complete programme designed to help the thousands of illegal immigrants, largely from North African countries, to legalise their situation in Spain, obtaining permits and access to Spanish health care and other services.

Then the Congress, fearing the wave of illegal immigrants pouring in from Africa, turned around and made the law stiffer again. In early 2005 they changed the law yet again. The Socialist government enacted measures to allow any immigrant with a work contract and already in the country for six months to apply for a legal permit. Hundreds of thousands of illegal immigrants applied, clogging the system so badly that thousands of "normal" foreigners find themselves waiting up to a year for a simple renewal of their residence card.

The Foreigners' Law deals with many of the areas discussed in this book, including entry formalities, resident status, work permits and penalties for foreigners living or working in Spain illegally.

It sets the criteria to use in granting a work permit, listing circumstances that will work in favour of the applicant, such as having been born in Spain, or being the spouse or child of a foreigner who already holds a work permit.

Another important section lists the circumstances under which a foreigner can be expelled from Spain, which include working without a permit, or having been convicted of a serious crime, either in Spain or abroad. The foreigner can appeal the decision. If he doesn't, he can be given 72 hours to leave Spain, and he will not be able to return for at least three years.

It also establishes a new system of "permanent" and "temporary" work and residence permits, especially designed to ease the situation of the immigrant workers, but which can also be applied to other non-EU citizens as well, such as Canadians and Australians.

GLOSSARY

Alcalde – mayor
Ayuntamiento – town hall
Censo Electoral – voter list
Certificado de Empadronamiento – certificate of residence
 in the municipality
Comisaría – police station
Concejal – municipal councillor
Demanda – lawsuit
Demandar – to sue
Denuncia – report to authorities of an infraction
Derecho - right
Diputación – provincial legislature
Juez – judge
Juicio – trial, hearing
Juzgado – court
Multa – fine
Plus valía – municipal capital gains tax
Proceso monitorio – procedure to recover debt without
 lawyer involved
Querella – criminal charge
Reclamación – complaint
Votar – to vote

HOW TO COMPLAIN

17

TOWN HALL   295
OMIC   296
HOJA DE RECLAMACIÓN   296
CONSUMER ORGANISATIONS   299
OMBUDSMAN   300
BANKS   300
DOCTORS   300
LAWYERS   300
REAL ESTATE AGENTS   301
TAX CONSULTANTS   301

SOMETIMES people will put up with mistreatment because they are confused and ignorant of how to go about protesting in their new country. But even though consumer protection in Spain still lags behind other countries, you can usually get a hearing when you have a complaint.

Town hall

Town halls maintain offices where you make a *reclamación* in writing if your complaint has to do with municipal services such as poor rubbish collection or cuts in the water supply.

The Law of Local Administrations requires the town hall to accept your complaint and register it as received for consideration. They are supposed to respond within a relatively short period of time, even if their answer is a refusal of your demand, but in prac-

JUNTA DE ANDALUCIA
Conserjería de Trabajo e Industria
Drirección General de Comercio. Consumo
y Cooperación Económica

CONTROL DE ENTRADA EN
LA OFICINA DE RECEPCION

FECHA

FIRMA RECEPTOR

HOJA DE RECLAMACION
COMPLAINT FORM

INSTRUCCIONES DE USO EN EL DORSO DE LA HOJA VERDE
PLEASE, FOR INSTRUCCIONS SEE OVER

1.- LUGAR DEL HECHO - PLACE OF OCCURRENCE

EN TOWN	PROVINCIA PROVINCE	FECHA DATE

2.- IDENTIFICACION DEL RECLAMANTE - DETAILS OF COMPLAINANT

1.ER APELLIDO SURNAME	2.ª APELLIDO	NOMBRE FIRST NAME

SEXO SEX	EDAD AGE	PROFESION PROFESSION	

D.N.I. PASSPORT N.º	DOMICILIO C/ ADDRESS ST.	

MUNICIPIO TOWN	PROVINCIA PROVINCE	COD. POST. POSTAL CODE

NACIONALIDAD NATIONALITY	TELEFONO TELEPHONE

3.- IDENTIFICACION DEL RECLAMADO-DETAILS OF PERSON UNDER COMPLAINT

2020103

NOMBRE O RAZON SOCIAL NAME OR COMPANY	

C.I.F. O D.N.I. FISCAL N.º	ACTIVIDAD ACTIVITY

DOMICILIO ADDRESS ST.	MUNICIPIO TOWN

PROVINCIA PROVINCE	COD. POST. POSTAL CODE	TELEFONO TELEPHONE

4.- HECHOS RECLAMADOS - DETAILS OF COMPLAINT

CONTROL

SERIE E

DOCUMENTOS QUE SE ACOMPAÑAN - DOCUMENTS INCLUDED
FACTURAS, ENTRADAS, MUESTRAS, ETC. - TICKETS, BILLS, SAMPLES, ETC.

5.- FIRMAS - SIGNATURES

CONSUMIDOR: CONSUMER:	RECLAMADO PERSON UNDER COMPLAINT

I271501

- **EJEMPLAR PARA ENTREGAR POR EL CONSUMIDOR EN LA ADMINISTRACION**
- THE CLIENT IS REQUESTED TO HARD THIS COPY OVER TO THE ADMINISTRATION

tice we find that many complaints are slow to produce results.

If your town hall has an office for foreign residents with staff who speak several languages, this would be your best starting point, of course. More and more towns with many foreign residents are opening these offices and some of them give excellent service.

You may follow up by asking for the appropriate *concejal,* or council member. Each councillor is assigned a particular area of responsibility, such as rubbish collection or street maintenance, and he will probably give you an appointment so that you can discuss your problem in person with him or her. If you don't speak Spanish, take an interpreter with you.

Sometimes you may even be pleasantly surprised when a simple telephone call about the broken streetlight brings a repair crew the same afternoon.

OMIC

This is the big one. Most towns maintain consumer information and complaint offices called *Oficina Municipal de Información al Consumidor* which can inform you about prices, quality requirements for merchandise, and also process complaints. These offices are sometimes located at the municipal market and sometimes they are in the town hall itself.

The OMIC offices are usually very helpful and make an effort to see that action is taken. The offices themselves have no legal power to compel the return of an item or punish offenders, but they see that the proper authorities are informed.

This is where you present your complaint sheet for processing almost any complaint about a commercial establishment, from a restaurant to an auto repair garage (see below).

We recommend the OMIC as the place to start almost every sort of complaint. Even if the problem does not come under their competence, they will help you to find the most effective method of dealing with it.

The OMIC is not limited to basic consumer problems such as defective goods or abusive prices. They can process complaints about timeshare, rentals, mobile phones and property purchase, too.

Hoja de Reclamación

Most foreigners first become acquainted with the *Hoja de Reclamación,* the complaints sheet, in a restaurant or bar, where a notice proclaims in Spanish and English that the sheet is available. All establishments are required by law to keep this official complaint sheet.

When a customer complains, they must produce the sheet for him to register his complaint. If the establishment refuses to produce the complaint sheet and you are really serious about your problem, you go outside and find the nearest policeman. Return to the shop with the policeman. If they do not produce the complaint sheet in his presence, they can be fined up to €6,000.

The sheet comes in three copies. It is in Spanish with a brief English translation (see the example on another page). Our example is the Andalusian one. Forms may differ from region to region. The establishment keeps one copy and the customer takes the other two, one to retain and the other to present at the local OMIC office for processing.

If you do not like confrontation with the establishment owner, you can simply go to the OMIC, where they have the forms on file. Staff will help you prepare your complaint correctly. You can then return to the establishment and drop off a copy for them. If the manager refuses to sign the form, this is not strictly necessary.

Each province has a consumer affairs department. If you want to make sure your complaint is heard, you can follow up your *Hoja de Reclamación* by checking back with the OMIC to see whether they have examined the sheet from the offending establishment.

Consumer laws in Andalusia, for example, require absolutely all businesses to keep such complaint sheets. They must respond directly to the client's complaint within 10 days. If they do not, the client can continue his case through the OMIC.

This includes automobile repairs, sales of appliances and restaurants, to name three typical areas of complaint.

You can also make a complaint to the tourist office which most towns maintain. Although these offices are primarily there to give information, they will direct you to the appropriate place for making your particular complaint known.

If you have a complaint about a shop regarding weight, quality, service or prices, you can direct this to the *Jefatura Provincial de Comercio Interior,* the Provincial Department of Internal Commerce, in your province.

This office is charged with seeing that weights are honest, that prices are within certain margins on controlled items, and that merchandise is up to standard. Although they probably will not oblige a market stall to replace the kilo of rotten oranges they sold you, these offices maintain a staff of inspectors who will visit an offending establishment. If they find any violations, the shop-keeper will be warned or fined.

European consumer directive

When you buy a washing machine or any home appliance in Spain, you should know that European Union consumer directives prescribe an obligatory guarantee for two years. This replaces Spain's former requirement of a six-month guarantee. Remember that you must fill in your guarantee form and have it stamped to assure this.

When you wish to return a defective appliance to the shop which sold it to you, they sometimes declare that they are not responsible and that you must deal with the manufacturer directly. This is simply not true. Recent Spanish consumer legislation obliges the seller to make good on the guarantee.

If you do not get satisfaction, you have recourse to the OMIC. If you are a serious consumer, you might consider one of Spain's consumer organisations, as described below.

See What To Do section for an example of how things might work.

Consumer organisations

There are a number of national consumer organisations, as well as others which operate in the various provinces or autonomous regions. These organisations generally require that you become a member and pay their yearly fees, which are not high, in order to benefit from their services.

One of the largest and most effective of the national organisations, with a good record of assistance to consumers, is the OCU, the *Organización de Consumidores y Usuarios*. Their head office is in Madrid and their telephone number is 91-300 00 45. Or send them a fax at 91-388 73 72.

They offer an advice service weekdays from 10am to Ipm on 91-388 74 24. Their Barcelona office also offers consumer advice on 93-218 06 11 from 10am to 12 noon.

The OCU publishes a magazine called *Compra Maestra,* which analyses different products, and another called *Dinero y Derechos,* which concentrates on legal and financial matters. Both of these publications are excellent sources of information for this book.

Other consumer organisations are found in the telephone book of your area. These locally-based consumer associations may be particularly effective in different areas. We give details on the OCU simply as one example.

Other defenders of consumers' and citizens' rights include:

Ombudsman

If your complaint to the town hall, as mentioned above, fails to bring the desired result, or if you feel that you have been unjustly treated by any government agency, you may have recourse to the *Defensor del Pueblo,* the regional or national ombudsman. You must have exhausted all normal administrative channels before he will accept your case. This Defender of the People is the last resort when you are convinced that justice has not been done.

Banking complaints

Every Spanish bank has its own central Defender of the Customer *(Defensor del Cliente),* who will hear your complaint when you do not get satisfaction from the branch office. If you are still unsatisfied, you have recourse to the complaints department of the Bank of Spain.

Ausbanc, the association of bank customers, is a consumer defence group which will advise you if you are a member with dues paid up. They also carry out campaigns against banking practices they consider abusive, such as high commissions and mortgage contracts which round off interest rates upwards. You can find your local Ausbanc affiliate by contacting their website at www.ausbanc.es.

Doctors

If you have a complaint against the treatment given you by a private doctor, you can present this to the *Colegio de Médicos,* the College of Physicians, which is the professional body overseeing doctors. If you feel that you have a case for malpractice, you can bring a civil suit against the doctor for damages and suffering. These cases are now appearing with more frequency in Spain, and courts have made large awards. There is also an association for the defence of the patient which has branches in major cities.

Lawyers

As mentioned in the section on lawyers, the Law Society, or body which controls professional standards and fees, is called the

Colegio de Abogados. Your best bet is probably to consult another lawyer and explain your case to him. The new lawyer will help you put your complaint in proper form. Nevertheless, you can go directly to the *Colegio* office in your province if you feel you have been over-charged or improperly treated.

Real estate agents

In some European countries, the responsibilities of real estate agents are very carefully regulated. Unfortunately, in practical terms, this is not the case in Spain. Anyone may mediate in property transactions and "buyer beware" is the only advice we can give. There are professional bodies for registered agents such as the API, the *Agente de la Propiedad Inmobiliaria,* which enforces standards. However, many property agencies are not registered and the law does not require this.

Tax consultants

If your Spanish *asesor fiscal,* or tax consultant, has given you bad advice which has cost you money, your only remedy is to bring a civil lawsuit against him. Many tax consultants have advanced training and are members of the various associations, but there is no professional oversight body so anyone can hang out his shingle and call himself a tax consultant.

GLOSSARY

Ayuntamiento – town hall
Compra – purchase
Comprador – purchaser
Concejal – municipal councillor
Consumidor - consumer
Demanda – lawsuit
Demandar – to sue
Factura – bill, invoice
Hoja de Reclamación – complaint form required of all businesses
OMIC - Oficina Municipal de Información al Consumidor – municipal consumer information office, receives complaints
Reclamación – complaint

YOU AND YOUR COMMUNITY

18

COMMUNITY OF PROPERTY OWNERS   *304*

BEFORE YOU BUY   *305*

YOUR RIGHTS AND OBLIGATIONS   *308*

THE PRESIDENT   *309*

THE ADMINISTRATOR   *310*

ANNUAL GENERAL MEETING   *311*

WHEN you buy a property in Spain — as more than one million foreigners already have — you automatically become a member of a community of property owners, whether you like it or not. Whether the property is your retirement home or a holiday flat, whether it is an apartment, a townhouse or a detached villa on an urbanisation, you will find your own interests affected by the community and the decisions of your neighbours. You will pay your community fees every year, and you will meet with your neighbours at the annual general meeting to argue about whether to paint the outside of the building or whether to fire the gardener.

If your building or urbanisation is new, you may even take part in the original organisation of the community, with all its problems of drafting the statutes, electing a president, fixing the amount of community fees, planning the budget and defining the relation of the property promoter and his still unsold properties to the rest of the community.

Only those who buy an individual house in a town street or a farmhouse on a large tract of rural land will not have to deal with belonging to a Spanish *Comunidad de Propietarios*. A well-run community can add thousands of euros of value to an otherwise unremarkable house, and a poorly run community can cut thousands off the value of even a very nice apartment.

Before you buy any Spanish property, find out as much as you can about the operations of the community. See the list of questions to ask in the Capsule Guide that follows.

Over the years problems arising from community life have produced hundreds of letters to my magazine columns and many, many telephone calls to my radio programme. People want to know if the annual general meeting can be held in English, how to fire an administrator who is not properly serving the interests of all the owners, how to form a legal community on an unregistered urbanisation, how to collect community fees from non-payers, and hundreds of other matters.

This guide and the following two chapters aim to answer these questions and:

· To help you understand your rights and obligations as a member of the community of property owners.

· To show you how to participate effectively in community life, both in and out of the annual general meeting.

· To make suggestions for dealing with problems that most frequently arise.

· To provide a ready reference to the complete English translation of Spain's Law of Horizontal Property, the law which regulates communities of property owners.

Beware, however. If the law itself were perfectly clear to the normal citizen, we would not need lawyers to help us interpret it. This is just as true of Spanish law as it is of any other country's law.

So we have provided explanatory comments for each article of the law, telling how the rules work out in practice.

Keep in mind also that the English translation of the law is only informative. The real law is the one in Spanish.

Remember also that this book can only guide you in a general way. If there are serious disputes within your community which involve legal action, do not hesitate to obtain the services of a Spanish lawyer skilled in community matters. Often, a group of members can share the expenses. The courts of law are not an appropriate arena for the do-it-yourselfer.

WHAT IS A COMMUNITY?

The Community of Property Owners - *Comunidad de Propietarios* - is the Spanish system for regulating the joint ownership of common property. In an apartment building this means the entranceway, the staircases, the lift, the roof space, the grounds and any other shared spaces used by all the owners. On an urbanisation it will include the roads, gardens, communal pools, lighting system, drains and other services.

This type of ownership is often called "condominium" in English, for co-ownership. The community sets out the manner in which all the co-owners manage their joint affairs for the best administration of the shared property. The co-owners must decide how much money they want to pay for the maintenance and management of their building, and how this money will be spent.

The law which regulates this system is called the Law of Horizontal Property (*La Ley de Propiedad Horizontal*). This law, originally passed in 1960 and amended in April, 1999, is actually more vertical than horizontal because it applies mainly to apartment buildings, although it also covers townhouse developments of attached units.

Communities of owners on urbanisations of detached villas do not come directly under the original Horizontal Law but provisions of the 1999 law make it easier for detached villas to use the Horizontal Law's protection.

Urbanisations are regulated by other laws included in several sections of the Land Law, the *Ley del Suelo*. These communities may be of several sorts, but the most effective are called *entidad urbanística colaboradora de gestión y conservación*. This mouthful translates as "collaborating urbanistic entity of management and maintenance," and is often shortened to EUC. Estates of detached villas may require a different body of law because they present different problems. The roads, drains and lighting installations of the urbanisation may serve the public as well as the residents, thus having a quasi-public aspect which requires collaboration between the urbanisation owners and the Town Hall authorities. This interaction between the town and the estate demands extra regulation not needed in the case of apartment buildings.

But in both cases the idea of the law is the same: to provide a framework in which the community becomes a legal force. It can go to court, enforce the payment of community fees and make contracts. It can also be sued itself. Many problems have arisen in communities of detached villas because they were not originally formed according to the correct laws.

SEE: Law of Horizontal Property, Articles 1 through 5, Article 24, and Legal Communities for Urbanisations.

BEFORE YOU BUY

When you buy property in Spain, you become a member of the Community of Property Owners. You should know five things about this community before you sign any purchase contract.

Ask these five questions:

1. How much will I have to pay each year in community charges?

Whether you buy an apartment, a townhouse or a detached villa, the property will have a participation share assigned to it, the *cuota*, which determines the amount of the yearly fees for community expenses. This can vary from as little as €50 a month in a modest apartment building up to €400 a month and even more on a luxurious urbanisation with many services to maintain.

These fees can be expected to rise with the general cost of living. The community members may have unexpected expenses, such as repairing the lift or the roof, or they may vote improvements which will add to the costs.

Keep in mind that community fees only cover the operating and maintenance of the building or estate. In addition, you will have to pay your individual annual real estate taxes and your water and electricity bills.

Ask your seller for his last paid-up community fee receipt. He is obligated by law to justify this or to declare the amount of the debt. If this is not possible, you can find out your property's share by asking the promoter of the building or the president of the community.

2. Are the community fees paid up to date?

The Horizontal Law requires the president of the community to produce a certificate stating that the property's fees are paid up, or listing the amount of the debt owed. The seller of the property should arrange for this. In any case, the buyer can be held liable only for the community fees of this year and last year. The law makes the seller responsible for unpaid community fees and for concealing any hidden debt which may attach to the property.

3. Can I see the community statutes?

Of course you can, and you can learn many things from them about life in your new property. Remember that the regulations of the statutes will be binding on you as a member of the community. If they prohibit dogs, you will not be able to keep Rover, for example.

Many sales contracts contain a clause in which the buyer states that he accepts the statutes of the community, understands them and agrees to abide by them. Even when there is not such a reference, the buyer is legally bound when he becomes the owner of the property. He cannot refuse to join a community which legally exists.

Ask your seller, the president of the community, or the real estate promoter of a new building for a copy of the statutes. If they are not available, it may mean problems ahead for you, which brings us to the next question.

4. Does the community legally exist?

Sometimes a community of property owners does not have a proper legal existence, even when required by law. This can occur in a new building or urbanisation when sales are not yet completed and the community has not yet been constituted and its statutes registered with the Property Registry, in the case of apartment buildings, or the Registry of Conservation Entities, in the case of an urbanisation. Yes, a properly constituted community is registered in the Property Registry. After all, it owns property, such as the garden spaces or the roads.

This legal vacuum can also occur when an established urbanisation either is illegal and unregistered or when the owners have formed their association under laws not properly designed for communities of property owners. Unless these associations of owners are registered and the new buyers agree in their contracts to abide by the statutes, their rules may not be legally enforceable. This does not mean that you don't have to pay your community charges. Spanish courts have often ruled that such associations have a *de facto* existence, and a right to collect the fees for the common good.

Ask to see the legal registration of the community in one of the registries listed above.

If the community does not yet exist or is not properly registered, you will sooner or later have problems to sort out, either in the formation of the community or in making it a legal body. In either case, lawyers will be involved and there will be fees to pay.

5. Is the community in debt? Check the minutes book

If the community has had to borrow money in order to pay for unexpected repairs on the building, you will assume your share of this debt when you become a member. Inform yourself in advance.

You can find out this and many other things by looking at the official minutes of the last annual general meeting of the community, along with the accounts. Your seller should have a copy of the minutes, called the *libro de actas,* and the accounts. If he has not, you can obtain them from the president of the community or from the promoter of the real estate where you are purchasing.

A reading of the minutes will give you an idea of the sort of problems and expenses that arise in this particular community. It should contain a record of the voting as well, so that you can see if one individual has voted the proxies of many others, as often happens in communities where many of the owners are absent from their properties much of the time.

If the minutes show that the principal business of the last meeting was how to deal with the persistent water problems or with the backlog of unpaid fees, you will know you have trouble ahead.

These official minutes will be in Spanish, but it will be well worth your time to have at least a rough translation made. The administrator or president of the community is obliged by law to keep these records at the disposal of the members.

SEE: For proper registration of community, Law of Horizontal Property, Articles 5 and 6 and Urban Regulations of the Land Law, Articles 25 and 26.

For community fees, see Amendment to Article 9 of Horizontal Law. For minutes of the meeting, see Law of Horizontal Property, Article 17.

Your rights and obligations

As a member of the community of property owners, you have the right to attend the annual general meeting, and any other meetings of the community, along with the right to be properly informed in advance of the dates and the order of business of any meeting called. If you are not correctly informed, you can protest and even have the results of the meeting annulled by a court.

At the meeting you have the right to voice your opinion, the right to vote, and to present motions for the vote of the other members.

You have the right to be elected and to hold office in the community. You may be the president, the vice-president or the secretary. You may be charged with administrating the affairs of the community.

You have the right to see all of the documentation and records of the community. The administrator or other officers are legally bound to keep these records and accounts at the disposal of the members. If they refuse to show them to you, you can obtain a court order to see the documents.

You have the right to hold and to vote proxies issued by other members who are absent from the meeting. This is common practice in communities where the foreign owners are absent much of the time. Most communities in fact have a standard proxy form on which an absent member can delegate his vote to another member.

If you feel that a decision voted by the majority of the community is illegal or contrary to the statutes, you, acting alone, can ask the local court to rule on the matter. If you feel that the decision is legal, but seriously prejudicial to your own interests, and you can unite 25 per cent of the owners and shares, you can petition the court to have the decision annulled, or you can oblige the president to call an extraordinary general meeting. You will need skilled legal counsel for either of these actions.

You are obligated to pay the *cuotas* — community fees which have been properly voted by the members at the annual general meeting. If you do not pay, the community can claim the debt in court and even have your property sold at auction.

You are obligated to abide by the statutes of the community. If these statutes require all owners to paint their properties white and forbid owners to keep dogs, then you must paint your property white and you may not keep a dog. If you violate the statutes, the community members can vote to ask the court to issue an injunction which will forbid you from entering your property for a period of up to two years. This seldom occurs but the threat is there and it has been carried out in a few isolated cases.

Both the Law of Horizontal Property and the statutes of most communities make provision for maintaining your property in good condition so that it does not cause damage to the other owners, and permitting workmen to enter your property when it is necessary for repairs on the building.

SEE: Law of Horizontal Property, Articles 9 and 10.

For violation of statutes, Article 19.

The president

The only community officer required by law is the president. He must be elected from among the members of the community, and he can carry out all the administrative work if no other officers are elected or appointed.

The president acts as the legal representative of the community in action. He signs contracts and cheques and can bring lawsuits in the name of the community when he is authorised by the vote of the general meeting. He himself can be sued by the community if the members feel his actions have prejudiced their interests. If the community is sued, perhaps by someone who fell through a badly maintained balustrade, the president, acting through a lawyer, will be their representative in court. The president gives orders to the administrator.

The president will prepare the notices of general meetings, along with the order of business. He will see that the notices are sent out well in advance. He will oversee the preparation of the accounts of expenditures and income and he will prepare the budget for the coming year. He makes sure that the minutes of the meeting are carefully kept and notarised. He presides over the meeting and informs the absent members in writing of the decisions taken. If they do not register any protest within 30 days, their agreement to the decisions is assumed.

The president, when acting as the sole officer of the community, will oversee the management of the common elements of the property, will hear the complaints of the community members, and has full responsibility for the operation of the community, subject only to the approval of the annual general meeting.

The president is so important that the law says the community must never be without one. The usual term of office is one year, although the statutes may specify other time periods. If the community does not act to elect a new president when the time is up, the old one continues in office until a new president is elected.

Many small communities where the president is the only officer find difficulty in persuading one of the members to take on this time-consuming responsibility. In many buildings, the flat owners take it in turn each year to be the president. Under the revised 1999 law, the president can even be paid for his services.

SEE: For duties of the president, Law of Horizontal Property, Article 13.

The administrator

Because so many details demand the attention of the person who runs a community, most communities choose to name a professional administrator for this job. The administrator is contracted to manage the services of the community and is paid a regular fee for this service.

Although many communities choose to employ a licensed *Administrador de Fincas,* or professional property administrator, or a licensed tax consultant or accountant, the community administrator need not hold any official title.

Many people think that the professional administrator is an elected officer of the community. This is not so. He is a hired professional, usually contracted for a period of one year. The community may vote to renew his contract, vary his payment, or name a new administrator at the annual general meeting. In extreme circumstances the president may terminate the services of the administrator at any time if he feels that the administrator is not carrying out the duties specified in his contract. This decision must be submitted to the general meeting for approval, but this can take place after the action.

Relations between communities and their professional administrators have caused many problems. The administrator's contract must be very carefully drafted to make sure that both parties know their rights and duties.

The administrator's duties are the normal ones of seeing to the proper management of the common elements of the community.

Unless otherwise specified in the statutes of a particular community, the horizontal law says that the administrator shall prepare the budget and present it to the meeting; maintain the building; inform the owners of his activities and carry out any other function conferred by the general meeting.

Many administrators carry out the work of the community effectively and rapidly, doing their best to keep all of the owners satisfied and well informed. They charge a reasonable fee for their services and they present the community members with clear accounts each year at the general meeting. These administrators are treasures.

In other cases, members complain that the administrators do not carry out the work for which they are responsible, that they arrange community affairs to suit themselves rather than the members, and that their accounts are vague and confusing. This leads the members to worry about where the money has gone. These administrators should be replaced.

Replacing the administrator, like electing the president, is an important step and will require the majority vote of the community members. This brings us to the annual general meeting, discussed below.

SEE: For duties of the Administrator, Law of Horizontal Property, Article 20.

Annual general meeting

The annual general meeting is the maximum authority of the community of property owners, who are required by law to meet at least once each year to elect a president, discuss issues affecting the community, to examine and approve the accounts of expenditures of the previous year. They must decide upon the budget - and the fees each member will pay - for the coming year.

The minutes book (*libro de actas),* which records details of the meeting and voting, is an official legal document which can be used in Spanish court proceedings. It must be stamped as authentic by a notary or a judge. This book establishes the right of the community president in court to bring a lawsuit against a community member who has not paid his fees, the *cuotas.* It should record the names of members who voted in favour of a measure, either in person or by proxy, and the names of those who voted against each measure. This listing is often ignored in practice but communities should take the trouble to do it.

The record of votes becomes important when a minority of community members wish to bring a legal protest against the decision of the majority, claiming that their interests have been seriously damaged, even though the majority vote was otherwise quite in order. In a court case, the dissenting minority must bring action against the majority. So the minutes book, as a legal document, establishes the names of those who voted on either side. The book is evidence in court, and decisions made by the community are serious matters.

Before you attend your first meeting, you should try to meet the president and the administrator of your community, as well as other members, to get an idea of the problems facing the members. If you already have a motion that you want passed by community vote, you can begin to assemble the proxy votes of members who support your position and who will be absent from the meeting. This proxy can be a simple written authorisation that enables you to cast the vote of the absentee.

You must be notified at least eight days in advance of the meeting's date, time and place. You should also receive a written agenda, the order of business to be transacted, though this is not strictly necessary. The members can bring up any new business they wish at the meeting. It need not be listed on the agenda. At the meeting, you will register your attendance, and any proxies you will vote, with the secretary or keeper of the minutes book.

The president will preside over the meeting. The first item will be the reading and voting to approve the minutes of the previous meeting. If the minutes do not meet with your approval, either because they are false or incomplete, you can vote against accepting them. Your protest will be registered in the book and can serve as evidence in court if you wish to make a claim.

The accounts of the previous year's income and expenditures will then be presented for the members' approval. You should have received your copy of these accounts before the meeting. Sometimes they are perfectly clear and other times they are quite incomprehensible. Ask the president, administrator or treasurer to explain any points not clear to you.

Then discussion will start on proposed plans and expenses for the coming year. Many issues can arise. Perhaps one group wishes to paint the building or to install a swimming pool, but others protest that this will raise the fees too high.

Tempers can run high at community meetings. They often degenerate into multilingual shouting matches when not properly managed. At one meeting a woman, enraged when she felt she was not getting her fair chance to speak, threw an ashtray at the table of the presiding officers. A heavy ashtray.

Even in the best of circumstances, meetings tend to be long-winded, as different members insist on discussing minor details. One community I know voted unanimously to limit each member's speaking time to five minutes, and to limit each member to two speeches.

When it is time to vote, you will vote according to your *cuota,* or community share. This *cuota,* based on the size of your property, determines both your share of community fees and the weight of your vote. Usually, the majority of members is also the majority of the *cuotas,* but sometimes a few members with large properties can dominate the workings of a community. This can happen on an urbanisation where the developer still controls the votes of the unsold parcels of land and runs the community to suit himself.

The votes of the members will be recorded in the minutes book and action will be taken accordingly. A new president will be elected by majority vote and the building will be painted or not, according to the majority decision. There is always the possibility of protest, remember, when a minority of members feel they have been mistreated by the majority.

If a decision requires a unanimous vote, such as a change in the statutes or a construction project which will alter the participation shares of the community members, this unanimity can be achieved by informing any absent members of the decision. If they do not respond negatively within one month the motion is considered as passed unanimously.

One recent amendment to the horizontal law provides that the installation of ramps and other facilities for the handicapped requires only a three-fifths majority, even when such an alteration of the building would normally need a unanimous vote. This does not exactly give the handicapped a free rein, but it does improve their negotiating position. The new law came from a court case in which one person in a building had blocked the installation of ramps. This was perfectly legal although not very nice, and the Spanish Congress voted, in July 1990, to amend the law.

Finally the meeting will be adjourned, with some members

pleased and others not pleased at all. This is truly democracy in action, with all its advantages and disadvantages.

When people are unhappy with their community, they refer to it as "they." The community is never "they". It is always "we".

SEE: For proxy votes, Law of Horizontal Property, Article 15. For annual general meeting, Article 14. For Minutes Book, Article 19.

THE LAW OF HORIZONTAL PROPERTY IN ENGLISH

19

NEW Text of Law 49/1960 of July 21, as amended by Law 8/1999 of April 6, published in the Official State Bulletin April 8, 1999

CHAPTER I:
GENERAL DISPOSITIONS

Article 1

The purpose of the present Law is the regulation of the special form of property ownership set out in Article 396 of the Civil Code, called horizontal property.

For the purposes of this Law, any part of a building which may be subject to independent use by virtue of an entrance either to the public thoroughfare or to a common area of the building itself shall be considered as "premises".

Article 2

This Law shall apply to:

a) Communities of Owners constituted under the provisions of Article 5.

b) Communities which fulfil the requirements established in Article 396 but which have not filed their charter or constitution as horizontal property. These communities shall be governed, in any case, by the dispositions of this Law in matters regarding the legal framework of ownership of the property, of its individual parts and of its common elements, as well as matters referring to the reciprocal rights and obligations of the community members.

c) Private real estate complexes (urbanisations or estates), in the terms established in this Law.

What it means

The big change in the 1999 law is that urbanisations, or private housing estates, can be governed by the Horizontal Law, even if they have never registered their statutes or constituted themselves legally as communities. If they meet the terms of Article 396 of the Civil Code, which basically means that the community shares some common elements, they can obtain the full force of the law in compelling the payment of debts and enforcing their rules.

Formerly, the only way for such non-registered urbanisations to obtain full legal status was through the complicated process of creating a Collaborating Urbanistic Entity. This still is necessary in some cases but the revised law now permits most urbanisations to function as real communities.

CHAPTER II:
REGARDING THE SYSTEM OF OWNERSHIP BY FLATS OR BUSINESS PREMISES

Article 3

In the system of ownership set forth in Article 396 of the Civil Code, the owner of each flat or business premises shall have:

a) The unique and exclusive ownership rights over an adequately delimited area subject to independent usage, along with the architectural features and all types of installations, apparent or not, which may be included within its boundaries and which serve the owner exclusively, as well as any ancillary property expressly mentioned in the property deed, even when they are located outside the delimited area.

b) Co-ownership, with the other owners of flats and premises, of the remaining common areas, appurtenances and services.

To each flat or commercial premises there will be assigned a share

*of participation (cuota) relative to the total value of the property,
expressed as a percentage of it. Said share (cuota) will serve as a
basis to determine participation in the expenses and earnings of
the community. The improvements or deterioration of each flat or
premises will not alter the assigned share, which can only be
changed by unanimous agreement.*

*Each owner may freely dispose of his property right, but he may not
separate the elements composing it and any transmission of the
property right shall not affect the obligations arising from this
system of property ownership.*

What it means

The provisions of Article 3 are quite clear, setting out the terms of
separate individual ownership of flats and the joint ownership of
the common elements of the building. In paragraph A, the reference
to "ancillary properties" means such things as garages or storage
space in the basement which go with each apartment.

The final section of paragraph B establishes the principle that
an owner may not subdivide his property. Later, in Article 8, we
shall see that he can indeed divide his property into smaller units,
but this requires the consent of the community, as it will affect the
participation shares.

Article 4

*The action of division shall not proceed to terminate the situation
regulated by this Law. It can only be effected by each co-owner in
regard to one flat or premises, is limited to that property, and providing that the joint ownership has not been established intentiona-
lly for the common service or use of all the owners.*

What it means

Article 4 makes it clear that any further action of subdivision of the
property will not affect the scheme of Horizontal Property regulating the building in general. The last line means, for example, that
a gardener who is given a flat in the building for his own use may
not subdivide it. This action of division usually occurs when a
property is inherited by several owners.

Article 5

The charter of constitution of the condominium (ownership by flats or premises) will describe, besides the property as a whole, each one of those units to which a correlative number is assigned. The description of the overall property must express the details required by the mortgage legislation and the services and installations belonging to it. The description of each flat or premises will express its area, boundaries, the floor on which it is located, and any ancillary properties such as garage, attic or basement.

This same charter shall determine the share of participation that pertains to each flat or premises, to be set by the sole owner of the building at the beginning of its sale by flats, by the agreement of all existing owners, by arbitration, or by court order. For this determination, the useful surface area of each flat or premises relative to the total area of the building, its exterior or interior emplacement, its situation, and the use it can reasonably be assumed to make of the common services and installations shall be taken as a basis.

The charter may also contain regulations for the establishment and exercise of this property right and other dispositions not prohibited by law relating to the use and purpose of the building, its various flats or premises, installations and services, expenses, administration and management, insurance, maintenance and repairs, forming private statutes which shall not prejudice third parties if they have not been registered in the Registry of Property.

In any modification of the property title and apart from what is disposed regarding the validity of community decisions, the same requirements shall be applied as for the charter of constitution.

What it means

In Article 5 we find several important points about the constitution of the community of owners. In the first paragraph the method of describing the property is set out. In the second paragraph, we find that each owner's *cuota*, or participation share, is fixed when the community is legally constituted and registered. Afterwards it can only be changed by unanimous vote of all members.

This paragraph also notes that the use each property makes of the common services shall be taken into account when setting the *cuotas*. This provision allows variation between flats and commercial premises, for example. Sometimes commercial premises pay a *cuota* per square metre higher than that of flats, on the grounds that the people they attract make extra use of common elements. In one case, the promoter of the building (who can set the *cuotas* when the flats are first sold) provided in the statutes of the community that the commercial premises would pay no *cuotas* at all until they were sold. This is because the flats always sell first and the commercial premises sometimes remain vacant for a year, or even more. By this means the promoter avoided paying any *cuotas* on his unsold business premises, and the community of owners had a lower income than they otherwise would expect.

This provision in the statutes — written by the promoter — is perfectly legal, even if unfair to the other new flat-buyers, and is only one of the little tricks available to the promoter when he constitutes the community. It is always wise to read the statutes of the building or urbanisation where you are going to purchase.

In the case of the community cited above, the flat owners were preparing to vote against the promoter's rule in the statutes, charging that their interests were prejudiced by it.

Article 5 continues to note that the private statutes of the community will not be binding unless they are registered in the Registry of Property as part of the registration of the building itself.

It is perfectly possible for a community to exist without private statutes, which means that it will be regulated only by the terms set out here in the Horizontal Property Law. These regulations are sufficient for the orderly government of the community, but most buildings also require some special statutes to suit their individual circumstances.

Article 6

In order to regulate the details of their co-existence and the proper usage of the services and common elements and within the limits established by the Law and the statutes, the body of proprietors shall be able to make internal rules binding on all owners unless they are modified in the manner set forth for making decisions regarding administration.

What it means

Article 6 is clear in itself. It allows the members of the community to make internal rules by majority vote. This would include matters such as the banning of pets or a requirement to make all awnings the same colour. This is the Horizontal Law for flats. In most urbanisations, such internal rules may only be enforceable when the new purchasers have specifically agreed to accept the statutes in their purchase contract.

However, as we shall see, the revised 1999 law allows urbanisations to register their communities under the terms of the Horizontal Law, making their rules binding on the members.

Article 7

1. The owner of each flat or business premises may modify the architectural features, installations and services of the flat, so long as it does not diminish or alter the safety of the building, its general structure, its form or its exterior condition nor prejudice the rights of another owner, reporting such alterations beforehand to the representative of the community.

In the rest of the building he may not make any alteration whatsoever and if he observes the need for any urgent repairs, he should communicate this to the administrator without delay.

2. The owner and the occupant of the flat or business premises are forbidden to carry on in the flat or in the rest of the building any activities which are not permitted in the statutes, which damage the property, or which violate laws regulating activities that are a nuisance, unhealthy, noxious, dangerous, or illegal.

The President of the community, either on his own initiative, or at the request of any of the owners or occupants, shall require the immediate ceasing of any of the activities prohibited in this section, under warning of appropriate legal action.

If the offender persists in his conduct, the President, upon authorisation by the General Assembly, duly convened for this purpose, can seek a court injunction against him, which, where not expressly provided in this section, shall proceed according to the "Cognisance Hearing" regulations.

Once the action is brought, along with the accreditation of formal notification to the offender and the certification of the resolution voted by the General Assembly, the court, as a precautionary measure, may order the immediate ceasing of the prohibited activity, warning that non-compliance will constitute contempt of court. The court may likewise order as many such immediate measures as deemed necessary to ensure the effectiveness of the cease and desist order. The action must be brought against the owner of the property or, in such case, against the occupant.

If the sentence is in favour of the plaintiff, the court may order, as well as the final ending of the prohibited activity and the awarding of damages involved, the deprival of the defendant's right to use the flat or premises for a period not to exceed three years, depending on the seriousness of the violation and the damages caused to the community. If the offender is not the owner, the sentence can terminate all the offender's rights over the flat or premises as well as order his immediate eviction.

What it means

Paragraph 2 of Article 7 sets forth the manner in which the community can protect itself from truly antisocial elements in its midst.

If one of the owners or his tenants is brewing poisons in his kitchen, with nasty fumes in the air vents, or if they insist on making loud noises all night long, or if they scatter garbage through the halls, the community can go to court against them and obtain an injunction order to cease the offending activity.

The community can also seek cash damages for the problems and suffering involved.

If the offender does not obey the order, he can be considered as in contempt of court, and ordered to leave the property for up to three years.

If he is a tenant, he can be evicted immediately, as well as losing any contractual rights he has over the property.

Included in the list of banned activities are those forbidden by the statutes. Thus, dogs may be prohibited, for example, and owners must abide by this.

If an owner ignores the statutory prohibition, the community, by majority vote, may take legal action against him. Article 7 also limits the owner's right to alter his property to interior elements only, and only when it does not threaten the structural soundness of the building or alter its appearance. One problem that arises here is the closing-in of the terraces. Because the enclosure of the terrace with glass panels alters the exterior form of the building and would change the pattern of participation shares because of the greater enclosed area, it is strictly prohibited by this article.

So, when an owner goes to the community president and asks for permission to glass in his terrace, this must be denied. As you may notice, however, about 75 per cent of all the terraces in Spain have been glassed in. You guessed it. None of these owners asked anyone's permission. They just went ahead and did it. If neither the community nor the town hall presents any complaint, the terrace remains enclosed. The possibility of protest does exist, however.

Article 8

Flats or commercial premises and their ancillary elements can be the object of physical division to form other, smaller independent units and made larger by the incorporation of adjoining units of the same building, or made smaller by the separation of some part.

In such cases, besides the consent of the affected property owners, there will be required the approval of the Annual General Meeting of the owners, to which pertains the determination of the new participation shares (cuotas) for the modified flats subject to the dispositions of Article 5, without altering the participation shares of the remaining properties.

What it means

We saw in Article 3 that the right of an owner to divide his property in smaller units is limited, but it can be done. It requires, however, the approval of the annual general meeting.

Article 9

The obligations of each owner shall be:

a) To respect the general installations of the community and any other common elements, whether for general or private use by any of the owners, whether or not they are included in his unit, making appropriate use of them and avoiding any damage or deterioration at all times.

b) To maintain his own flat and private installations in a good state of order in conditions that do not prejudice the community or the other owners, making good any damages caused by his lack of care or that of any persons for whom he is responsible.

c) To permit in his flat or premises the repairs required for the service of the building and to permit in his flat the necessary rights of passage required for the creation of common services of general interest, voted according to the terms of Article 17, having the right to be indemnified by the community for any damage and prejudice.

d) To allow entry into his flat for the purposes stated in the three preceding paragraphs.

e) To contribute, according to the participation share(cuota) determined in his property title or according to any system especially established, to the general expenses for the proper upkeep of the building, its services, taxes, charges and responsibilities that are not subject to individual allocation.

Amounts due to the community deriving from the obligation to contribute to the payment of the general expenses which correspond to the fees assessed for the period up to date of the current year and for the previous year shall be deemed preferential debts under the terms of Article 1923 of the Civil Code and take preference for their settlement over those listed in paragraphs 3, 4, and 5 of that law without prejudicing the preference in favour of salary charges in the Workers' Law.

Any person acquiring a dwelling unit or commercial premises in the system of horizontal property, even with a title inscribed in the Property Registry, is held responsible, with the acquired property as guaranty, for the amounts owed by previous owners to the community for the payment of general expenses up to the limit of fees charged for the period to date of the year in which the purchase took place and for the immediately preceding year. The property itself is legally encumbered for the fulfilment of this obligation.

In the public contract or deed of sale by which the property is transferred in any way, the seller must declare that he is up to date with payment for general expenses of the community, or he must list what he owes. The seller must present certification of the state of his balance with the community, coinciding with this declaration, without which no public title can be authorised, unless the buyer should expressly waive the seller from this obligation. This certification shall be issued in a maximum of seven days from the request by the person acting as Secretary of the Community, with the authorisation of the President. In the case of fault or negligence, they shall be held liable for the accuracy of the information and for damages caused by delay in its issue.

f) To contribute, according to their respective participation shares (cuotas), to the reserve fund which shall exist in the community for the maintenance and repair of the property.

The reserve fund, which is held by the community to all effects, shall be supplied with an amount that in no case shall be less than five per cent of the last ordinary budget.

The community may use the reserve fund to take out an insurance policy covering damages to the property or to undertake a permanent maintenance contract for the building and its general installations.

g) To observe due care in the use of the property and in their relations with the other owners and to be responsible to them for any infractions committed or damages caused.

h) To notify the person acting as Community Secretary, by any means which allows evidence of service, of their domicile in Spain for the purpose of receiving citations and notifications of any sort related to the Community. In the absence of this notification, the flat or premises in the Community shall be considered the domicile for receiving communications from the Community, and delivery to its occupant shall constitute full legal notification.

Should notification to the owner prove impossible at the place indicated in the previous paragraph, it shall be deemed to have taken place if the notice is posted on the notice board of the community, or in a visible place set aside for this purpose, indicating the date and the reasons for which this form of notification has been employed, signed by the person acting as Community Secretary and endorsed by the President. Notice served in this way shall produce full legal effect in three days.

i) To notify the person acting as Secretary of the Community, by any means providing certification of delivery, of any change in ownership of the unit.

Any owner who fails to comply with this obligation will be held liable to the Community jointly with the new owner for debts incurred after the transfer, without prejudicing his right to claim repayment from the new owner.

These terms shall not apply when any of the governing bodies of the community established in Article 13 have been notified of the change of owners by any other means or by definite actions of the new owner or when the transfer is publicly known.

2. For the application of the preceding regulations, expenses will be deemed as general when they are not imputable to one or several flats, nor shall the non-usage of a service bring exemption from the fulfilment of the corresponding obligations, subject to the terms of Article 11.2 of this Law.

What it means

The first paragraphs of this article set out owners' obligations clearly enough.

Paragraph E tells us that the new buyer in a community is held responsible only for the community fees of this year and the year before, with the property itself acting as the final guaranty for payment.

This paragraph also tells us that the seller is obliged to present certification of payment up to date or the amount of his debt at the time of signing the contract, which means at the Spanish Notary's office. The president of the community must vouch for this certification.

Further, without the certification of payment or debt, the notary will not stamp the contract of sale, unless the buyer specifically waives the requirement.

Paragraph F provides for the establishment of a reserve fund in all communities, which must be at least 5 per cent of the normal operating budget, and sets out the obligation of each owner to contribute to this fund. The fund can be used for an insurance policy or a maintenance contract, thus protecting the installations.

Paragraph H requires every member to notify the community of the address in Spain where he wishes to receive any legal notices. One way to do this is to use the Burofax system of the Spanish postal service. They will certify both the content of the message and its delivery. Lacking an address, the community can notify the owner at the property itself, and, if for some reason this cannot be done, simply posting the notice on the notice board will take full legal effect within three days.

This is a big change from previous practice, which made the notification so complicated that communities just gave up trying. The procedure used to be so difficult and time-consuming that it was hardly worthwhile in most cases. The community had to prove that the defaulter had received in a certified manner each of the unpaid bills, and that he had been informed of the debt and had acknowledged receipt, and every stage of the process was complex.

The last paragraph of this article settles another common dispute. Sometimes an owner will declare that, because he does not use the swimming pool, which he voted against in the meeting, he will not pay this portion of his community charges. This line says he is obliged to pay, abiding by the majority decision.

Even so, in many communities, the members will vote to exempt non-users from the payment for a particular amenity.

Article 10
1. The Community is obligated to carry out work necessary for the

proper upkeep and maintenance of the building and its services to ensure adequate structural, waterproof, habitability and safety conditions.

2. Any owners who unjustifiably oppose or delay the execution of orders issued by public authorities shall be held responsible individually for any administrative fines that are charged as a result.

3. Disagreements concerning the nature of works to be carried out shall be resolved by the General Assembly of Owners. The parties may also apply for arbitration or for a technical report in the terms established by law.

4. The payment of expenses arising from maintenance work referred to in this article shall attach to the flat or premises in the same terms and conditions set out in Article 9 for general expenses.

Article 11

1. No owner can demand new installations, services or improvements not required for the adequate maintenance and habitation of the building, in accordance with its nature and characteristics.

2. When decisions are lawfully made to carry out improvements not required in accordance with the terms of the preceding paragraph and the proportionate cost of installation exceeds the amount of three ordinary monthly payments for common expenses, a dissenter shall not be obligated, nor shall his fee be altered, even in the case that he cannot be deprived of the improvement or innovation.

If the dissenter wishes at any time to take advantage of the improvement he must pay his share of the expenses of installation and maintenance, brought up to date by application of the legal interest rate.

3. Innovations which render any part of the building unserviceable for the use and enjoyment of an individual owner shall require his express consent.

4. Special assessments for improvements made or to be made in the community shall be charged to the owner of the property at the time when such payments fall due.

What it means

Article 11 requires some careful interpretation and amplification. There is more in it than it seems to say.

The first paragraph seems clear enough. No single owner or minority group can demand unnecessary improvements. The definition of "necessary" is here related to the building's category or standard of luxury. Central air-conditioning may be "necessary" in a luxury building. A swimming pool or satellite TV will not be necessary in a modest block of flats, and no single owner can demand it. Majority rules.

It's what this paragraph doesn't say that is more important. It implies that one single owner can demand "necessary" improvements, with legal right on his side. That is, there exists in law a principle that the property must be properly maintained. If the majority of owners refuses to repair the broken lift, fix the broken windows or doors, one single owner can demand of the court that the community be obliged to carry out this normal maintenance. He can cite this article, along with Article 16, to back up his case.

He will find additional support if the building has become a health or safety hazard, as the community's decision to let it fall into ruin will then run contrary to law.

Of course, honest dispute is also possible about what constitutes "necessary" and people can spend hours arguing this in the community meeting.

In the second paragraph of Article 10, we find another sore point relating to "necessary" improvements. If the annual general meeting votes to carry out some improvement which is clearly not required for adequate maintenance and the cost of this improvement exceeds the amount of three months community *cuotas*, a dissenter can legally refuse to pay for it. This could be a new swimming pool, for example.

Even though the next two lines make reference to his eventual payment should he wish to make use of the improvement, Spanish courts have ruled that the dissenter cannot be deprived of the use of the improvement even though he does not pay for it.

Paragraph 3 gives the individual owner the power to block any change in the building which would affect his use and enjoyment of the property. This would include the building of a wall in front of his window, for example.

Paragraph 4 settles an area where confusion may arise. The new owner of the property might refuse to make the next payment on a new swimming pool which was voted before he bought his flat. He can't do that. He assumes all the community expenses and projects when he becomes a member.

The same principle applies if the community has previously voted to make special assessments in order to pay off a debt which existed before our new buyer came in. He must pay his share as he is the owner when the payment comes due.

He cannot charge the debt to the previous owner, even if the debt was incurred in the previous owner's time and has nothing to do with the new owner.

Article 12

The construction of new floors and any other change in the support-ing structure or walls of the building or in the common elements affect the charter of constitution and must be submitted to the pro-cedures established for modifications of it. The resolution which is adopted shall determine the nature of the modification, the alterations it produces in the description of the property and the flats or premises, the variation of the participation shares (cuotas) and the owner or owners of the new premises or flats.

What it means

Article 12 is clear enough. When it says that any major modifica-tion of the structure must be submitted to the same procedure as for changes in the community's charter, it means by unanimous vote. The resolution so passed must be specific and completely detailed.

Article 13

1. The governing bodies of the Community shall be the following:

a) The General Assembly of owners.

b) The President and, when applicable, the Vice-Presidents

c) The Secretary

d) The Administrator

The Statutes or a majority vote by the General Assembly may establish other governing bodies for the Community but these may not detract from the functions and responsibilities with regard to third parties which this Law confers on those mentioned above.

2. The President shall be chosen from among the owners in the Community by election or by turns in rotation or by drawing lots. Acceptance shall be compulsory, although the designated owner may request the Court to relieve him of the office, within one month of taking office, citing his reasons for it. The Court, following the procedure established in Article 17.3, will rule on the matter, desig-nating in the same ruling which of the owners will substitute for the

President in the office, until a new President is chosen in a time set by the Judge.

Likewise, the Court may be approached when it has proved impossible for the Assembly to choose a President for some reason.

3. The President legally represents the Community both in and out of court and in all matters affecting it.

4. The existence of Vice-Presidents is voluntary. They shall be chosen by the same procedure established for the designation of the President.

The Vice-President or Vice-Presidents in the order prescribed, shall replace the President in cases of absence, vacancy or incapacity and assist him in carrying out his duties according to the terms established by the General Assembly.

5. The functions of secretary and administrator shall be carried out by the President of the Community, except when the Statutes or the General Assembly, by majority vote, provide that such office be held separately from the presidency.

6. The posts of Secretary and Administrator may be vested in the same person or separately chosen.

The posts of administrator or secretary-administrator may be held by any owner or by individuals with sufficient professional qualifications or legally licensed to carry out such functions. The post can also go to a company or other corporate entity in the terms set out by law.

7. Unless otherwise provided by Community Statutes, the term of office of all governing bodies will be for one year.

The persons designated to can be removed from their offices before the expiry of their terms by a resolution of the General Assembly, convoked for an extraordinary meeting.

8. When the number of owners in the community is no more than four, they can govern themselves by the administrative system of Article 398 of the Civil Code, if their Statutes expressly establish this.

What it means

Article 13 states that the president must be a member of the community. A simple majority vote in the annual general meeting suffices to elect him, and a simple majority vote can put him out, along with any other officer of the community.

There is nothing in the rule book that says the president must speak Spanish, or be Spanish, or even an official full-time resident of Spain. It would be difficult for an absentee president to serve his community well, of course, but the only requirement is that the president be a member of the community.

By law, the president is the only officer that a community must elect. He can combine in himself the duties of the secretary, treasurer and administrator, and in many smaller communities this is the case. In larger blocks — sometimes numbering more than 100 members — communities may elect a vice-president to stand in for the president when he is absent, a secretary to keep the official minutes book of the meetings, a treasurer to take charge of the funds, and appoint a professional administrator to handle the maintenance of the property. The professional administrator, paid for his services, may not in principle be a member of the community as this would be an obvious conflict of interests.

The community can see that the president's expenses are covered and they can even pay him a wage if they choose.

The president's responsibilities include:

Convening the annual general meeting, giving reasonable advance notice, along with the order of business. Any owner who was not properly notified of the meeting can later protest and have the results of the meeting annulled by a judge.

Presiding over the general meeting, seeing that the order of business is followed and making sure that each person gets a fair hearing. This can be a very arduous task.

Representing the community in its relations with the individual members. That is, if you have a complaint about water dripping from the terrace of your upstairs neighbour, you take this complaint to the president.

Representing the community to all third parties, which would include the company contracted to paint the building. It is the president who signs the contract in the name of the community.

Carrying out any legal action for which he has been authorised by the majority vote of the owners assembled in the general meeting.

It is a serious matter to be president of a legally-registered community of property owners. The president cannot simply resign his office, for example, if things do not go well. He officially holds the post until a new president is elected. This is because the community can never be without a legal representative. So, if the president wants out, he must convene an extraordinary general meeting for the election of his successor or petition the court to relieve him.

Further, if the community members feel that the president, through negligence or error, has seriously damaged their interests, they can bring suit against him for monetary damages.

Normally the president is elected for one year, unless the community statutes specify a longer term of office. At the end of this year, his mandate will continue unless the general meeting votes to replace him. So it is perfectly possible for a president to continue in office year after year without any new elections.

If any member of the community wants to contest this continuance, he can either ask for an election notice to be included in the agenda of the meeting, or he can call for elections in the meeting itself. Remember that the annual general meeting is the supreme authority of the community. It can, by majority vote, elect a new president whenever it desires to do so. The normal procedure would be to convoke an extraordinary general meeting for this purpose. Remember also that, whenever 25 per cent of the members agree, they can call for such an extraordinary general meeting.

This unpaid job of president is often so unrewarding that, in some buildings, rather than actually hold elections, the community members agree to take the post in turns, with a different member taking up the task each year. When your turn comes, you are unanimously "elected" and this is shown in the minutes book.

If the community chooses to contract a paid professional administrator, the president can hire and fire this administrator, subject always to the specific contract made, giving account later to the community.

Sometimes community presidents act in a high-handed manner, spending the funds incorrectly and favouring one group of owners over another. This might happen when one member controls many votes. Far more often the president is a civic-minded spirit who is willing to take his turn at handling the problems which arise in any community, only to discover that his co-owners find fault with every decision he makes and are utterly ungrateful for his efforts to help the common good. So he is vastly relieved when his term of office ends and he absolutely refuses to be elected again.

If the community chooses to name a secretary, his function will be the normal work of a secretary in any organisation: to send or deliver the notices of meetings; to take the minutes of the meeting and see that they are recorded in the official minutes book, which is stamped by the Notary; to keep the records, correspondence and documents of the community and to show these to any member who wishes to inspect them, and to send out notification of the decisions taken in the annual general meeting to any absent members. This is obligatory. Members who were absent from any meeting must be reliably informed of any decisions taken at that meeting. They then have 30 days starting from the date they received the notification, in which to make a protest if they are opposed to the decision. If they do not make a written protest, they are considered as accepting any action taken by the meeting. If the meeting has adopted a measure needed unanimous approval, the non-reply of the absentees is included as approval, thus making the vote "unanimous".

Although the law of horizontal property does not require a vice-president or a treasurer, the community statutes can provide for the election of these officers, or the members may vote at the annual general meeting to create the offices and elect members to carry them out.

The treasurer would prepare the proposed budget of expenses for the forthcoming year for the approval of the meeting; would collect and keep the funds of the community; would be responsible for the accounts, and make payments and prepare the yearly accounting for the members' approval. He might also order an independent auditing of the accounts, especially if the community is a large one with important sums of money coming in and going out.

An important point to note about a possible vice-president in a community is that this office must be specifically mentioned, with its powers, in the statutes or in the official minutes book of the community. If not, the vice-president will not be empowered to use the faculties of the president in his absence. He will not be able to sign cheques, represent the community or take legal action.

Article 13 closes with a mention of Article 398 of the Civil Code, which provides a much simpler legal framework for organizing the affairs of communities with four or fewer members.

Article 14
The functions of the Annual General Meeting are:
a) To appoint and to remove the persons who hold the official posts mentioned in the preceding article and to settle any complaints

which the property owners may bring against their actions.

b) To approve the budget of foreseeable expenses and income and the pertinent accounts.

c) To approve bids and the carrying out of all repair work on the property, whether ordinary or extraordinary, and to be informed of any urgent measures taken by the Administrator in accordance with the terms of Article 20, paragraph C.

d) To approve or change the statutes and to make bylaws for internal management.

e) To be informed and to decide on the other matters of general interest to the community, taking any necessary or advisable measures for the best common service.

What it means

Article 14 states the basic functions of the annual general meeting. The general meeting, ordinary or extraordinary, is the supreme authority of the community. Its decisions, either by majority vote or unanimous vote when necessary, are binding on all officers and members of the community.

Majority vote will elect the officers and also put them out if necessary. If the members are unhappy with the president, for example, they themselves can convoke an extraordinary general meeting, and vote him out. If they have contracted a professional administrator for one year, they can vote at the meeting not to renew his contract.

The meeting will hear the budget of expenses prepared for the coming year. They must approve the expenses or the officials will not be empowered to spend the money. It is here that the fighting often starts. Does the community need a full-time gardener? Should they paint the building or let it go another year? Each point of view will have its backers. They present their opposing arguments, a vote is called, and majority rules. If a dissenter feels his own private interests are seriously damaged by a decision of the majority, he has the power to protest before a court.

The community must also approve the accounts presented for the preceding year. Here again there are often many protests, as some presidents and even some professional administrators often fail to keep adequate records. This is sometimes due to concealment of payments to the administrator but more often results from careless bookkeeping. Many larger communities are beginning to require an independent audit of the accounts as a regular yearly practice.

The third item of the functions of the annual general meeting is probably the one that causes most fireworks: the execution of extraordinary works and the necessary funding. In every community there is someone who wants a swimming pool, or a new lighting system, or satellite television. And in every community there is someone who does not want these things and says he will refuse to pay for them.

Remember that a dissenter can refuse to pay — legally — if the improvement is not "necessary" and if his share of it comes to more than a three months' *cuota*.

The annual general meeting has the power to change the statutes, but only by unanimous vote, and to make internal regulations. These would include things like the prohibition of pets in the building, for example, or the denial of permission to hang out laundry on the roof terrace.

Of course the members must have information in order to decide matters of general interest to the community, as noted in the final section. This means that the administrator and president must present complete information to the meeting. It is their legal obligation to allow community members to examine the community's accounts and documents.

Paragraph C makes special mention of the assembly's right to be informed by the administrator of any urgent measures he has taken. Administrators sometimes treat communities as their own property and fail to keep the members well informed of their actions.

Article 15

1. Attendance at the general meeting of owners shall be in person or by legal or voluntary representation, a written authorisation signed by the owner being sufficient to accredit this representation.

If a flat belongs jointly to several owners, these shall name one representative to attend and to vote in the meetings.

If the flat is held in usufruct, the attendance and the vote belong to the original owner who, except for his manifestation to the contrary, shall be held to be represented by the holder of the usufruct, this representation requiring to be specifically expressed when the vote is on the matters referred to in the First paragraph of Article 17 or on extraordinary works or improvements.

2. Owners who at the time of the Assembly are not current in the payment of all their debts owed to the Community, and who have not legally challenged these debts or deposited the amount of them in court shall be allowed to take part in discussion but shall not have the right to vote. The minutes of the meeting will show the names of the owners deprived of their voting rights and neither the person nor the participation share shall be computed when calculating the majorities required by this Law.

What it means

The first paragraph of Article 15 makes provision for the representation of a community member by proxy if he cannot attend in person.

A simple "written authorisation" is sufficient to establish this proxy legally. There is no specific form required. All it need say is that you authorise such-and-such a person to vote in your name at the meeting of the community on such-and-such a day, and it should include the phrase "any postponement of that meeting". This is because very often the community does not have a full quorum when the meeting is first called and so it will be held on the 'second convocation", usually specified as half an hour later.

This sort of open proxy can be dangerous if you do not fully trust the person exercising it. He can vote against your best interests if he chooses. You can also make a specific and detailed proxy, which authorises its holder to cast your vote only in certain ways. That is, the proxy can declare that its holder must vote "yes" on items three and five of the meeting agenda and can vote "no" on items one and four, and that he must abstain from voting on the other issues. The secretary of the meeting will ask to see the proxy forms when he registers each member's attendance at the meeting, so he will know this.

Most communities have proxy forms already printed and available from the secretary, but they are the open sort, so you must make your own if you want to be specific. There is no provision for absentee voting by post.

The holder and voter of your proxy does not have to be a community member. He can be anyone you choose to name.

Proxies have caused many problems in communities. Foreign owners absent from Spain tend to give their proxy to some influential person in the community. This person is often the developer of the building, who still has unsold units, and so is a member of the community. He votes the shares of the unsold flats still in his name, along with the proxies he has been given, and can often control the operations of the community in this way. Or it may be the president who keeps himself in office with these proxies. In one case, it was the representative of a rental agency which owned some flats in a building and managed others. With the proxies the agency controlled, they ran the building to suit the renters and to the disadvantage of the permanent residents. So there are many tricks available with proxies.

Article 15 also refers to flats held in usufruct. This means that the owner has granted the right to occupy the flat to another person, as sometimes happens when the property is held in the name of a son or daughter. The son or daughter, by a legal document, grants to the parent the lifetime right, the usufruct, to inhabit the property. This is sometimes done in order to skip over one generation of inheritance taxes. When the parent dies, the son or daughter simply takes possession of the property which has always been his. The holder of this usufruct is considered the owner's representative at the community meeting for all normal matters. If, however, the community is voting to change its statutes or to authorise extraordinary works, then the holder of the usufruct will need a specific written authorisation from the owner of record.

Paragraph 2 of the article contains the real change in the revised law. For the first time, community debtors are both deprived of the right to vote and are listed for all to see. Unless these debtors have impugned the court decision against them and deposited the funds, they cannot vote.

Article 16

The General Meeting of proprietors will be held at least once a year to approve the budgets and accounts and at any other time the President considers it advisable or when one quarter of the owners request it, or any number of owners who represent at least 25 per cent of the participation shares.

The President shall convoke the meeting and, in the absence of this, the promoters of the meeting, giving notice of the agenda of business, the time, day and place of the meeting for the first call, and, when applicable, the second call. Notification shall be given in the form set out in Article 9. The notice of meeting shall contain a list of the owners who are not current in the payment of debts to the Community and will warn of the loss of the right to vote under the conditions expressed in Article 15.2

Any owner can request the General Meeting to examine and resolve on any matter of interest to the Community.

For this purpose he should present to the President in writing the clearly specified points he wishes dealt with. The President shall include them in the agenda of the following General Meeting.

If the majority of owners, representing at the same time the majority of participation shares (cuotas) are not present at the time of the first call, the meeting shall be convened again on second call, without the need for a quorum.

The meeting shall be held on the second call at the time, date and place indicated in the first notification. It can be held on the same day, as long as at least half an hour has passed since the first call.

Failing this, it shall be convened again, according to the forms established in this Article, within eight days following the meeting not held. In such case, notification must be made at least three days before the meeting.

3. Notification of the ordinary Annual General Meeting will be given at least six days beforehand and, for extraordinary meetings with as much advance notice as possible so that it can come to the attention of all the parties involved. The general meeting can lawfully take place even without the convocation of the President, providing that all of the proprietors agree and decide this.

What it means

Article 15 states that, by law, a general meeting must be held at least once a year. The only item of business legally required is the approval by the members of the accounts and budget. It is not strictly necessary to hold elections for a new president because the old one will continue in office until he is replaced by majority vote.

But the expenses must be approved by a legally-registered vote of the community members. It is perfectly possible for them to decide that they will not pay out any money for the next year. This means, of course, that the electric company will cut off the lights and the building's insurance policy will lapse. But no money can be spent without the majority vote of the members.

This annual general meeting is the ordinary meeting. Other

meetings, known as extraordinary meetings, may also take place. The president may call such a meeting at any time, giving adequate notice. This question of what constitutes "adequate" notification is a little tricky, especially when three quarters of the members of the community are residing in another country at any particular moment, but any president will try to give sufficient notice because he knows that a member who feels he has not been correctly warned of the meeting can protest and a court may rule the results of the meeting void.

An extraordinary meeting can also be called whenever one quarter of the members of the community, or people who represent one-quarter of the participation shares, request it. The president is then obligated to convene the meeting. In the case of the president's absence or incapacitation, the promoters of the meeting may also convoke it.

The law mentions one-quarter of the participation shares, or *cuotas*, because in many cases one or two owners may control a much larger share of the building than the owner of a single flat. One such example would be a large department store that holds more than one-quarter of the *cuotas* all on its own. Another would be the developer himself, who controls and votes all the shares of the unsold flats. This situation, in which one owner holds great voting power, has caused problems in more than one community.

It is common practice for the second calling of the meeting to appear on the original notification, usually set for a half hour after the first calling.

This means that, if a majority of members or *cuotas* is not present — and often it isn't — the meeting can still take place, no matter how few owners or shares are present. Their decisions will be perfectly valid if not protested by the other owners within 30 days after they are notified of the actions.

Article 17

Decisions of the general meeting shall be subject to the following rules:

1. Unanimity shall only be required for the validity of those resolutions which involve approval or modification of rules contained in the charter of constitution of the property or in the Community Statutes.

The establishment or elimination of the lift, janitor, reception desk, security services or other common services of general interest, even when they involve modification of the charter of constitution or the Community Statutes, shall require the vote in favour of three fifths of the total number of owners, who at the same time represent three fifths of the cuotas, or participation shares. The leasing out of common elements which have no specific use assigned them in the building shall also require the favourable vote of three fifths of the total number of owners who, at the same time represent three fifths of the participation shares, as well as the consent of the owner directly affected, should there be one.

Work executed or new common services established to eliminate structural barriers which hinder the access or mobility of handicapped persons, even when this involves the modification of the charter of constitution or the Community Statutes, shall require the favourable vote of a simple majority of the owners, who at the same time represent the majority of the cuotas.

For effects established in the preceding paragraph, the votes of correctly notified owners absent from the meeting shall be computed as favourable when, having been informed of the decision taken by those present, in accordance with the procedure set out in Article 9, they did not express dissent to the person acting as Community Secretary within 30 days, by any certified means of delivery.

Decisions validly taken according to the dispositions of this rule are binding on all owners.

2. The installation of common facilities providing access to telecommunication services regulated in Royal Decree-Law 1/1998 of February 27, or the adaptation of existing systems, as well as the installation of solar energy systems, whether common or private, and facilities necessary for obtaining new collective energy sources, may be agreed, at the request of any one owner, by one third of the members of the community representing one third of the cuotas.

The Community shall not charge the cost of the installation or adaptation of the above-mentioned facilities, nor the costs arising from its conservation and maintenance, to those owners who did not expressly vote in the meeting in favour of the decision. Nevertheless, if they later request access to the telecommunication system or to the energy supplies and this requires the use of the new facilities or the adaptations carried out on the pre-existing systems, this can be granted, providing that they pay the amount which would have corresponded to them, correctly brought up to date by applying the corresponding legal interest.

Without prejudice to the above-mentioned expenses of upkeep and maintenance, the new facilities shall have the status, to all effects established by this Law, of common elements.

3. For the validity of all other resolutions, the favourable vote of the majority of the owners which at the same time represents the majority of the cuotas shall suffice.

On the second calling of the meeting decisions voted by the majority of those present, provided that they represent more than half the participation shares present, shall be valid.

When a majority cannot be achieved by the procedures established in the foregoing paragraphs, the Court, at the petition of one of the parties within a month of the date of the second meeting, and hearing any dissenters, who must be duly notified, will rule in equity within 20 days of the petition, and will rule on the assignment of legal costs as well.

What it means

Under the previous Law of Horizontal Property, a unanimous vote was required for any modification of the building, which led to necessary and useful action being blocked by one or two dissenters.

The new law sets out very carefully the sort of actions which now require only a three-fifths majority.

It also notes that your vote will be counted as favourable if you were absent from the meeting and did not protest within 30 days of being informed, and you will then be bound by the decision of those present at the meeting.

Sometimes a very small number of owners really make the decisions for the community.

If you are baffled by references in this article to access to telecommunications, don't worry. They mean communal television aerials, which require only a one-third vote in order to bind all of the owners. The same goes for work to install any renewable energy source.

All other community votes require only a simple majority, including the election of the president.

And if you are puzzled by the requirement that this majority must be a majority of the number of owners present as well as a majority of the amounts of participation shares, or *cuotas*, this is understandable.

The law stipulates this double majority because a conflict can arise when one owner controls many shares because he owns 10 apartments in the building or for some other reason. Spanish courts usually rule in favour of the number of owners rather than the amount of *cuotas* when deciding a contested vote.

Article 18

1. Decisions voted by the Annual General Meeting may be challenged in court, following the provisions of the general procedural law, in the following situations:
a) When such decisions are contrary to the law or to the Community Statutes.
b) When they are seriously damaging to the interests of the Community itself and benefit one or several owners.
c) When they cause serious harm to an owner who has no legal obligation to suffer this harm, or when the decisions have been made by abusing the law.
2. Owners who expressly registered a dissenting vote in the meeting, those who were absent for any reason, and those who were incorrectly deprived of their right to vote are legally entitled to impugn these decisions. To challenge a resolution of the Meeting, an owner must be current in his payment of debts owed to the Community or he must deposit the amount of the debt with the Court beforehand. This rule shall not apply when challenging a decision regarding the establishment or alteration of the participation shares referred to in Article 9.
3. The action lapses three months after the decision taken by the general meeting unless the decision is contrary to law or to the Community Statutes, in which case the period is one year. For those owners who were absent this period is counted from the date of notification of the decision according to the procedure set out in Article 9.
4. Impugning a decision of the general meeting does not suspend its being put into force unless the Court orders so, as a precautionary measure, at the petition of the plaintiff and having heard the community of owners.

What it means

Article 18 means that even one owner can challenge a community decision in court, if it seriously harms the interests of one of the members, or if it seems to benefit a few people to the detriment of the community as a whole, or if it is contrary to law or the statutes of the community.

Dissenters, be warned that you should have your vote against the measure reflected in the official minutes book if you want to impugn the decision.

Absentees have three months in most cases, and they had better have their fees paid up.

Article 19

1. Decisions of the general meeting shall be recorded in a book of minutes stamped and validated by the Property Registrar in the form set out by law.

2. The minutes of each meeting must express at least the following circumstances:

a) The date and place of the meeting

b) The name of the caller of the meeting, or the names of the owners who promoted it.

c) Whether it was ordinary or extraordinary and whether it was held on first or second call.

d) List of all those attending and their respective offices, as well as those owners represented by proxy, with the cuotas of each one.

e) The agenda for the meeting.

f) Decisions taken, showing, where it is relevant for the validity of the decision, the names of those owners who voted in favour and those who voted against them, as well as the participation shares they respectively represent.

3. The minutes book should close with the signatures of the president and the secretary at the end of the meeting or within 10 days after. At the signing of the minutes book, the resolutions of the meeting shall be in force, unless the law disposes otherwise.

The minutes shall be sent to the absent owners, following the procedure set out in Article 9.

Errors or defects in the minutes are rectifiable, provided that the book unmistakably indicates the date and place of the meeting, the owners in attendance, either present or represented by proxy, the decisions taken, with notation of the votes for and against, as well as the participation shares represented and that the book has been signed by the president and secretary. Said rectification should be made before the following general assembly, which must ratify the corrections.

4. The Secretary will keep the minutes books of the general meeting.

He will likewise retain, during a period of five years, the convocations, communications, powers of attorney and other documents relating to the meetings.

What it means

The official minutes book described here must be kept in Spanish because it is a legal document, registering the acts of the community. This *libro de actas* must be stamped by the Registrar of Property and its contents can be cited in court.

The book must record the names of the members present and the proxies present at the meeting; tell who presided; when and where the meeting was held; give the agenda for the meeting; mention the main points of view discussed in the debate; list the resolutions taken and record the voting results.

If any member or group wishes to contest a resolution of the community, either in person or by certified post, this also should be recorded.

This minutes book establishes the powers of the president and any other officer to act for the community, and justifies the actions by its recording of the community's votes.

The annual general meeting usually begins with the reading of the minutes of the previous meeting, which must be approved by the members. If any member has a protest against the book, it must be registered officially in the book itself. It sometimes happens that the official record does not agree with one person's version of what actually happened, so it is necessary to be attentive.

Article 20

It is the function of the administrator:

a) To ensure the proper management of the house, its installations and services and, to this effect, provide the owners with timely information and warnings.

b) To prepare the budget of anticipated expenses sufficiently in advance and submit it to the general meeting, proposing the necessary measures to cover the expenses.

c) To attend to the conservation and maintenance of the building, arranging for the ordinary repairs and taking urgent measures regarding extraordinary repairs, giving an immediate report to the general meeting or, as the case may be, to the property owners.

d) To carry out resolutions taken regarding works and to make any

payments and receive any monies as properly disposed.
e) To act, when the case arises, as secretary of the general meeting and to keep custody, at the disposition of the owners, of the documentation of the community.
f) Any other functions conferred by the general meeting.

What it means

Contrary to popular belief, the administrator, when he is a paid professional, is not an elected officer of the community. He is contracted for his services, usually for one year, and the community may choose not to renew his contract at its termination, and to employ another paid professional administrator.

Of course, a community member, the president or another, may carry out the many duties of administrating the building, and he may even be paid for it.

Article 20 lists the functions of the administrator. He must run the building properly and keep the owners informed about it. If there is no treasurer, the administrator prepares the budget for the coming year, attends to repairs in the building, makes payments and receives money, acts as secretary and keeps the community records safe and at the disposition of the members, and any other functions voted to him by the community.

Because the administrator may be a volunteer member of the community, the law sets no requirement for carrying out this mission. The administrator needs no professional title or special qualifications. He does not have to be Spanish or even to speak Spanish.

Nevertheless, many of the paid professional administrators hold titles as lawyers, gestors or, best of all, as an *administrador de fincas*, a professional property management expert.

Most administrators try to give good service to the community, charge reasonable fees, and put up with many petty complaints from the members. But others are not so honest, and more than one community has had bad experiences with administrators who seem to feel that the community works for them, rather than the other way around.

Sometimes promoters, in order to maintain their influence in the community, even have the names of administrators written into the original community statutes when they register the building. They are counting on the fact that any change in the statutes requires a unanimous vote, which is very difficult to achieve, so the members could not put out the administrator. Their legal position here is quite shaky, though, as the law also says that the annual general meeting has the power to change the president and the administrator.

In any case, if the community feels that the administrator is not presenting proper accounts, or his fees are too high, or he has purchased supplies from his cousin when he could have got them more cheaply from another source, they can vote him out.

The administrator, whether professional or volunteer, can also be sued in court for damages caused by his misconduct or negligence in office.

Article 21

1. The obligations referred to in paragraphs e) and f) of Article 9 must be fulfilled by the owner of the flat or premises in the time and form determined by the General Meeting. If not, the President or the Administrator, if so disposed by the General Meeting, can seek legal redress by the procedure established in this Article.

2. Use of this procedure will require the prior notification of the decision of the General Meeting approving the claim of the debt with the Community by the person acting as Secretary, with the endorsement of the President, providing that this decision has been notified to the owners affected in the form set out in Article 9.

3. Territorial jurisdiction shall correspond exclusively to the Court of the place where the property is located. Representation by a lawyer or procurator shall not be compulsory, subject to the dispositions of paragraph 10. of this Article.

4. Proceedings begin with a simple claim form, accompanied by the certification referred to in Number 2. of this Article. In case the previous owner of the property is liable jointly for the debt, without affecting his right to claim repayment from the present owner, action should be brought against him jointly with the present owner. In any case, the action must be brought against the registered owner.

5. Once the claim has been presented and accepted for procedure, the judge shall summon the defendant and order him to pay the plaintiff within 20 days and accredit this to the Court, or to appear before the court and present his allegations justifying that he does not owe, either in whole or in part, the amount claimed. The summons should be served at the domicile in Spain previously designated by the debtor, or in its absence, at the flat itself, with the admonition

that, if he neither pays nor appears to declare his reasons for refusal to pay, the Court will rule against him in the manner set out in the following Number.
6. *If the defendant does not appear before the Court and does not oppose the claim, the Judge shall issue a writ of execution*
which shall proceed according to the provisions for court rulings, for the amount owed plus interest and foreseeable costs and for prior extra-judicial costs for the notifications of the debt if the services of a Notary were used.

The plaintiff in this procedure and the debtor acted against shall not be able to respectively claim the amount or seek the refund of monies paid out in a subsequent ordinary civil action.

From the time the writ is issued, the debt will draw interest at the legal interest rate plus two per cent.
7. *If the debtor pays upon the demand for payment, as soon as he accredits this to theCourt, he will be given the document registering the debt and the case will be dropped.*

Nevertheless, the legal costs cited in Number 10 of this Article and the expenses set out in the preceding Number will be for his account.
8. *If the debtor opposes the claim, giving reasons for refusal to pay, in whole or in part, the Judge, after transmitting the opposition plea to the plaintiff, shall follow the procedure for oral hearings from the time of the summons. However, once opposition is declared, the plaintiff may seek a lien or attachment on assets of the debtor of sufficient value to cover the amount claimed, interest, and costs.*

The Judge will dispose such lien in any case without the necessity of the creditor posting bond. The debtor can avoid the lien by presenting a bank guarantee for the amount set in the preventive lien.
9. *If the debtor appears on time in Court and opposes the payment only in part, alleging overcharging, his plea will be admitted only when he accredits having either paid or placed at the disposition of the plaintiff, before the claim was made, the amount he recognises as his debt. If the opposition is based on overcharging, the lien can only be sought for the amount not paid by the debtor.*
10. *The Court's ruling will have the force of "final judgment".*

Costs will be charged to the party whose claim is totally rejected. If the claim is partially granted, each party will pay its own individual costs and half of the common costs. The order to pay costs will include legal fees to lawyer and attorney of the winning side, if they have used these professional services in their claim or opposition.

11. Community fees which fall due while the case is in process can be added to the amount without having to recommence the proceedings, considering them as common to the debt and affected by the procedural stages which went before. This faculty shall extend through the execution of the writ.

This addition during the process of community fees falling due after the presentation of the claim shall require prior accreditation by a new certification of the community decision approving the claim, issued according to the provisions of Number 2.

12, No appeal against the ruling will be admitted to Court unless the defendant accredits having settled the debt or deposited the amount of the judgment with the Court before he brings the appeal.

If the ruling orders the payment of certain sums for late payment or for unpaid fees due, the appeal will be annulled if the appellant ceases to pay or to deposit with the Court on time the payments of the same class which continue to come due during the procedure.

What it means

This article sets out the real changes in the 1999 law which at last put some real teeth into the community's ability to compel payment of debt.

The community can now certify the debt and go immediately into court for a lien against the debtor's property. If the debtor does not pay up, the court will order some of his assets seized to pay the debt. If the debtor chooses to fight the bill, he himself must put up either his assets or a bank guarantee for the amount. Formerly, the community was required to make a deposit with the court when they sought to collect the back fees. No longer.

Furthermore, any community debts that accumulate during the procedure are simply added into the original debt. No complications.

Furthermore, if the debtor fights to drag out the case, he will be liable for the community's legal costs if he loses.

Article 22

1. The Community of Property Owners will be liable with all its assets and credits for any debt to third parties. In addition, the creditor can act against each individual owner who took part in the process for his proportional share of the unpaid amount, after

serving a demand for payment on such owners.
2. Any owner can oppose the claim by justifying that he is fully current in the payment of all debts due to the community at the time the demand referred to above was made.
If the debtor immediately pays the demand, he will be charged the proportional part of the costs involved.

What it means

It happens with a certain frequency that communities of property owners cannot pay their debts to suppliers or service providers simply because their members have not paid their annual community fees.

This article gives community creditors a handle on direct action. They can proceed against the members themselves as individuals. Those members who are fully paid up cannot be made to pay.

Article 23

The legal structure of horizontal property (condominium) is terminated:
1. By the destruction of the building, unless there is agreement to the contrary.
Such destruction shall be deemed to exist when the cost of rebuilding exceeds 50 per cent of the value of the property at the time the event occurs, unless the amount in excess of the aforesaid cost is covered by insurance.
2. By conversion into ordinary ownership or joint ownership.

What it means

Clearly, the horizontal property scheme must be terminated when the building is destroyed. By fire, for example. The second paragraph refers to the sale of the building to one owner or several joint owners. Yes, the community can even vote — unanimously, of course — to sell itself and divide the cash among the owners.

CHAPTER III:
REGARDING PRIVATE REAL ESTATE COMPLEXES

Article 24

1. The special scheme of property ownership set out in Article 396 of the Civil Code shall be applicable to those private real estate complexes which meet the following requirements:

a) Being made up of two or more buildings or independent plots whose principal use is dwellings or commercial premises.

b) The owners of these buildings or properties or of the units into which they are divided horizontally, with an inherent nature for this right, participate in an indivisible co-ownership of other real estate elements, such as roads, installations or services.

2. Private real estate complexes referred to in the previous Number may:

a) Constitute themselves as one only Community of Owners by means of any of the procedures established in the second paragraph of Article 5. In this case they will be subject to the dispositions of this Law, which will be fully applied to them.

b) Constitute themselves as a grouping of Communities of Owners. To this effect, the Charter of Constitution of the new grouped Community must be granted by the only and single owner of the complex or by the Presidents of all the Communities to compose it, previously authorised by majority vote of their respective general meetings. The Charter of Constitution will contain the description of the real estate complex in its setting and descriptions of the elements, roads, installations and common services. Likewise, it will fix the participation shares (cuotas) of each of the component Communities, which will be jointly liable for the obligation to contribute to the general expenses of the group macro-community. This title of charter and the Statutes of the Community can be inscribed in the Property Registry.

3. The grouping of Communities referred to above shall, to all effects, enjoy the same legal situation as Communities of Owners and will be governed by the dispositions of this Law, with the following special provisions:

a) The general assembly of owners, unless otherwise agreed, will be composed of the Presidents of the communities forming the group, who will represent the individual owners of each Community .

b) The making of decisions for which the Law requires qualified majorities will require, in all cases, the prior vote of the majority required in each of the individual Communities that compose the grouping.

c) Except by agreement of the general meeting otherwise, the dispositions of Article 9 of this Law regarding the reserve fund shall not apply to the group community.

The jurisdiction of the governing organs of the group community cover only the real estate elements, roads, installations and common services. In no case shall their decisions prejudice the faculties corresponding to the governing bodies of the Communities of Owners which make up the grouping of Communities.

4. The dispositions of this Law, with the same special provisions, shall be applicable to those private real estate complexes which do not adopt any of the legal forms indicated in Number 2 as a complement to agreements made by the co-owners among themselves

What it means

This is the big one. For the first time, the Horizontal Law takes account of urbanisations of detached houses, or groupings of townhouses, flats and detached villas.

The full protection of the new Horizontal Law is now available for these urbanisations, with very little effort on their part. They can vote for it, write themselves a set of statutes, and go straight to the Property Registry.

Until now, urbanisations had to form themselves as Collaborating Urbanistic Entities, a complex process which often proved extremely expensive for the owners and involved long and tortuous negotiations with the town hall.

Sometimes the formation of an EUC will be the only possibility for an urbanisation, but many of them will now find their way smoothed to legality and the power to enforce debt collection.

ADDITIONAL DISPOSITION

1. Without prejudice to any dispositions which, using the powers conferred on them, the Regional Governments may make, the constitution of the reserve fund regulated in Article 9.1.f) shall comply with the following rules:

a) The fund must be created when the General Meeting approves the ordinary yearly budget, corresponding to the year immediately following the putting into effect of this Law.

New Communities shall create the fund when they approve their first ordinary budget.

b)When constituted, the fund shall be endowed with no less than 2.5 per cent of the ordinary budget of the Community. To this effect, the owners must make in advance the necessary contributions proportionally to their participation shares.

c) When the ordinary budget for the financial year following that in which the fund was established is passed, the amount of the reserve fund should reach the minimum quantity established in Article 9.

2. The amount of the reserve fund at no time during the budget period shall be less than the minimum legally established.

Amounts drawn from the reserve fund during the budget period in order to pay the expenses on maintenance and repairs of the property permitted by the present law shall be computed as an integral part of the fund for purposes of calculating its minimum amount.

At the beginning of the following financial year there shall be made the contributions necessary to cover the amounts drawn from the reserve fund in accordance with the terms of the preceding paragraph.

What it means

The last disposition requires communities to establish and maintain a reserve fund to deal with any emergencies.

COMMUNITIES OF DETACHED VILLAS

20

THOSE who live in urbanisations of detached villas have a more complicated set of problems than those living in flats. Before 1978 it was very difficult for them to form any sort of community with the legal power to enforce its statutes and compel payment of fees.

The inhabitants of these housing estates, or urbanisations, a rather new invention in Spain at that time, had to find ways of financing their roads, lighting, security, gardens, etc, as well as establishing the basic services of water, electric power and rubbish collection.

Even when they can now come under the protection of the Horizontal Law, they still have these basic problems not related to the pure legality of their existence.

In addition, the urbanisations often had complex relations with the town hall of their municipality. If the road passing through the estate continues on to other properties and is used by the general public, who pays for its maintenance? Can the inhabitants cut this road and seal off the community, or are they obliged to permit the public to use it? Will the town hall rubbish collectors enter the estate, or must all rubbish be placed at a central point for collection? A thousand questions arise.

What is basically important for the formation of a community is Royal Decree 3288/1978 of August 25, which sets forth the regulations for urban administration based on the existing *Ley del Suelo*, the Land Law. Even the 1978 regulations are complex and confusing, but they can provide a framework for setting up an effective community.

These regulations establish the figure of the *Entidad Urbanística Colaboradora de Gestión y Conservación*, the Collaborating

Urbanistic Entity of Maintenance and Management. A real mouthful to describe the quasi-public functions of the urbanisation of detached villas. This is often shortened today to EUC.

In a perfect world, you would find that your dream villa was located on an urbanisation where all roads, lighting and services were carefully provided by a benevolent and foresighted municipal administration, just as they are in many countries. But you are more likely to encounter a situation where the developer is no longer maintaining the roads and services, where the town hall refuses to help because all the requirements in the original building permission were not fulfilled by the developers, and the owners are unable to establish an effective community.

You need to start with Article 25 of the 1978 regulations. If you are lucky, your situation will come under Section 3 of this law which provides for the forming of collaborating entities which group all owners in a certain zone, whether they want to join or not. Without the power to compel all owners to belong to the entity, it would be meaningless.

Then you can study Article 67, which provides that the town hall will take charge of maintaining and providing all normal services once these have been ceded to the town hall. That is, the association of owners or the developer will transfer the roads, sewage, lighting and perhaps some common green zone to the town hall.

The catch here is that the town hall may very well refuse to accept this transfer until the roads and other services have been put into good condition. Guess who must pay for this. Right. Either the developer, or the owners as a group. Some parts of the regulations can even oblige the urbanisation to pay all costs for establishing connections to the nearest town roads, sewers and lighting systems.

The great advantage of the collaborating entity is that the urbanisation then becomes a normal part of the municipality for the provision of basic services, and, if one of the members refuses to pay his share of community fees, the town hall itself may act against him with the threat to seize his property or bank account to satisfy the unpaid debt. This procedure is much more effective and rapid than going through the courts.

So you begin to see that the collaborating entity must work closely with the municipal authorities because the urbanisation is not separated from the rest of the world the way an apartment building is. In fact, the authorisation of the town hall is required for the formation of this entity.

All these negotiations between the owners and the municipal authorities will require the counsel and representation of a Spanish lawyer or property administrator who is knowledgeable in this area. In one recent case on the Costa del Sol, the backers of a very large estate worked closely with the existing owners and the town hall. First the existing owners voted unanimously to form an association. Then the developers, acting on the requirements of the town hall, put all the services in good order. Costs were shared by the owners and the developer. Then the backers had to pay the town hall a fine of €120,000 for not fulfilling all their original obligations. (The town hall first wanted €480,000, but were argued into the lower figure.) Finally, the town hall accepted the transfer of the roads and other services, and authorised the formation of a collaborating urban entity. This was properly registered in the registry of such entities, which exists at the provincial urban office, giving it a legal personality.

Any new purchaser in this zone must now become a member of the entity by virtue of his purchase. This is clearly stated in each sales contract. Both the developer and the present owners have bound themselves to include such a clause in any sales deed. Even if they didn't, the legal personality of the entity requires it.

Now the members only have to squabble among themselves about how much to pay for the security patrol, whether they want an extra tennis court and how to act against the owner with the barking dogs. Of course they also have to fight with their new partners in the town hall about the size of their assessment for the sewage repairs, compared to the urbanisation just down the road. The problems will never end, but at least they have a clear and coherent system for dealing with them.

These particular members are now up in arms because they feel they are being charged twice for municipal services. That is because they pay their annual real estate taxes to the town hall, the IBI, just like other owners. But they also pay their annual fees to the EUC, which, they argue, covers basically the same services, so they are being forced to pay twice. The argument is still going on.

Things can be much worse in a situation where the owners cannot agree at the beginning and where the developer is not willing to help. But if the whole thing seems like too much trouble, remember that a well-run community can add thousands of euros to your property's value and a poorly maintained urbanisation can cut thousands off your price.

The following section contains an English translation of the Spanish national legislation affecting the formation of conservation entities. It is not complete because many different bodies of law can come into play. The Land Law is frequently modified and each region, such as Valencia or Andalusia, has its own land law as well. Nevertheless, the basic 1978 law still gives a good idea of the legislation.

LAW FOR DETACHED VILLAS

Land Law Regulations III
Regulations of Urban Administration
TITLE I General Dispositions CHAPTER 1. Subjects and Means of Administration SECTION 6.

Article 24
1. Affected parties may participate in urban administration through the creation of Collaborating Urban Entities.
2. Collaborating Urban Entities are:
a) Compensation Boards.
b) Administrative Associations of owners in the co-operation system.
c) Entities of Conservation.
3. Collaborating Urban Entities will be governed by their Statutes and by the dispositions of this section, without prejudice to the application of the specific precepts contained in Chapters 11 and III of Title V of these Regulations for Compensation Boards and Administrative Associations of owners in the co-operation system, nor to the provisions established in Chapter 1-V of Title III for the conservation of the works of urbanisation.

What it means
These regulations establish a legal basis for private citizens to participate in public administration. Keep in mind that streets, lighting, main drains, sewage systems and electric conduits passing through the land of the urbanisation to the next property will be of public nature. It is not like a building of flats, in which the

services are simply connected and do not pass on to other properties.

This article of the regulations allows private persons to share administration of these services with the municipal authorities through the formation of one of three types of collaborating urban entities.

The first mentioned, the compensation board, is created when land is being re-zoned or subdivided and where several owners may be involved. The situation can get complicated. Imagine an area which includes a large working farm, a small factory with lots of land around it, nine or 10 homes built on large rural plots, and maybe a developer who has bought a big tract which he wants to urbanise. The nearby town is expanding and a new road is being put in. The entire zone will be declared building land.

The compensation board is the legal structure created for the purpose of sorting out all the problems that will arise and for seeing that each participant is fairly treated. The town hall is represented, too, as it will be expropriating land from some of the owners for the road and other services. The members of the board will squabble and negotiate until they agree on each party's share of the rights and obligations. This is one form of urban entity.

The compensation board operates principally as a forum to ensure the equitable distribution of problems and profits in such a re-zoning situation. But what happens after the subdivision is complete?

One scheme set up in law is the second structure mentioned in this article: the administrative association of owners in the co-operation system. Here the owners co-operate with each other and with the town hall to organise smooth functioning of the services in the area they share. This is much like the conservation entity, but its legal underpinnings are different, involving several different ownerships.

Both the compensation board and the administrative association are designed to serve in the early stages of a transformation in the ownership pattern of land. Either of them can be changed into a conservation entity, the legal framework for the ongoing maintenance of an established urbanisation.

Article 25

1. The constitution of the Compensation Boards and of the Administrative Associations of owners in the co-operation system shall be adapted to the provisions of the regulations contained in the respective schemes of action.

2. Entities of conservation of the works of urbanisation may be constituted as a result of the transformation of some pre-existing Entity of those set out in the previous number or, specifically for these purposes, without previously having constituted any Entity for the execution of the works of urbanisation.

3. The constitution of a conservation Entity will be obligatory whenever the duty of conservation of the works of urbanisation falls upon the owners included in a determined zone or unit of action by virtue of the dispositions of the town urban Plan or the bases of the urban action programme or if it results expressly from legal dispositions. In such cases membership in the conservation Entity will be obligatory for all owners included in its territorial range.

What it means

The big news comes here in the last sentence of paragraph 3, which provides that membership in the conservation entity shall be obligatory for all owners in the zone, and that the formation of the conservation entity shall be obligatory when provided by law, meaning that it may be set out in the town urban development plan, or in a Plan of Urbanistic Action, a development plan for a restricted area, or it may simply be a regulation passed by the Town Council. Any legal disposition will suffice.

In practice this means some urbanisations will find that the law requires them to form a conservation entity and that all must be members, and other urbanisations will find it is not legally necessary for them to do so.

Article 26

1. Collaborating urbanistic entities shall have an administrative character and shall be dependent in this order on the acting urbanistic Administration.

2. The legal personality of collaborating urbanistic entities shall be understood as acquired from the moment of their inscription in the corresponding Registry.

What it means

The first paragraph of this article grants to these entities powers to act legally, and notes that this power depends on the entity's relation to the public administration involved, which would usually be the municipality, though it could also be the province or a special authority ruling some particular piece of terrain.

The second paragraph reminds us that there exists a special Registry for these entities and they cannot act with legal force, to compel payment of debts, for example, until the entity is properly registered.

Article 27

1. The constitution of collaborating urban entities, as well as their Statutes, must be approved by the acting urban Administration.
2. The document approving this constitution shall be entered in the Registry of Collaborating Urban Entities which is kept by the respective Provincial Urban Commissions, where likewise shall be kept an example of the statutes of the entity authorised by the competent official.
3. The appointments and dismissals of the persons charged with governing and administrating the entity shall also be inscribed in said Registry.
4. Modification of the statutes shall require the approval of the acting urban Administration. The respective resolutions, with the content of the modification, in such case, must be entered in the Registry.

What it means

This article points up the importance of the co-operation required of the local town hall or other urban administration body which has competence over the zone. These official bodies must approve the formation of the entity and its statutes.

The names of its officers, and any changes in its rules, must be registered in the Registry. Any major changes of the statutes will require approval from the municipal authorities.

Article 28

The transfer of title which determines membership in any of the types of collaborating urbanistic entities shall carry with it the termination of the rights and obligations of the transferring party and the acquirer shall be understood as incorporated into the Entity from the time of transfer.

What it means

This of course applies only when the Entity is legally constituted and registered. If the owner's community is not an Entity, but only a civil association, then each new buyer's contract must contain a clause stating that he joins the community and agrees to abide by its statutes.

Article 29

Resolutions of Collaborating Urbanistic Entities shall be adopted by simple majority of participation shares, unless a special quorum is established in the Statutes or other regulations for certain cases. Such resolutions can be impugned in appeal to the acting urbanistic Administration.

What it means

Each urban entity can make its own statutes with provisions on where unanimous vote may be required. If they do not, this article of the regulations will apply and a simple majority decision will be sufficient to take action. Any owner who feels his interests have been prejudiced can appeal the vote to the town hall or other official administration acting in the case.

ARTICLES 30 THROUGH 57 are of a highly technical nature and do not bear directly on the formation of communities.

Article 58

The owners of properties affected by an urbanistic action programme shall be obliged to pay the costs of urbanisation specified in the following articles in proportion to the area of their respective properties, or, as the case may be, to the area figuring in the documents referred to in Article 53 of these regulations.

What it means

This means that owners shall be assessed payment participation shares according to the size of their properties. Big properties pay more, small properties pay less. The Article 53 referred to relates to various forms of documenting property ownership, such as the *Registro de la Propiedad*, and others.

Article 59

1. The cost of works of urbanisation which are charged to the account of the owners of a determined zone or unit of action shall include the following:

a) Street works, including works of levelling, compacting and paving of roadways, construction and kerbing of pavements and channelling which must be constructed in the subsurface of the public way for services.

b) Sanitation works, which include general and partial collectors, connections, sewers and culverts for rain-waters and purification installations, in the proportion that they affect the action unit or zone.

c) Water supply, in which is included works of obtaining the water, when such are necessary, the distribution to homes of potable water, of irrigation water and of fluid for fire-fighting.

d) Supply of electrical current, including its conduction and distribution and public lighting.

e) Gardening and tree-planting in parks, gardens and public ways.

2. Private parties involved in works of urbanisation in a zone or urban action unit may be reimbursed for the expenses of installation of the networks of supply of water and electricity, charged to the concession-holding companies, to the extent that, according to the regulation of such services, these expenses must not be charged to the users. The costs of installation shall be accredited by certification issued by the acting administration.

What it means

Have they left anything out? The owners on an urbanisation can find themselves liable for any of the expenses mentioned here. If the developer has failed to carry out all requirements set by the town hall, either in the urban plan itself or other subsidiary legislation, the owners can be stuck for it in most cases. It pays to check up first.

Article 60

Any indemnities owed to the owners and renters of buildings or constructions of any sort which must be knocked down for the correct execution of the plan, as well as indemnity payments arising from the destruction of plantings, works or installations incompatible with the plan being carried out shall likewise be charged to the account of the property owners in the proportions set out in Article 58.

What it means

Yes, they left something out. Owners are also liable for any payments made to persons suffering loss from the execution of the urbanisation plan.

Article 61

Also for the account of the owners of land included in the zone or relevant action unit shall be the cost of preparing and processing the Plan of plots and the projects of urbanisation and the total cost of expenses of subdivision or compensation.

What it means

This expense would fall on the owners of land which is in the process of being subdivided, and will produce profits for them when they sell. It is not likely to affect purchasers on an already-established urbanisation; but be alert because legal expenses can also be charged to the owners.

Article 62

If agreement exists between the Administration and the affected owners, the payment of all or part of the expenses noted in the three previous articles can be made by the owners ceding to the Administration, for no consideration and free of all charges, buildable land in the amount deemed sufficient for the compensation of such expenses, whose value shall be determined in the agreement itself.

What it means

That's good of the administration. If you can't pay, they will accept your valuable land instead. In fact, this situation normally arises when the town itself is re-zoning land. The new building permissions mean large profits for the existing owners so it is expected they pay for it, either in cash or by the transfer of part of the land to the town hall.

Article 63

Owners of non-programmed developable land which is the object of a Programme of urbanistic action, besides paying the costs of urbanisation set out in the previous articles and satisfying any supplementary charges which the programme may impose on them, must pay for the complete execution or the supplement necessary for the exterior works of infrastructure on which the urbanistic action is based, such as road networks connecting with population centres, installation or amplification of the channels of services of water supply, drains and sewage, purification stations, supply of electricity and any other services necessary for the land subject to the urbanistic action programme to be duly connected through these general systems with the structure of the Municipality in which the programme is carried out.

What it means

Owners of land which is improved or made more valuable by any action of the town hall can find themselves liable even for these expenses.

ARTICLE 64 has been left out, as it does not bear directly on communities.

Article 65

Incompliance by the owners of the land with the obligations and charges established in these Regulations will give rise to:
a) The collection of the urbanisation costs by executive order under threat of embargo and legal seizure of the property.
b) Expropriation by the Administration of the lands affected by compliance with the charges, the Administration itself, or the Compensation Board, as the case may be, being beneficiaries of the expropriation.

What it means

This article is what makes the conservation entity such an effective form for communities of owners of detached villas in an urbanisation. The executive order to seize property of non-payers is a far easier and swifter process than going to court against them, which can take many months, and even years.

ARTICLE 66 has been left out, as it does not bear directly on communities.

CHAPTER IV -
MAINTENANCE OF
THE URBANISATION

Article 67

The conservation of the works of urbanisation and the maintenance of the equipment and installations of the public services will be the charge of the acting administration, once the transfer of these services has been made.

What it means

Yes, this is the dream paradise in which the town hall provides and maintains all the basic services of the urbanisation. This article obliges them to do so. The catch is that they have to accept the transfer of these services from the private developer or urbanisation first. And they will not accept — and have not done so in many cases — these services until everything is properly installed and functioning. Sometimes this works quite well and the community, the services and the town hall co-operate in harmony happily ever after, with the occasional non-payer of fees being forced to produce the money by the threat of executive order. Far more often, the town hall finds many deficiencies in the installations and services and will not take over their administration and maintenance until the owners' community has put them right, at great expense. Be warned.

Article 68

1. Regardless of the dispositions of the preceding article, the owners of the land included in the zone or action unit will be subject to the aforesaid obligation when it is imposed on them by the Urban Zoning Plan, or by the bases of a programme of urban action or results expressly from legal dispositions.
2. In the case of the preceding number, the owners must form themselves into an Entity of Conservation.

What it means

Even though it is clear from both principle and law that the owners will be obliged to maintain the installations, this article exists to remind us of that fact. Even when no specific provision is made for this, that last phrase of Article 68 paragraph 1 — "results expressly from legal dispositions" — gives the town hall the power to pass a resolution requiring the owners to maintain their roads in good repair, and the community will be bound by law.

Article 69

1. The participation of the owners in the obligation of conservation and maintenance of the works of urbanisation, equipment and installations of the public services, when this is not the charge of the acting administration, shall be determined as a function of the participation share set for them by the Compensation Board, in the subdivision plan, or, as the case may be, in the share specified in the Entity of Conservation.

2. If systems of horizontal property have been constituted over the properties, the contribution of the owners to said obligation of conservation and maintenance shall be determined by the participation share (cuota) with relation to the total value of the property which is assigned in each community.

What it means

This article determines the way in which each owner's share of the payment is calculated, and provides also for calculating the shares of apartment dwellers who already have horizontal property systems operating in their buildings located on the parent urbanisation.

Article 70

1. Whosoever shall be the subject to whom corresponds the obligation of maintenance referred to in the preceding articles, the Town Hall or the acting administration, in its condition as owner of the lands of public domain, works, equipment and installations of obligatory cession, may require by executive order under threat of embargo the payment of the shares owed, whether acting on its own initiative or at the instance of the collaborating urbanistic entity.

2. The amount of the payment share will be delivered by the Town Hall or acting administration to the entity charged with the conservation, when this obligation does not pertain to the Administration.

What it means

Paragraph 1 here repeats the power of the town hall to carry out an executive order of garnishment or embargo in order to compel payment of participation share fees. It notes that the town hall may do this either on its own initiative or when requested by the conservation entity. Paragraph 2 makes it clear that the town hall is to deliver this money to the conservation entity, unless the town hall itself is charged with the maintenance of the services. This means the town hall can collect the money and provide the services, or collect part of the money and provide part of the services.

Because the town hall itself is often a member of the entity, because of its own installations on the 10 per cent of the land which the promoter must transfer to the Town, this gives rise to a situation where the town hall may have to collect debts from itself.

"LEGALITY" OF COMMUNITIES

A final note here on the "legality" of communities. Throughout this text we refer to the inscription of the community in the Property Registry or Registry of Conservation Entities. We point out that the Statutes must be registered in order to be fully legal, and we insist on every point of the law being observed.

This is all well and good. In the real world, however, we find groups of houses built in the property boom that do not really make up an urbanisation, where the owners have simply agreed to organise and pay for some basic services among themselves. We find urbanisations that were never registered as such, where no community statutes exist, but the owners hold annual meetings and pay dues. We find other urbanisations, where the community has formal statutes and regulations, but these are not registered.

Are all these other forms of communities "legal"?

Well, in one sense they are not legal because they are not registered. But if you, as an owner in one of these situations, think you can get away with not paying your fees, perhaps you should think again.

Spanish courts have ruled on a number of occasions that these communities, although not registered, have acquired a legal personality simply by existing through the years, that they function for the benefit of the owners and society in general, and so they can in fact compel the payment of fees and bring a case against a non-payer, even seizing his property and having it sold at auction.

INDEX

205 Procedure	*63*
220 volts	*22*

A

Abogado	*40, 82, 267*
Accountants	*274*
Administrador	*317*
Administrador de Fincas	*275*
Agencia Estatal de Administracion Tributaria	*192*
Agente de Aduana	*25*
Agente de la Propiedad Inmobiliaria	*37*
Ajuar	*259*
Alcalde	*286*
Annual General Meeting	*311*
Annuities	*191*
Aparejador	*99*
Architect	*98, 99*
Arrienda de Temporada	*110*
Arrienda de Vivienda	*109*
Asesor Fiscal	*274*
Asistencia Jurídica Gratuita	*270*
Auction	*65*
Audiencia Provincial	*288*
Autoescuela	*142*
Automobile accident	*138*
Automobile insurance	*135*
Autónomo work permit	*213*
Autonomous regions	*282*
Ayuntamiento	*280, 295*

B

Bandera	*101*
Bank accounts	*157*
Bearer cheques	*154*
Birth Certificate	*236*
Boletín Oficial	*55, 75*
Bonded client account	*48*
Burial insurance	*240*

C

"C" leaflets	*22*
Camino Real	*96*
Car on foreign plates	*122*
Car on Spanish plates	*127*
CAPITAL GAINS TAX	*166*
Capital gains tax 1	*3, 66*
Catastral reference	*42*
Catastro	*45, 97*
Cemetery	*239*
Censo electoral	*282*
Certificado de Antecedentes Penales	*34*
Certificado Catastral	*86*
Certificado de Empadronamiento	*34, 239, 282*
Certificado de Equivalencia	*128*
Certificado de Ley	*255*
Certificado de Nacimiento	*236*
Certificado final de obra	*102*
Certificate of non-residence	*58, 87*
Cesión	*118*
Circulation Permit	*149*
Civil marriage	*241*

Coeficiente de actualización 169
Colegio de Abogados 301
Colegio de Arquitectos 100
COMMUNITY OF PROPERTY
OWNERS 301, 304
Compulsory heirs 249
Comunidad de Propietarios 301
Concejal 280
Consejería de la Vivienda 109
Constitution 291
Constitutional Court 288
Consular inscription 291
Consulate 18, 291
Consumer information office 297
Consumer organisations 299
Councillor 280
Court of First Instance 287
Cremation 239
Cuenta ajena 209
Cuenta extranjera 157
Cuenta propia 209
Cuota 308

D

Dar de alta 102
Death certificate 238
Declaración amistosa 138
Declaración de obra nueva
41, 42, 61
Demanda 289
Denuncia 286
Deposit 109
Devolución 192

Diputación 282
Dirección General de
Transacciones Exteriores 153
Divorce 243
Domiciliado 160
Driving licence 14, 140, 143
Dual Nationality 244

E

E-121 18
ESCRITURA 43
Escritura de compraventa 51, 81
Escritura pública 42, 43, 61, 81, 85
Estate agent 37, 80
Estimación directa 210
EU citizen 18
EU workers 207
Expediente de dominio 63
Expropriation 74
Extracto de inscripción de
Nacimiento 236

F

Factura 82, 229
Financing purchase 67
Fiscal representative 175
Five per cent deposit 58
Foreigners Law 291
Form 210 162, 175
Form 211 180
Form 212 182
Form 213 184

Form 214 — *173, 186*
Form 714 — *174, 175*
Form 750 — *32*
Form E-121 — *18*
Funeral director — *238*

G

Gay marriage — *242*
Generalitat Valenciana — *282*
Gestor — *273*
Gestor Intermediario de Propiedades y Edificios — *37*
Gestoría — *273*
Gibraltar — *177, 242*
Guardia Civil — *285*

H

Hacienda — *49, 58, 249*
Hipoteca — *76*
Hoja de Reclamación — *296*
Home insurance — *71*

I

IAE — *213, 219*
IBI — *41, 44, 61, 85, 174*
Importing possessions — *21*
Impuesto de Actividades Economicas — *213, 219*
Impuesto de Transmisiones Patrimoniales — *47, 76*
Impuesto sobre Bienes Inmuebles — *41, 44, 61, 85, 174*
Impuesto sobre Valor Añadido — *48, 76*

Incremento de Patrimonio — *203*
INEM — *212*
Inheritance tax rates — *261*
Inspección Técnica de Vehiculos — *138*
Instituto Nacional de Empleo — *212*
ITP — *48*
ITV — *138*
IVA — *163, 220, 228, 229*

J

Jefatura de Costas — *41*
Jefatura de Tráfico — *131*
Jefatura Provincial de Comercio Interior — *297*
Juez de Paz — *287*
Junta de Andalucía — *282*
Jurado de Expropiaciones — *75*
Justice of the Peace — *287*
Justiprecio — *74*
Juzgado de Primera Instancia — *287*

L

Law of Horizontal Property — *322*
Law for the Rights and Freedoms of Foreigners — *291*
Law of Urban Lettings — *106*
Lawsuit — *289*
Lawyer — *40, 82, 267*
Legal domicile — *254*
Legal separation — *244*
Ley de Arrendamientos Urbanos — *106*
Ley de Costas — *41*
Ley de derechos y libertades de los extranjeros — *291*

Ley Horizontal	322
Ley de Ordenación de la Edificación	102
Ley de Sucesiones	257
Ley de Suelo	99
LRAU	99
LUV	99
Libro de Actas	298
Libro de Familia	246
Licencia de Apertura	213, 218
Licencia de obra	93, 102
Licencia de primera ocupación	60, 102
Licencia fiscal	213

M

Memoria de Calidades	100
Minimum wage	226
Ministerio de Economía y Hacienda	222
Ministerio de Obras Públicas y Transportes	74
Módulos	210
MOPT	74
Mortgage	67
MOT	124
Motorcycles	134
Multa	145. 148
Municipal vehicle tax	129

N

Nationality	244
NIE	33
Non-EU citizen	19
Non-resident bank account	157

Non-returnable deposit	48
Nota Simple	42, 43, 57
Notario	81, 274
Número de Identificación de Extranjero	33, 175

O

Oferta Vinculante	68
OMIC	296
Obligatory heirs	249
Offshore company ownership	64, 176
Oficina liquidadora	49
Oficina Municipal de Información al Consumidor	297
Ombudsman	300
Organización de Consumidores y Usuarios	299

P

PADRE	192
Padrón	34
Pago fraccionado	210
Patrimonio tax	171, 172, 203
Perito judicial	272, 288
Permanencia	28
Permiso de trabajo	210
Pets	25
PGOU	42, 93
Plan General de Ordenación Urbana	42, 93
Plan Parcial	41
Plus valía	48, 88
Poder	52, 81, 263
Policía Nacional	283

Por temporada 114
Power of attorney 52, 81, 263
Precintar 124
Private contract 81
Proceso Monitorio 289
Property Registry 45
Proxy 312
Proyecto de urbanización 94

R

Reclamación 296
Referencia Catastral 45, 61
Registro Central de Ultima
Voluntad 256
Registro Civil 246
Registro de la Propiedad
55, 57, 61, 85
Rejas 71
Renta Vitalicia 191
Rental contract 109
Rental tax (Form 210) 113
Representante Fiscal 175
Resident status 29
Residence application 32
Residential rental contracts 109

S

Saldo medio 198
Servidumbre de paso 96
Short-term contract 110
Smoking law 15
SOCIAL SECURITY 215
Social Security 228, 230
Sociedad Anonima 221
Sociedad Limitada 221

Solicitud 223
Spanish Consulate 18
Statute of Limitations
Subsidised housing 70
Sub-Delegado del Gobierno
Supreme Court 288

T

Tasación 90
Testamento Abierto 256
Testamento Cerrado 256
Law of Horizontal Property 311
Law Regulating the Rights of
Rotational Enjoyment 72
Title Deed See *Escritura*
Tourist plates 126
Tourist status 28
Town Hall 280, 295
Tráfico 131
Transfer tax 47
Traspaso 118

U

Urbanismo 93
Usufruct 168, 250
Utilities bills 47

V

Valencia land law 14, 99
Valor Catastral 44, 85
Value Added Tax 48, 76
Vehicle inspection 132
Vehicle transfer 131
Visado de Residencia 21

Vivienda de Protección Oficial
(VPO)   70
Vivienda secundaria   26

W

Wealth Tax   *171, 203*
Wills   *248*
Withholding tax   *157, 192*
Work permit   *211*